Constructing Civility

RICHARD S. PARK

Constructing Civility

The Human Good in Christian and Islamic Political Theologies

UNIVERSITY OF NOTRE DAME PRESS
NOTRE DAME, INDIANA

University of Notre Dame Press
Notre Dame, Indiana 46556
undpress.nd.edu

Published in the United States of America

Library of Congress Cataloging-in-Publication Data

Names: Park, Richard S., 1975– author.

Title: Constructing civility : the human good in Christian and Islamic political theologies / Richard S. Park.

Description: Notre Dame : University of Notre Dame Press, 2017. | Includes bibliographical references and index. |

Identifiers: LCCN 2017024323 (print) | LCCN 2017032084 (ebook) | ISBN 9780268102753 (pdf) | ISBN 9780268102760 (epub) | ISBN 9780268102739 (hardcover : alk. paper) | ISBN 0268102732 (hardcover : alk. paper)

Subjects: LCSH: Religion and politics. | Common good—Religious aspects. | Religious ethics. | Religion and sociology. | Catholic Church—Doctrines. | Islam—Doctrines.

Classification: LCC BL65.P7 (ebook) | LCC BL65.P7 P38 2017 (print) | DDC 201/.72—dc23

LC record available at https://lccn.loc.gov/2017024323

∞ *This paper meets the requirements of ANSI/NISO Z39.48-1992 (Permanence of Paper).*

To my wife, Christine,
whose strength and dignity
are my sine qua non

CONTENTS

ACKNOWLEDGMENTS

The gratitude one has for the benefits one receives can be difficult to put into words. While recognizing this difficulty and risking some (possibly obvious) omissions, I would like to acknowledge the help that I have received in this effort of "constructing civility." First and foremost, I thank my parents, Brian and Soo, who have taught me, more through life than with words, the virtues of a disciplined mind, a joyful spirit, and a God-fearing disposition. They have sacrificed much; they have shown even more.

I am deeply indebted for the always wise, never tiring, ever kind feedback and friendship of Mark D. Chapman at the University of Oxford. He never let on that he knew all of the answers to the questions he posed to me; surely, such is the mark of a brilliant educator. The wisdom and moral courage of Os Guinness and David Horner—who are themselves graduates of Oriel College, Oxford—have helped me to see what true mentors are. Their strength of character, their care for this world, and their devotion to following the Way are virtues I seek always to emulate.

For various aspects of this multidisciplinary work, I thank, in political theory, Monica Duffy Toft (Blavatnik School of Government, Oxford); for my appreciation of social theory and modernity critique, Os Guinness; in legal theory and Catholic social thought, Paul Yowell (Oriel College, Oxford); for Islamic legal and political thought, the scholars at the Center for Muslim-Christian Studies, Oxford, including Shabbir Akhtar, Ida Glaser, and Martin Whittingham; and for the incredible capacity of seeing how all of it fits together, my doctoral supervisor, Mark Chapman. Through extensive feedback and collegial encouragement, these distinguished thinkers have contributed greatly to my academic journey at Oxford and beyond.

I am very grateful to those who participated in the interviews I conducted in Mindanao, Philippines: Albert Alejo, SJ; Angel Calvo, CMF; former Archbishop Fernando Capalla, DD; Sebastiano D'Ambra, PIME; Myla Leguro of Catholic Relief Services; Moner Bajunaid and Amina Rasul of the Philippine Center for Islam and Democracy; and Mohagher Iqbal, Peace Panel chairperson of the Moro Islamic Liberation Front. Their work has undoubtedly contributed to the peace of the southern Philippines; I hope that I have done justice to their insights.

Fellow sojourners who have enriched my soul include Max and Michelle Baker-Hytch, Jonathan and Tricia Brant, Britton and Michelle Brooks, Charlie and Anita Cleverly, James Crocker, Geoff Dargan, Harry and Minerva Edwards, Pete and Angela Howard, Kurt and Michaela Jaros, Peter and Gina Kim, Peter and Jennifer Kim, Jon and Susan Knoche, Roy and Jean Lee, Jeremy and Sarah Livermore, Luke Martin, Shaun McNaughton, Nazirudin Mohd Nasir and Azrifah Zakaria, Thomas and Nary Oh, Esther Park and Mijin Park, Ryan and Jen Pemberton, Bobby and Clare Ryu, and Jeff and Solange Siribandan. I also thank my parents-in-law, Young and Helen, who are a constant and kind source of encouragement and prayers.

I am immensely grateful to the University of Notre Dame Press, especially Stephen Little, Rebecca DeBoer, and Sheila Berg, whose encouragement and expertise have made the publication process extremely efficient and deeply delightful. I also thank the anonymous reviewers for the press for helping to make the arguments herein stronger and clearer.

Finally, I thank my wife, Christine, who gave up nearly everything to allow me this opportunity to flourish, fail, and finally find myself standing on this side of the City of Dreaming Spires with my head high, heart humbled, and hand held. I cannot thank you enough, my love; but every day I will try. From early morning prayers to midnight feasts, you will always be my line in the sand, my queen, my everything.

INTRODUCTION

With religion's global public resurgence, increasing social unrest and rampant violence have sounded a clarion call for a peaceable framework for a common public life. Crucial to the task of constructing such a framework within advanced modernity is (1) a critical look at the *ideas* that have helped to shape the modern outlook; and (2) a critical appreciation of the *social contexts* in which the advanced modern world is situated. The overarching aim of this book is to consider ways of constructing a framework of what I call *public civility*, specifically within liberal democratic societies. More specifically, I am interested in constructing this framework between two of the world's largest faith communities, Roman Catholicism and Islam.

By "public civility," I mean the attitudes, affirmations, and actions consonant with a just and peaceable common public life. The deeply fragmentizing effects that modernity has had on plural societies tend to exacerbate instances of the increasingly pervasive religious conflict. In order to counteract such fragmentation in the context of religiously divided societies, we must examine (among other things) the relevant political theologies of the religious groups in question. Yet given the social, political, legal, and theological dimensions pertinent to constructing a framework of public civility, this work is necessarily multifaceted, involving sociology (theories of modernity and multiculturalism), political science (studies on religion and violence), philosophy (analyses of legal pluralism and moral relativism), and an exploration of Roman Catholic and Islamic political theologies.

Secularist frameworks such as multiculturalism and legal pluralism have been put forward as approaches to constructing public civility. Yet insofar as these approaches fail to take seriously an objective moral dimension they are relativistic and thereby lack the resources needed to ground a universal public civility. Within the faith communities of Roman Catholicism and Islam, a common approach to constructing a "just society" is based on the notion of *the common good.* The problem with these approaches is that the so-called common good is defined such that the "good" is ineluctably un-"common." In this work, I suggest that a more promising basis on which to construct a universal framework of public civility is found in the wisdom of an ancient thinker—Aristotle—who articulates a notion of *the human good.*

The argument proceeds in three main stages. First, I engage in a critical assessment of ideological and sociological forces that have resulted in the deep fragmentation of modern society and the decline of public life (chs. 1–3). Second, I provide a detailed delineation of the human good (ch. 4) on the basis of which I construct a framework of public civility between Roman Catholic and Islamic traditions (chs. 5–7). (Here I explore the Roman Catholic doctrine of the *imago Dei* and the Islamic notion of *fiṭra* as conceptual counterparts to the human good.) I then consider an illustration of the proposed framework in an area that represents one of the longest-standing internal conflicts in human history, Mindanao, Philippines (ch. 8). The overarching argument is that, when reframed in terms of the human good rather than the common good, Catholic and Islamic political theologies can contribute positively and invaluably to the construction of public civility.

I offer some concluding remarks (ch. 9) on the implications that follow from this investigation: (1) what I call "dialogical friendships" is crucial to constructing a global framework of public civility; and (2) global moral responsibility is indeed justified and required. Thus my aim is to show how the Aristotelian notion of the human good serves as a promising basis for constructing public civility in liberal democratic societies among two of the largest faith communities in our world today.

CHAPTER 1

RELIGIOUS DIVERSITY AND PUBLIC CIVILITY

If we are to analyze and propose a framework for robust and sustained peace between the world's two largest faith communities, Islam and Christianity, we need first to understand the prior relationship between religion and society. More specifically, we need to grasp just how religion sits and fits (or doesn't fit) within the contemporary, allegedly secular societies of advanced modernity. Modern secularization theory, as originally articulated by thinkers such as Karl Marx, Max Weber, and Émile Durkheim, suggests that as modernity advances religion will decline. Yet religion has been on the rise, in an increasingly public way. The sociologist Peter Berger—once a prominent proponent of the secularization thesis—notes, "The world today . . . is as furiously religious as it ever was, and in some places more so than ever."[1]

Given that such "furious" religiosity far too often spills over into deadly religious conflicts, what the world urgently needs is a framework of what I call *public civility*—the attitudes, affirmations, and actions consonant with deep mutual moral concern, which originates and persists in particular locales but extends to the global scene. Moreover, given the trends of modern globalization along with mass global migrations, religious diversity within modern societies is becoming the predominant social condition. Consequently, for the foreseeable future, plural societies across the globe will be in desperate need of constructing this framework of public civility.

SETTING THE SCENE

The political scientist Timothy Shah points out that in the past a variety of religious traditions including Christianity have been complicit in acts of tremendous incivility and fatal violence; however, in the present century, "Islamist extremism and terrorism pose one of the gravest threats to peace, security, and freedom."[2] Other political scientists, drawing on the Global Terrorism Database, show that between 1998 and 2004 Muslim terrorist groups "accounted for the overwhelming majority of attacks"—98 percent involved "Islamic ideas as a motivation for violence"—and of the forty-two religious civil wars between 1940 and 2000, thirty-four involved one or both parties claiming the religion of Islam.[3] One place where such fatal incivility exists is in the religiously plural and conflict-ridden region of Mindanao, Philippines.

The overarching aim of this book is to examine various ways of constructing a framework of public civility, especially among Christian and Muslim communities, using Mindanao, Philippines, as an illustration. In the Republic of the Philippines, Mindanao makes up one of the three major island groups, alongside those of Luzon and Visayas. On the Philippine archipelago, Mindanao has the largest Muslim population, whose origin dates to the thirteenth century. Since the arrival of Spanish colonizers in the sixteenth century and up to the time of this writing, there has been continual, often fatal conflict between Muslims and Catholics, making it the second oldest religious conflict in recorded history next to the Sudan.

While there are other places of long-standing conflict, such as the Middle East, the Indian subcontinent, or the Republic of the Sudan, Mindanao is a particularly illuminating example because of the key insights that thinkers and practitioners there have to offer with regard to interfaith conflict and resolution, insights that result from their centuries-long struggle for public civility. In addition, my experience in, connections to, and knowledge of the southern Philippines give me a platform from which to illustrate my theories. I reserve for chapter 8 an extensive historical sketch of the conflict in Mindanao as well as a discussion of my findings from the interviews I conducted there.

THE ACADEMIC LANDSCAPE

The Mindanao example illustrates the need to address questions that challenge the construction of public civility in similarly situated plural societies. Given the religiously driven nature of deep social conflicts, what practicable conceptual basis might there be to ground peaceful coexistence and social solidarity? Rising above social separatism and moving beyond peacebuilding, how might a framework of public civility be constructed, especially across Muslim and Catholic traditions? Is full independence, favored by many Muslim groups, the most promising route to constructing such civility? Is the *common good* approach, taken up within both Catholic social thought and Islamic jurisprudence, the most viable basis on which to construct such a framework? Or is there some other conceptual basis on which to construct public civility across divergent and often antagonistic communities?

Since at least the time of Aristotle, thinkers have studied the issues of religious-cultural plurality and hostility. Contemporary scholars of political theory, social theory, and legal theory have made insightful contributions to this truly global issue.[4] In the course of this book, I engage and build on the work of key scholars as I lay out my case for public civility across Muslim and Christian communities.

The objective of the present work is not to seek a legal solution to the problem of pluralism, although aspects of legal theory are considered. Nor is it to offer a specifically political solution to the problem. Rather, the challenge of public civility involves the human problem of living together across divergent communities, especially given the conditions and constraints of advanced modernity. As the renowned social and political theorist Jürgen Habermas notes, in the context of political society a purely secular modus vivendi is not sufficient for "solidarity among citizens"; rather, the prospect of civil "coexistence within a democratic system must also be founded on convictions," including religious ones.[5]

Relatedly, within various academic disciplines there has been a resurgence in considerations of religious convictions and the actors who hold them. Thus the deeply religious character of the Mindanaoan conflict serves to illustrate the importance of considering the political theologies of the communities involved in peacebuilding efforts. This theological dimension of analysis is but one (albeit crucial) aspect of the fuller notion of public civility. In the next section, I explore in detail the concept of civility in order to set foundations for the rest of this work.

TWO KINDS OF CIVILITY

The idea of civility can be thought of in two ways. First, there is the "civility" of *civil society*, which can be analyzed as follows. In modern liberal democratic societies, with a growing political sphere on the one hand and a private sphere shrinking in its public significance on the other, there is a crucial need for some structural link between state and self. Civil society, which consists of family, neighborhood, religious communities, and volunteer associations, is that link which helps to buttress the realm of the private sphere against the impersonal structures of the public sphere (the state, corporations, etc.). As one theorist puts it, "We can speak of civil society wherever the ensemble of associations can significantly determine or inflect the course of state policy."[6] In brief, civil society is distinct from and helps to mediate between the spheres of statecraft and private life. Second, civility may be understood as having to do with the "other" or "stranger" in society.

To distinguish between these two kinds of civility, I characterize the first as having to do with the *vertical dimension*—in view of the mediatory role it plays between the state and the self—whereas the second has to do with what I call the *horizontal dimension*. This horizontal dimension of civility is captured well by the social theorist Zygmunt Bauman: "The main point about civility is the ability to interact with strangers without holding their strangeness against them and without pressing them to surrender it or to renounce some or all the traits that have made them strangers in the first place."[7] In other words, horizontal civility enables individuals in society to treat their fellows with respect and dignity, regardless or perhaps precisely because of their differences, whether racial, religious, cultural, or otherwise.

In sum, vertical civility has mainly to do with social institutions that primarily fulfill a mediatory role of influencing state policies; horizontal civility concerns the plurality of divergent groups within a given society and those activities of preventing or at least minimizing the alienating effects of social anomie in a fragmented modernity. We must ask what, aside from the etymological commonality between vertical civil society and horizontal civility, connects these two distinct ideas. More specifically, how are the contemporary understandings of horizontal civility related to the historical development of vertical civil society?

A BRIEF HISTORY OF CIVIL SOCIETY AND THE NEED TO RECOVER CIVILITY

In classical Greece, civil society was the political realm (i.e., the city-state, or polis), and civility described the kind of virtuous citizenship characteristic of true citizens in the polis. Into the medieval period as well, civil society was synonymous with the political realm; and even in the early modern period civil society was equated simply with "political society." Whether it was Thomas Hobbes's "commonwealth" or Jean-Jacques Rousseau's *la société polie* (polite society), civil society was basically identical to the political state. It was only during the Enlightenment that civil society came to be understood as that enterprise which protects citizens' recently realized personal rights against state intrusions.[8]

Through the developing discourse on civil society, an important historical question arose as to whether civil society includes the realm of economic activity. For Marx, since a common economic life was the essence and end goal of civil society, "the anatomy of civil society" was to be sought within the "political economy." Such a view is unsurprising given Marx's famous aphorism, "The first historical act is . . . the production of the material life itself." Similarly for Immanuel Kant, a common economic life had quite literally a civilizing effect: "The commercial spirit cannot co-exist with war, and sooner or later it takes possession of every nation." In the same vein, Montesquieu's notion of *le doux commerce* (the gentle trade) connects economic activity intimately with civil society: "The natural effect of commerce is to lead to peace."[9] Accordingly, economic activity, which demanded civil social interaction, was a central, if not defining, feature of civil society. In light of this exchange, it is clear how *civility* and *civil society* are historically and conceptually linked: civil society required civil economic exchange.

Similarly, drawing on thinkers from Aristotle to Montesquieu, the Scottish philosopher Adam Ferguson locates civil society within the sphere of the market economy. Ferguson writes that since "the care of subsistence is the principal spring of human actions, [civility is needed in] every department of public business [lest] man . . . be classed with the mere brutes."[10] Civility, which is necessary for economic exchange, was understood to be the backbone of a civilized common life. In view of this historical development, then, Hegel's characterization of *bürgerliche Gesellschaft* (civil society) was novel: it included not only economics but also religious and educational associations.[11] Over time, discussion about civil society began focusing primarily on the latter (associational groups), at times even to the exclusion of the former (economic dimension).

More recently, in view of growing global market capitalism, political and social theorists have argued for the idea of locating economics outside of civil society. For example: "Only a concept of civil society [as] differentiated from the economy . . . can become the center of a critical social and political theory in market economies."[12] That is, with the separation of economic activity from civil society and the rise of global market capitalism, far too much civility has been removed from civil society, for face-to-face economic exchange—which initially produced the need for civility—became increasingly less common and necessary.

Thus, given an increasingly public economic life—wherein the economy has moved from the private household to the public sphere (a phenomenon I discuss further in ch. 3)—civility among members of society has become even more crucial in view of its absence. So a construction of public civility would function both to prevent an expanding political state (vertical civility) and to provide the geographic and metaphorical space within which to conduct civil social interaction (horizontal civility).

The political theorist Michael Edwards provides a helpful summary of the notion of civil society since the time of classical Greece: "Civil society has been a point of reference of philosophers since antiquity in their struggle to understand: the nature of the good society, the rights and responsibilities of citizens, the practice of politics . . . and, most especially, how to live together peacefully by reconciling our individual autonomy with our collective aspirations, . . . marrying pluralism with conformity so that complex societies can function with both efficiency and justice."[13] It would seem, however, that Edwards's conception of civil society does not go far enough. While the aims of balancing "individual autonomy with collectivity" (liberty with equality) and "pluralism with conformity" (multiculturality with solidarity) are important for any society, in deeply conflictual societies even striking these balances is not sufficient to the task of peacebuilding, let alone that of constructing public civility. What is missing is a robust recovery and articulation of the essential attributes of humanity—in a word, human teleology. That is, to ground public civility, we must resource a notion that is truly universal to every human person, regardless of religious tradition or community, a notion that can be articulated in terms of the essential attributes of humanity. This notion I call *the human good* (which I unpack in detail in ch. 4). Allow me for now, then, to continue to outline the nature and scope of public civility.

THE NATURE AND SCOPE OF PUBLIC CIVILITY

In addition to vertical and horizontal civilities, there is another kind that one might call *personal civility*, distinct from but connected to my notion of public civility. In a landmark work, the social historian Norbert Elias shows how throughout medieval and Renaissance Europe the notion of *civilité* had to do mainly with "*curtois* [courtly] society," whereby *gentilhomme* (gentlemen) both made and made up *Kultur* and *Zivilisation*.[14] In short, the mark of "civilized" society was its artistic, intellectual, and religious achievements (e.g., in Germany) as well as its political, economic, and social progress (e.g., in England and France). Anything less than such "civility" was considered naïveté or barbarity, or both. Civility, in other words, consisted mainly in the manners and monuments of the knights, kings, and courtly society of high *Kultur*. I call this personal civility given that, while visible and therefore "public" in one sense, its origin lay largely in the high culture of refined dining and demeanor rather than in the robust civic engagement of citizens qua citizens of plural societies.

The focus on personal civility is illustrated poignantly in the sixteenth-century work of Desiderius Erasmus, *De civilitate morum puerilium* (a manual of "good manners for children"). The historian Philippe Ariès describes the particular context in which Erasmus's text and early modern personal civility are set: "The word 'civil' was roughly synonymous with our modern word 'social.' The word 'civility' would thus correspond to what we call 'good manners.' . . . Civility was the practical knowledge . . . necessary to have in order to live in society . . . : [It is] what colloquially might be called etiquette[, i.e.,] the older name of 'courtesy.'" This personal civility was codified in "manuals of civility or manuals of etiquette," which ranged over three broad categories: courtesy, morality, and "arts of love." Such manuals were meant for and read not only by schoolchildren being trained to assimilate into the "civility" of adult life but also by adults who were considered "insufficiently versed" in the courtesies appropriate to social life. Civility was about speaking, dressing, and acting like adults.[15]

Personal civility is related to but distinct from public civility. They are related in that they share an etymology with words like *civilized*, *civilization*, and *city*, an etymology whose Indo-European root refers to "members of the household." Thus personal as well as public civilities have to do with the manners to which one adheres when engaging with other members of the household—whether in the private *oikos* (household) or the larger public polis. Public civility, in this way, marks the manners and mode of interaction between members of a polis. As Aristotle notes, a balance between personal "liberty" and communal "equality" marks the essence of democracy. The legal scholar Stephen Carter picks up this idea: "To be civilized is to understand that we live in society as in a household, and that within that [civic] household . . .

our relationships . . . are governed by standards of behavior that limit our freedom."[16] Civility, in this sense, is the practice of living with the tension between individual liberty and communal equality. Thus what I call public civility characterizes the attitudes, affirmations, and actions of participating in the common life of a plural society—a life that conduces to just peace and social harmony.

That said, there is a marked difference between personal and public civilities. Here it is important to note the meaning of the word *politeness* and its connection to the polis. It shares its etymological root with the words *polity*, *politics*, and *policy*. In French, "courtly" people used the term *civilisé*—as nearly synonymous with *cultivé*, *poli*, and *police*—to mean a particular type of behavior.[17] I suggest that this private politeness, like personal civility, must be reconnected with a kind of political politeness proper to a life lived in the polis. That is, what demands the civility of the person living in the polity is her status as a member of a civic household: accordingly, the activity befitting and demanded of citizens of the polis is the construction of a public—not merely private—civility.

We should also note that public civility is not strictly limited to the political realm of the nation-state; rather, public civility has to do with the attitudes and actions that human persons ought to have toward one another qua human persons, thereby rendering the scope of public civility as ultimately no less than global. While I unpack this idea of a global public civility in detail in chapter 9, I would like here to develop, preliminarily at least, the idea of what I shall call "moral cosmopolitanism" before moving on. So, having discussed the nature of public civility, I would like now to discuss its scope.

The moral philosopher Anthony Appiah writes, "Each person you know about and can affect is someone to whom you have responsibilities"; "to say this is just to affirm the very idea of morality."[18] And, in connection with the present study, "the very idea of morality" is intrinsic to our notion of public civility, for public civility must be shown to, or rather must be constructed with, persons to whom we have responsibility, that is, members of our civic household. But questions arise: How large is this household? Who are its members? And where, if at all, do we draw its boundaries? At this point in the investigation, we should remember that I am focused on securing a basis for public civility specifically across Christian-Muslim divides.

That said, I am also interested to see whether this basis—which I shall argue can be found in the human good—also could serve for constructing a global framework of public civility. For, if the human good, as noted above, is those attributes which inhere in every human person, then the scope of public civility must be applicable not only to Christian-Muslim divides, but to divides found across all of humanity. Indeed, to augment Appiah's apt definition of morality, I might add that the "very idea of morality" includes not only those whom one knows but also those whom one simply knows *about*. As one peace studies scholar writes, "The moral imagination has a capacity . . . to understand that the welfare of my community is directly related to the welfare of your community"; and this capacity "create[s the moral] connection between the local and the [global] public."[19]

HOW PUBLIC CIVILITY IS NOT (MERELY) PEACEBUILDING

A final notion may help to illuminate the significance of public civility and differentiate it from a somewhat similar term: namely, *peacebuilding*. A leading expert in peace and conflict studies, John Paul Lederach, articulates what he sees as the fundamental challenge to the project of peacebuilding: "*How do we transcend the cycles of violence that bewitch our human community while still living in them?*" Similarly, though specifically with regard to religiously conflictual societies, the historian R. Scott Appleby notes that religious actors whose "*ultimate goal*" is "*peaceful coexistence*" play a crucial role in peacebuilding.[20] Drawing on though in some tension with these ideas, I characterize public civility as going beyond "peaceful coexistence": it involves an active, continual construction of a common public life in plural society, a construction crucially based on a recognition of the universal human good in "the other."

In a coauthored work, Appleby and Lederach describe the activity of peacebuilding in a way similar to that of public civility: "The practices of peacebuilding that help bring about this desired state of affairs [namely, "justpeace"] must become routinized in the society." According to this view, peacebuilding is not merely a "cessation of violence," but a participative activity that members of society continually engage in for the sake of constructing "justpeace." It is worth noting that Appleby too at points construes peace in terms of "civility": "A workable peace is not the absence of conflict but the conditions of structural civility that obtain when a society has developed culturally appropriate and effective ways of adjudicating and resolving conflict nonviolently."[21] It seems that for Appleby peacebuilding efforts go beyond nonviolence to a sort of structural emergence of social civility.

In light of this discussion, it might be suggested that *public civility* is conceptually no different from *peacebuilding*—the latter of which is used more widely in current academic literature. However, I submit that there is one fundamental difference between these concepts, a difference that underscores the central contention of this work: namely, that rather than framing the dialogue between Islamic and Catholic political theologies on the basis of *the common good*, the construction of public civility is more promising when this engagement is reframed on the basis of *the human good*. This crucial difference can be seen especially when considering a model proposed more recently by Appleby and Lederach.[22] They characterize their idea of "strategic peacebuilding" as follows: "an approach to reducing violence, resolving conflict and building peace that is marked by a heightened awareness of and skillful adaptation to the complex and shifting material, geopolitical, economic, and cultural realities of our increasingly globalized and interdependent world." That is, peacebuilding involves a set of activities by myriad actors and institutions throughout various social sectors on multiple levels of engagements. I would note: so far, so similar. But for Appleby and Lederach these activities of peacebuilding count as such only insofar as they are "conducive to *the common good*." While my account of public civility overlaps significantly with that of peacebuilding, it departs precisely with regard to the conceptual ground on which the accounts are based. That is, while for Appleby and Lederach the ground is "the common good," I argue that approaches based on this ground are inadequate to provide the resources needed for a universal framework of public civility in plural societies. The "good" that is assumed to be "common" is, precisely in plural societies, only purportedly so. As I argue (see chs. 5–7), the idea of the common good is subject to either an inescapable relativism at best or a conceptual incoherence at worst; and the idea of the human good offers a universal and thereby more promising basis for constructing public civility.

PUBLIC CIVILITY, LIBERAL SOCIETIES, AND MORAL TRADITIONS

Before concluding this chapter, I need to make several qualifications regarding the notion of public civility. First, public civility requires more than simply democracy. The political theorist and commentator Fareed Zakaria poses this insightful question: "What if democracy produces an Islamic theocracy?"; for technically it is possible that the *demos* might freely favor and thereby vote in a theocratic political order. Democracy, after all, concerns the freedom of the expression of the will of the people to elect officials who in turn enact and enforce this will. So what is to preclude such leaders from imposing an order of un-freedom? For it is "liberty [that has] led to democracy, and not the other way around." In other words, liberty is prerequisite to a flourishing democracy, for democracy in and of itself does not preclude the possibility of un-freedom. For this reason, it must be stipulated that the kind of political orders with which I am concerned are specifically *liberal* democratic societies. Without a liberal democratic ethos, public civility is neither an ideal nor a possibility.[23]

A second qualification worth reiterating is that public civility requires more than a well-functioning vertical civil society. Constructing civility solely for "associational life," as some theorists such as Michael Edwards want to suggest,[24] suffers a crucial problem: namely, that of providing the morally normative grounds of public civility. Edwards himself argues that "associations" such as the Italian mafia or al-Qaeda must not count as part of civil society. For this reason, when constructing civility we must consider a society's "normative goals"—obvious candidates, he suggests, being "love," "compassion," and "solidarity." But on what grounds, we must ask, must it be these ideals rather than others that supposedly serve as "normative goals"? Civil society in and of itself lacks the moral resources to ground such normativity; all that civil society can afford is the prizing of associational life—nothing less and tragically nothing more. Morally normative civility requires, rather, the underpinning of a moral tradition. Islam and Christianity, which are more than (and certainly not less than) moral traditions, do possess the conceptual resources needed to ground the evaluative (i.e., moral) capacities of a normative public civility.[25] Hence we must seek a basis of public civility that has a normativity, so to speak, built into its moral resources.

Nevertheless, these attempts at constructing public civility give way to their own share of problems when the communities based on such moral traditions collide. Paradoxically, precisely those traditions that provide the resources needed for grounding a morally normative public civility often become the breeding grounds for deep and sometimes fatal incivility. There remains, then, a need to secure and articulate some fundamental, transcommunal basis of public civility.

Securing a firm and fundamental basis for constructing a common life marked by public civility is a necessary though not entirely novel goal. From ancient Greek thinkers to modern European philosophers to contemporary scholars of civil society, various explorations have been undertaken. Since the classical period, efforts to secure a just, peaceful, and civil society have been based predominantly on *the common good* approach, an approach I find problematic. As for the more recent considerations of "civil society," they seem to suffer the problem of grounding moral normativity, as just discussed. An altogether different (though again not novel) approach is needed—one that is rooted in classical Aristotelian ethics and politics and that finds resonance also within the religious traditions of Catholicism and Islam.

In the next chapter, I consider the task of constructing public civility vis-à-vis another major "tradition" that has become increasingly relevant in the context of advanced modernity: namely, the tradition of modern secularism. Modern secularism, I argue, is a tradition of a sort, specifically in its entailing certain ideological commitments; but these commitments are ones that constrain rather than conduce the construction of public civility. In order to understand the impact that secularism has had on political theory and on the public sphere, we first need to consider several key concepts that have been transmuted in modern political theoretical discourse. To this task I now turn.

CHAPTER 2

MODERNITY'S MAYHEM AND THE NEED FOR MORAL POLITICAL THEORY

If we are to construct public civility between Muslim and Christian communities, then we must address the ideological "tradition" of modern secularism, a tradition that cuts across both of them. Secularism influences the construction of civility insofar as it makes a definite, largely detrimental impact on the modern condition. That is, since the condition of modern public life is so deeply marred by a "radical secularity," to ignore the impact of secularism as an ideological force is to fail to do justice to the task of civility construction.

Late in his career, Peter Berger underwent a complete change of mind regarding secularization theory: "the assumption that we live in a secularized world is false"; "the whole body of literature . . . labeled 'secularization theory' is essentially mistaken." As noted previously, the secularization thesis has been found to be a myth. That said, models of what is now called "desecularization" must still take into account a secularized and "globalized elite culture" found largely within the "faculty club culture."[1] That is, there is an academic *secularism* that brings with it certain modernistic conceptions—crucially for our purposes, of human freedom and of the state—that bear negatively on the prospect of civility construction. As one scholar puts it, "Secularism builds on a particular conception of the world [according to which] religious practice and belief [should] be confined to a space where they cannot threaten political stability."[2] It is to a critique of this ideology of modern secularism that I turn in this chapter.

SECULARIZATION AS PRIVATIZATION

With the arrival of the novel and distorted public and private spheres of social life, modernity has brought with it certain ideological and social shifts that have led to a saliently sentimentalized and privatized view of religion. The privatization of religion, to be sure, is part of the more general privatization found in modernity: it results from the deep social fragmentation characteristic of modern society.[3] This social fragmentation has yielded a social "department" for just about every area of life: family life here, religious life there, work life over yonder, and political life further afield still. The upshot is that in advanced modernity religion is, in many ways, reduced to a mere private meaningfulness.

This privatization represents a marked departure from the traditional task of religion, which is to serve as a *sacred canopy*—"a common universe of meaning" in society.[4] As one renowned sociologist writes, "If before, it was the religious realm which appeared to be the all-encompassing reality within which the secular realm found its proper place, now the secular sphere will be the all-encompassing reality, to which the religious sphere will have to adapt."[5]

Yet, privatization qua secularization is only (the sociological) half of the picture: privatization must also be understood qua secularism, an ideology that has been proffered by political philosophers such as Robert Audi and John Rawls. So, for example, while Audi allows deliberation over political matters to derive from religious convictions, a necessary condition for the expression of such convictions is that it be supported with "secular reason."[6] Religious convictions must be given a *secular reason* in order to count as valid political reasoning.

Also, in constructing his political theory of justice in plural contexts, Rawls seeks an "overlapping consensus" among "reasonable comprehensive doctrines" that converge on issues of "basic justice." Central to his project is the notion of *public reason*, according to which "comprehensive doctrines of truth [are to be] replaced by an idea of the politically reasonable," which in turn is addressed to "citizens as citizens." According to this arrangement, public reason is incompatible with "the zeal to embody the whole truth in politics." In short, political matters must be "expressed in terms of the political values of public reason" instead of those found in "comprehensive [e.g., religious] doctrines."[7]

Rawls's public reason is (slightly) less stringent than Audi's secular reason in that the former recognizes that the approach of secular reason itself subscribes to a comprehensive doctrine of a kind, namely, a "comprehensive nonreligious doctrine." Nevertheless, by insisting that only "the politically reasonable" be addressed "to citizens as citizens," the problem arises as to who or by what criterion one decides what is "politically reasonable." For Rawls, the solution is political liberalism itself, which he contends is "liberal," "self-standing," and noncomprehensive. Yet, as Alasdair MacIntyre has shown, liberalism itself is a tradition possessing its own standards of (Enlightenment) rationality and of (radically individualistic) justice.[8]

Continuing my critique of the tradition of secularism, by way of background I offer a (somewhat technical) analysis of what it means for any human act—political speech, the exercise of religion, the pursuit of life plans, and so on—to be considered public or private. In doing so, I lay the foundations for a larger critique—a critique of modernism—which is needed to evaluate properly the (il)legitimacy of the ideology of modern secularism and its effect on a common public life.

THE PRIVATE, THE PUBLIC, AND THE POLITICAL

What does it mean for religion to be private or public? What is it for any social phenomenon (SP) to be private or public? Drawing on the insights of the political theorist Jeff Weintraub,[9] I submit that there are several important distinctions and sets of criteria that may clarify issues surrounding these questions.

Weintraub notes two important sets of distinctions regarding what is to be considered "private" and "public." The first set of distinctions involves the *visibility criterion*, whereby an SP might be "hidden or withdrawn," that is, private, or "open, revealed, or accessible," that is, public. The second distinction has to do with the *collectivity criterion*, whereby what is private "pertains only to an individual" and what is public "affects the interests of a collectivity of individuals." Thus, consider some SP—call it SP1—that is private in the first sense (i.e., hidden from view): it does not follow that SP1 could not count as public in the second sense (i.e., affecting a collectivity). Weintraub gives the example of an electoral vote: while voting may be done in private away from the public's eye (visibility criterion), it is an act that can and does affect the collective public (collectivity criterion). Alternatively, SP2 may be private in the second sense (affecting an individual) yet public in the first sense (visible to others). For example, consider an individual's religious beliefs and practices: while such beliefs and practices may pertain to an individual, it often is and arguably should be visible to others, say, in the form of religious garb or in corporate (visible) worship.

A crucial implication of these distinctions is that, contrary to the mistaken idea that only the "public" aspects of human life constitute matters that are properly "political," as Weintraub writes, "there is no necessary connection between the notions of 'public' and 'political.'" By keeping these distinctions clear one could see how the affairs of the private domain can involve the political—and some of these affairs involve religion. Thus, to exclude religion from the political realm (i.e., to privatize religion) is to restrict unjustifiably the public (visible) expressions of religion—a restriction that is simply yet tragically a confusion of categories. Moreover, such a restriction is not only unjust but also endangering: as a number of political scientists have shown, privatizing religion far too often has had gravely counterproductive consequences for civility construction.[10]

Privatization of religion, then, is the result not only of the sociological shifts in modernity but also of the ideological forces of secularism; as such, privatization is antithetical to the construction of public civility. Below I continue my critique of modern secularism by considering modernist notions of human freedom and thereby arguing for the allowance of the free and public exercise of religion.

PUBLIC CIVILITY AND A CRITIQUE OF MODERNISM

An analysis of the impact of certain crucial ideological commitments of modern secularism on the construction of public civility requires a substantial treatment of aspects of political theory. For to understand properly the impact of modernity on the task of civility construction, what is needed is a critique of modernism, especially with regard to the notions of human freedom and the role of the state.

In the next chapter I explain further the term *critique of modernism*. For now, suffice it to say that it is a critical analysis of particular *concepts*—in this case, human freedom and political structures—that arguably have undergone distortions due to a modernist political ideology. Also in the next chapter I differentiate this term from a similar one—*modernity criticism*—which focuses more on the *lived realities* of individuals in modernity. In short and roughly speaking, if what follows is a critical look at the *political theory* of modernity, the next chapter is a critique of modernity's (seismic) *sociological shifts*.

MODERNISM AND HUMAN FREEDOM

In analyzing the problem of privatized religion, it is helpful to understand what it means for human persons to be free to express religious beliefs in public life; and in order to analyze this matter, it is necessary to consider the more fundamental question of what human freedom is. In the following, I consider the two most common conceptions of human freedom: *negative freedom* as connected to modern political liberalism; and *positive freedom* as characteristic of the communitarian tradition. Then I evaluate these respective views, along with the modernist transmutations of the concept of freedom, and their concomitant impact on public civility.

Since at least the time of the Enlightenment, there have been two main conceptions of human freedom. Broadly considered, on the one hand, social contract theory serves as a foundation for what has been called the "civic republican tradition," which emphasizes positive freedom—that is, freedom to contribute to a common public life. On the other hand, John Locke's "natural rights" view has served as a basis for modern political liberalism with an emphasis on negative freedom—that is, freedom of choice without interference.[11] In brief, while the civic republican tradition construes political life and its attendant political freedoms as a natural extension of "the good life," a Lockean view takes them as necessary to withstand political corruption. In considering how certain ideological commitments of modernism have distorted the notion of human freedom, it is important to distinguish between positive and negative freedom.

In his classic "Two Concepts of Liberty," Isaiah Berlin articulates a distinction between positive and negative liberty, or freedom. According to Berlin, negative liberty is interested in the question, "What is the area within which the subject . . . is or should be left to do or be what he is able to do or be, without interference by other persons?" By contrast, positive liberty is concerned with the question, "What, or who, is the source of control or interference that can determine someone to do or be, this rather than that?"[12] Berlin's distinction has been challenged most notably by Gerald MacCallum, who argues that both senses of freedom are really two different ways of understanding the "same triadic relation" whereby freedom obtains where "some agent *x*" is free from "some constraint *y*" in order to "do or become something *z*."[13] However, under MacCallum's conception of freedom, a crucial question remains: What is one free to "do or become"? For, even under MacCallum's view of freedom, it seems that a nonarbitrary answer to this question cannot be given: for without an objective telos—some definitive aim—that is proper to positive freedom, and given the range of viable "life plans" to which negative freedom can apply, there results multiple, sometimes incompatible forms of freedom. Modernistic notions of human freedom are so freestanding that they cannot be grounded.

It must be said, that negative freedom is a bona fide aspect of human freedom; however, it alone does not provide a full account. What is needed is a robust view of human freedom grounded in the classical view of human persons, which in turn requires a recovery of the notion of *the human good*. What is needed, as I shall argue further, is a *moral* political theory of freedom. What follows is a consideration of the merits and shortcomings of negative freedom. Then, building on recent "modernity critics," who argue for positive freedom, I conclude that aspects of both views of freedom are necessary to capture the notion of the human good. Furthermore, I argue that this notion of the human good (the essential attributes of which I unpack in ch. 4), which is foundational to the construction of public civility, transcends the traditions of Islam and Christianity and thereby grounds a framework of universal public civility between them.

Modern Liberalism and Negative Freedom

Negative freedom forms the basis of liberalism's modernist conceptions of freedom. Grounded in the idea of autonomous choice, it can be summarized as the individual's freedom to choose whatever she wills, without interference, so long as her freedom does not impinge on that of others. Recall here John Stuart Mill's famous dictum, "The only freedom which deserves the name, is that of pursuing our own good in our own way, so long as we do not attempt to deprive others of theirs, or impede their efforts to obtain it."[14] It is modern in that its articulation comes from Enlightenment thinkers, explicitly in Locke and Hobbes. It is liberal in that it purports to protect the liberties of individuals: Hobbes writes, "No liberty can be inferred of the will, desire, or inclination, but the liberty of the man; which consisteth in this, that he finds no stop in doing what he has the will, desire, or inclination to do." Similarly, Locke argues that freedom for humans is the "freedom to order their actions, and dispose of their possessions and persons as they think fit . . . without asking leave, or depending on the will of any other man."[15]

Such is negative liberty. Notably in the writings of Jeremy Bentham and John Stuart Mill, recent proponents of modern liberalism include Friedrich Hayek, John Rawls, and (though with significant departures) Robert Nozick. I raise three objections against negative freedom: (1) its alleged value-free status, (2) its rejection of human teleology, and (3) its assumption of human autonomy. I take each in turn before moving on to consider the positive freedom of communitarianism.

Objections to Negative Freedom

Alleged value-free status. Noninterference is the *condicio sine qua non* of negative freedom. That is, a necessary condition of freedom is that freedom be value-free: there can be no value given once-for-all about the ends of human life. Yet this begs the question, Does not such a condition itself presuppose a certain "value"? Does not this requirement—neutrality with respect to value—presuppose a particular understanding of human nature that in turn attaches a certain value to a particular view of human flourishing: namely, that human persons are "blank slates," value-free beings, with no teleology or proper end to determine their flourishing? Why should one suppose that noninterference is the telos of human freedom and of flourishing? On pain of self-referential incoherence, there necessarily cannot be a value-free view of human freedom. One political philosopher writes, "Because the negative view of liberty concentrates on freedom from external constraints, it does not specify [explicitly] any ends or purposes that the individual should be free to pursue"[16]—though it cannot help but do so implicitly. Furthermore, on this account of freedom, there will always be incompatible views of "the good" among members of society, yielding a situation inimical to a universal framework of public civility.

Rejection of human teleology. If, on the contrary, there indeed are standards by which to judge human acts as authentic instances of freedom, a question arises, Which standards? To this point, I draw on two important points made by the philosopher Charles Taylor: first, the purposive character of human life; and second, the degreed quality of the goals of human freedom.[17] Taylor writes, "Freedom is important to us because we are purposive beings." In other words, freedom is a function of human purposiveness: for freedom is construed always against a backdrop of considering "what is significant for human life." Put differently, the idea of a "good human life" is coherent only if there is some objectively human way of being. It follows, then, that the aims of freedom must be in accordance with some objective account of human flourishing. That is, for freedom to be genuine, we must presuppose a kind of flourishing that is natural and essential to human persons such that we could judge between "good" and "bad" human aims. And negative freedom does not, indeed cannot, afford such a view, since it is fundamentally committed to a rejection of human teleology, that is, the fact that human persons are made for certain (and not other) aims and ends.

Second, aims of human freedom come in degrees. That is, human acts are construed always against an understanding that certain human aims are in fact more significant than others. "There are," as Taylor puts it, "discriminations to be made" whereby certain restrictions to freedom are unquestionably "more serious than others." A view of purely negative freedom makes equal all claims to freedom, when clearly they are not all equal. For surely: "Restricting the expression of people's religious and ethical conviction is more significant than restricting . . . movement around . . . the country; and both are more significant than the trivia of traffic control." Not all human aims are equal. This truth can be seen in the fact that, as in the example above, not all restrictions to such aims are equal. There are certain aims that accord with human life and are thereby intrinsically more valuable for freedom and ones that do not and are not. Without objective human teleology what remains is modernity's "*privatized* individuality" with its myriad human aims. Without an objective telos in virtue of which humans are able to flourish, "freedom" is no freedom at all; and negative freedom rejects this necessary teleology.

Presumption of autonomy. It is not too much to say that a view of strictly negative freedom prizes the self as sovereign. For Bentham, "There is no-one who knows what is for your interest so well as yourself." Mill concurs: "People understand their own business and . . . interests better . . . than the government . . . [and] one ought to condemn every kind of government intervention that conflicts with [this truth]." Elsewhere, Mill argues that in any area which "concerns himself," one's "independence is . . . absolute"; in areas concerning "his own body and mind, the individual is sovereign."[18] More recently, Rawls has argued for the importance of individual autonomy, contending that the only legitimate conceptions of "the good [are] conceptions as one's own good."[19] Autonomy and self-arbitration are the hallmark of negative freedom. Yet this modernist view of autonomy is radically different from the classical understanding of human teleology, as noted above.

Exactly how this modernist outlook became a predominant one is a complex issue. While not simply a matter of intellectual articulation leading to wider social acceptance, neither was this transformation merely a matter of a shift in social practices. There is a dialectical interplay between the ideational and social forces of modernity. One of the most significant forces bringing about this transformation is the modernist conviction that human freedom is self-directed. Even as a proponent of the negative view, Berlin concedes, "Every plea for civil liberties and individual rights" derives from an "individualistic ... conception of man."[20] A modernist view of freedom, then, is incompatible with an objective human teleology, which I argue is crucial for establishing a universal basis for constructing public civility.

Communitarianism and Positive Freedom

By contrast, positive freedom may be understood as being grounded in a Rousseauian *social contract* whereby free citizens, in order to avoid a constant "state of war," are "compelled" to rise above individual interests in favor of the "general will" of a given community; by and only by such a process could citizens be free, even if "forced to be free."[21] The cost of this paradoxical coercion is counted as being worth the dividend of freedom. This communitarian view of freedom reaches back further than Rousseau to the works of Aristotle. It is called the *civic republican tradition*: it is civic in its presumption per Aristotle that "man is by nature a political animal,"[22] and as such he is most free when involved in civic affairs; and it is republican insofar as it insists on citizenship in res publica. In this tradition, community is hierarchically prior to the individual, a priority to which members of the republic are committed allegedly naturally.

This political communitarianism goes by other names (e.g., "positive libertarianism," "classical republicanism," and "contractarianism") and has been articulated in the works of thinkers like Kant and Hegel, continuing (though with differences) in Marx and T. H. Green. More recent theorists in this tradition include Michael Sandel, Charles Taylor, and Dana Villa. Green's view of positive freedom captures its central notion: "When we ... speak of freedom, ... [w]e do not mean merely freedom from restraint or compulsion.... [Rather], we mean a positive power or capacity of doing or enjoying something worth doing or enjoying, and that, too, something that we do or enjoy in common with others. We mean by it the power which each man exercises through the help and security given by his fellow men and which he, in turn, helps to secure for them."[23] Positive freedom is a freedom to be some *one* or do some *thing*, the pursuits of which obtain best within and for the sake of community.

The Objection from Totalitarianism

Among the objections to the communitarian tradition and its view of human freedom, there is one that, if true, would be fatal to it: namely, the objection that communitarianism ultimately collapses into totalitarianism.[24] As Isaiah Berlin would put it, to hold to a purely positive freedom is "to ignore the actual wishes of men or societies, to bully, oppress, torture in the name, and on behalf, of their 'real' selves."[25] That is, in the communitarian pursuit of equality, individual freedom is undercut, and this totalitarian push is entailed by the logic of positive freedom—or so goes the objection. Is it so?

In response to the charge of totalitarianism, the political theorist Adam Swift proffers a modified version of communitarianism that he suggests rebuffs the "slippery slope" objection. According to Swift, since "different ways to live are rational for different people," it is reasonable to take the role of the state as that of helping "its members towards freedom not by getting them all to live the same way, but by doing what it can to help them to live in ways which are rational for them." There is, after all, only "a limited core of things it is rational for all people to do and not to do"—so says Swift. The state, therefore, may "make us do and not do *those* in the name of our own freedom." That is, for freedom's sake, the state may interfere with the individual pursuits that are considered not "rational." Swift concludes that this modified communitarianism would escape the charge of totalitarianism.[26]

This nuanced argument, though laudable, suffers a crucial flaw captured in these questions: Who or what determines this "limited core of things" that ought and ought not to be done? What makes certain acts rational or irrational? And against which standards or on what basis would any conflicting claims of freedom be adjudicated? As I shall argue, without the idea of the human good there would be no legitimate framework of adjudicating intercommunal disagreement. Thus, if a modernist communitarianism escapes the tag of being an all-encompassing totalitarianism, it does so only too successfully in that it invites an unbounded view of freedom that affords no nonarbitrary adjudicative parameters.

Given the potential problem of relativism, a communitarian view of strict positive freedom is inadequate to ground human freedom. This inadequacy results from the modernistic privileging of individual autonomy because of which there emerge multiple and conflicting views on what freedom is for. This discussion, then, brings me to the second half of my critique of modernism, which has to do with modernist conceptions of the role of the state: that is, that the particularly modernist views of the state, like those of human freedom, occlude the construction of public civility.

MODERNISM AND THE ROLE OF THE STATE

A typical modernist statement on the role of the state is found in the political theorist Michael Walzer, who argues that "the good life" is that activity "pursued by individuals" over which the state "presides" but in which it does not "participate."[27] Under modernist liberal theories, law and politics are to be neutral with respect to conceptions of the good life. Thus, the state has gone from promoting "the good life" to merely providing benefits and preventing harms in allowing individuals to determine their own conceptions thereof. Modern politics has become a matter of social pragmatic utility at the expense of teleological human flourishing. Politics, as one legal theorist puts it, has become "*nomocratic*, concerned with rules and rights, rather than *teleocratic*, which would be concerned with a set of common goods and purposes."[28] *Rights* rather than considering *what is right* is what matters, according to the modernist.

Yet a modernist articulation of the role of the state admits of no universal conception of the human self and thereby of the political self. In the following, I discuss several key considerations with regard to the role of the state that bear on the construction of public civility. Then I return to a discussion of the tradition of secularism before summarizing the chapter.

TRANSFORMING THE "POLITICAL" SELF

A diversity of conceptions of the good life have marked human society since at least the time of the ancient Greeks, as evidenced in the writings of Aristotle, and presumably even before. The individualizing effects of modernity have exacerbated the problem of diversity: for the atomism that marks the political culture of modern democratic societies has helped to create a so-called political self who is, if ironically, an allegedly free individual untethered to the polis.

The resultant and reigning public philosophy of modernity is one according to which government "should provide a framework of rights that respects persons as free and independent selves, capable of choosing their own values and ends."[29] This outlook is captured in what has been famously dubbed *possessive individualism*,[30] whereby individual political rights trump the shared human good. Accordingly, political theorists like Chandran Kukathas (cheerfully) note that the state is "no more than a transitory political settlement whose virtue is that it secures civility" among divergent groups in society.[31] That is, given that individuals in plural polities have multiple identities, the primary function of the nation-state is ensuring "civility" (arguably of a weaker form than what I describe above). However, to ground a viable framework of robust public civility, what needs recapturing is an account of the attributes that are essential and common to all human persons, irrespective of their political status.

Yet, as so-called modernity critics help us to see, in modernity there has emerged an "independent morality," a nontheistic individualized ethics, that was previously unavailable. Accordingly, there has occurred a shift away from viewing society as a community "united in a shared vision" in fulfilling human teleology to viewing it as "an arena in which individuals seek to secure what[ever fulfills] them." Thus, modern society lacks the capacity to acknowledge, let alone articulate, "the good" as anything other than the "summing of individual interests." The good is whatever the self decides. In advanced modernity individual subjective fulfillment has come to eclipse objective human flourishing. Whereas once the good was defined by an objective view of the self, it is now decided by the subjective self.[32]

Consequently, public morality is reduced largely to social agreements on rule following. Such a view of political ethics is starkly different from the classical view that a whole-life orientation to human excellence is the proper aim of the moral life. Yet, without an objective view of moral human teleology, such rule-based moralities are an unsurprising substitute for public morality: if one cannot tell another how it is to be good (virtue ethics), at least they might agree on what counts as "good" interaction (utilitarianism). Without an objective human teleology articulated and acknowledged, any liberal political structure is bound to fall short of providing the needed resources for public civility. As the social critic Os Guinness puts it, the modern vision of the liberal state "has no commitment to virtue of any kind at the center of its free society"[33]—and it cannot have one without an account of objective human teleology. A truly just politics requires a truly human ethics.

In sum, only with a recovery of a classical understanding of the fundamental human identity, along with its moral nature, can there be the resources needed to both envision and engender a public civility adequate to bridge the divergent communities of Islam and Christianity. The upshot of this modernist transformation of the political self is summarized well by MacIntyre: "In a world of secular rationality religion could no longer provide . . . a shared background and foundation for moral discourse and action." And what religion is no longer allowed to do, moral philosophy is no longer able to do since it rejects an objective human teleology—that is, the view of humanity "as having an essence which defines [its] true end." This is why the Enlightenment project of founding a basis of public morality "had to fail."[34]

SECULARISM AS A POLITICAL TRADITION

My critique of modernist views of the state agrees with Aristotle's critique about the harmful effects of political atomism of his day. In the

Greek city-states, "there has arisen a false idea of freedom": namely, "that freedom means doing what a man likes." Aristotle's critique of negative freedom prophetically picks out the fundamental problem with modern political life: the totalizing and distorted view of human freedom as *freedom from*. For Aristotle, this view of human freedom produces democracies in which "every one lives as he pleases, or in the words of Euripides, 'according to his fancy.' But this is all wrong."[35]

What Aristotle feared the effects of modernity have transmuted into a secular ideology: that is, given the modern explosion of so-called freedoms, the political state took its place as the final arbiter of the principles and parameters of public life. With its continuous push toward uniformity, the forces of political modernity had brought about a near-omnicompetent state whereby social institutions are to be "state-established, state-endowed or state-licensed." "Because the modern nation-state seeks to regulate all aspects of the individual life—even the most intimate, such as birth and death—no one . . . can avoid encountering its ambitious powers"; consequently, "all social activity requires the consent of the law, and therefore of the nation-state." In other words, the politics of modern public life has yielded what one scholar calls a "secular liberal agnosticism."[36]

In sum, modernistic conceptions of human freedom and of the role of the state have resulted in a secular modernism—as reflected and reinforced in the set of political assumptions and structures consonant with a nearly all-encompassing secular political ideology; hence, secularism as the political tradition of advanced modernity.

In this chapter, I argue that secular modernity has yielded (among other things) fundamental conceptual transformations of human freedom and of the role of the political state; a transmutation of the political self as a possessor of anarchic "rights"; and a loss of an objective view of human teleology. These distortions and transformations bear negatively on the prospect of constructing public civility in plural societies, especially ones such as Mindanao, which comprise deeply divisive religious communities. In view of such ideological shifts, what is needed in political theory is a recovery of the classical notion of human teleology. In a word, what is needed is a specifically moral political theory.

Building on this premise, in the next chapter I consider another dimension that is crucial to the prospect of constructing public civility: the modern public sphere. Since the task of constructing public civility, like all human endeavors, is necessarily embedded in a given social-cultural context, its prospect must be considered against the social reality of the profoundly secular public sphere of advanced modernity. Given, on the one hand, modernist misconceptions of both human freedom and the role of the state and, on the other, the social-cultural context of advanced modernity as marked by radical individuality and secularity, any attempt to construct a framework of public civility requires both a critique of modernism, as given above, and a concomitant modernity criticism, to which I now turn.

CHAPTER 3

THE DECLINE OF PUBLIC LIFE

In analyzing the advanced modern world, especially in the context of religiously plural societies, it is crucial to not only engage in a critical examination of the concepts that represent the ideologies of modernism. A social history is also needed in order to understand the lived contexts against the background of which such concepts are expressed. To this end, in this chapter I suggest a reappraisal of several key social realities characteristic of advanced modernity, namely (1) the decline of public life; (2) the distortions of the public and private spheres; and (3) the rise of what I call the modern *professional sphere*. These social realities crucially constrain the viability of constructing public civility in the advanced modern world; for this reason, an examination of them is in order.

Before laying out my critique, I offer a brief explanation of the meanings of various terms related to the methodology that I employ in this chapter.

CIVILITY AND CRITIQUE

The notion of *critique* has a significant connection to the ancient Greek term *krisis*, which originally described any violent rupture within the polis; that is, in the classical world, to critique was to offer a corrective to a crisis. Through the modern period, the "critical" project was taken up by Enlightenment thinkers such as Friedrich Schiller, Pierre Bayle, and Immanuel Kant who criticized religion and its connection to absolutist forms of government, doing so within the alleged final court of arbitration: human reason. While used by such thinkers to characterize the "error" or "burden" of religious and political authority, more recently the term *critique* has been adopted by so-called modernity critics for expressly different purposes: to critique secular modernity.[1] Thus, while historically *critical theory* has been characterized by its suspicion of religious metaphysics and epistemology, we see that secular critiques themselves have ideological commitments that unjustifiably privilege secularity. Hans-Georg Gadamer writes famously, "There is one prejudice of the Enlightenment that defines its essence: the fundamental prejudice of the Enlightenment is the prejudice against prejudice itself."[2] That said, enlightened prejudice is no less a prejudice. For my purposes, then, I use *modernity criticism* to refer specifically to a critical reappraisal of the social contexts that have hosted a modern and particularly secular outlook.

In the previous chapter, I used the term *critique of modernism* when analyzing the ideological forces of secular modernism. In this chapter I use *modernity criticism* when evaluating the sociological context of secular modernity. A critique of modernism is based primarily on a *history of philosophy* under which perspective the ideological commitments of modernism are in focus; by contrast, modernity criticism, under a *sociology of knowledge* perspective, explores the social contexts in which modern forms of life are situated. The construction of a peaceable framework of public civility involves a methodology that considers both history of philosophy (intellectual history) and sociology of knowledge (social history). Having considered much by way of the former, I turn to the latter.

Other thinkers have pointed out the need to consider the lived realities of social change in addition to tracing the history of ideas. Norbert Elias, for example, argues that history does not unfold as a result of the "'rationally' planned" projects of individual thinkers; yet neither is social change "irrational." Rather, a given social reality typically results from a multiplicity of the "plans and actions of people [that] give rise to changes and patterns that no individual has planned or created"; and from this interplay "arises an order sui generis." In short, the modern social order consists in the attendant social "habitus" produced through a series of specific but mostly unplanned historical change.[3]

Similarly, Armando Salvatore and Dale Eickelman, scholars of Islam, offer this helpful commentary in applying a sociology of knowledge perspective to modern Muslim contexts: "It is important to incorporate historical and contextual accounts [which always involve both the] notions and practices of public life ... in the Muslim majority world and elsewhere. ... Ideas of the public are historically embedded and have strong links with culturally shared senses of self and community. They are situated at the strategic intersection of *practice* and *discourse*."[4] An assessment of both "practice" and "discourse"—that is, modernity criticism and a critique of modernism—is needed for a robust understanding of the impact of secular modernity on contemporary plural societies. Having already considered various aspects of "discourse" (the modernist distortion of freedom, the role of the state, and conditions of public civility), what follows is a critique of the social "practices" of advanced modernity. Specifically, I explore some of the most significant social transformations in modernity that constrain the prospect of public civility among divergent religious communities, especially those of Christianity and Islam.

THE PUBLIC AND PRIVATE SPHERES OF MODERNITY

I begin my exploration of certain major sociological forces that have helped to produce the modern public sphere and a concomitant decline of public life, and which thereby problematized the task of public civility in advanced modern plural society, by outlining several crucial features of the social "life-world"[5] of secular modernity. I then consider several major social transformations that constrain the task of constructing interreligious public civility, namely, (1) the decline of public life; (2) the distortions of the public and private spheres; and (3) the rise of what I call the *professional sphere*. The implications of such transformations have detrimental effects on the forging of public civility in religious plural societies. What is needed, therefore, is a corrective outlook on public life and the public sphere, an outlook that aligns with and requires a recovery of the notion of the human good (see ch. 4).

A BRIEF HISTORY OF THE SPHERES OF LIFE

In the classical world, the public life of the polis consisted in interaction among citizens that took place in the marketplace (agora), in open forum discussions (*lexis*), and in common action (praxis), examples of the latter being both war and athletic competitions. Such was the classical public sphere of liberty, equality, and virtue. By contrast, the private sphere consisted in activities such as slave labor, domestic duties, birth, and death that were associated with the household. Accordingly, it was largely in the public sphere that civility was a necessary and ongoing practice. Moving, however, to the public sphere of early modernity, coffeehouses, salons, and table societies became the main sites of public life, providing spaces in which individuals gathered to discuss political matters.[6]

Arguably, then, in order to understand the decline of public life in advanced modernity, it is important to consider the following: what the modern public sphere is, how it is uniquely modern, and the transformations that the private and public spheres have undergone since early modernity and even antiquity. I shall explore each of these points.

One philosopher helpfully defines *public* as that which is "commonly recognized as of common concern"; accordingly, what constitutes the public sphere are those individuals, institutions, and instruments "by which the society comes together as a body and acts." Put another way, in the public sphere a "shared anticipation" sets the scene for social interaction, and this shared anticipation, especially now in the advanced modern public sphere, includes not only face-to-face interaction but also new media such as mass communication.[7] What makes the public sphere especially modern, then, is this particular dimension of sociality: namely, sociality at a distance and across time.

Interestingly, there are two peculiarly novel features of the modern public sphere. The first, and crucial to its initial emergence, was *print culture*, the newspapers, magazines, political journals, and other print media that gave rise to a collective consciousness because of which public debates became important and possible. The second is the location of these public debates: whereas debates over public affairs in the Greek polis were carried on mostly by the same "free men" in various contexts (academic symposia, public forums, and political assemblies), the modern public is largely extrapolitical. That is, whereas in the Greek polis the persons deliberating in the agora were those who decided in the *ekklesia* (assembly), in the modern public sphere these constituencies are distinct and often disparate. Thus, while the modern public sphere might shape society to form a common public opinion, it does so, technically speaking, outside of the bounds of political power. In short, public discourse became distinct and distanced from political deliberation.

In classical Greece, between the private sphere of the *oikos* and the public sphere of the *ekkclesia* stood the agora. Aristotle describes the location of the agora as being notably below the "common tables of the magistrates" and the "buildings appropriated to religious worship," yet above the sphere of the *oikos.*[8] Arts, crafts, trades, and leisure were practiced in the freeman's agora, thus providing a place for "communication" between the *oikos* and the polis. In this way, the agora maintained a mediatory role between the political and private spheres of life (vertical civility). Since the classical period, however, a shift in sociality has led to a nearly complete disappearance of the agora, a shift arguably brought on by distortions of the public and private spheres—a brief history of which I sketch immediately below.

THE RISE OF THE MODERN PUBLIC SPHERE AND THE DECLINE OF PUBLIC LIFE

In the late Middle Ages there emerged an understanding and use of land according to which estates and manors were under "public," that is, state, authority—an authority that reigned largely unchallenged. As kingship and lordship came to be represented publicly, the public sphere was constituted mainly by political rule and action. So the political state largely subsumed the public space, relegating to the private sphere the activities of "production and reproduction." Over time, even leisure activities such as festivals, dance, and theater that were once publicly accessible began to retreat from public places, moving into the palaces of courtly society.[9] The private sphere, thereby, became the place for biological life and physical survival; the rest of life, while in a sense public, was hidden within the remit of the new political. Accordingly, the terms *public* and *private* came to take on a more modern usage as conceived in terms of geography rather than collectivity, more about literal space than political action. The public sphere was simply that which was visible to the people rather than a body acting in unison to inflect and inform political affairs. Thus was the scene of the English modern public sphere.

A similar though slightly different social history can be traced in France. The early modern *public* was understood initially in terms of the *body politic*, suggesting a strong connection between the public and the political. Soon thereafter, against a backdrop of the ever-increasing Parisian diversity, *le public* came to refer essentially to strangers and acquaintances brought together through urbanization. Indeed, the paradigmatic French cosmopolitan was one who was able to move about "comfortably in diversity," and for whom the "focus of public life [was] the capital city."[10] The so-called public man was the social chameleon. Thus, as in England, the French *le public* became a matter of geography (the capital city) rather than one of political significance.

So, through the course of modernity, social life in the geographic public became largely a matter of performance among strangers—except now such strangers, unlike the civic friends of a polis, remained strangers. Moreover, the modern public individual chose never to express herself, that is, her true self. Indeed, she could not do so, given that she was meant to be a malleable cosmopolitan. Such secret sociality became the principle of modern social interaction. Accordingly, the decline of public civility can be traced both in the distortion of the terms used to describe it and in its attendant social practices.

The sociologist Richard Sennett insightfully summarizes this decline of public life through the course of early to late modernity: while in the private sphere of family and friendships man "*realized* his nature," in the modern public sphere "man *made* himself."[11] That is, in relegating real life to the private sphere, in public man became an actor. This social schizophrenia had developed in response to the unique sociality of modernity: as modern man encountered the demands of civility in the public sphere, he "made" himself into a public personality, and banished his "rights of nature" (i.e., his true self) to the private sphere.

In the following, I trace various social shifts that commenced with the emergence of the modern public sphere, the implications of which constrain and thereby make all the more important the task of public civility. In addition to building on certain key modernity critics, I draw out Sennett's analogy between the changes in the world of performative arts and those in the wider society. Here, I consider (albeit somewhat briefly) four major shifts brought on by modernity that helpfully elucidate and illustrate the origins of the decline of public life: (1) the attire and speech of modernity; (2) the modern world of work; (3) the modern conception of social space; and (4) the shift in modern politics.

Modern public attire and speech. The loss of physical public squares (e.g., the Greek agora, the Roman forum, the Piazza Obliqua) both reflects and reinforces a loss of the hierarchy of social groups that, like the public square, was once physically visible. What has resulted is a modern amalgam of strangers exacerbated by the social anomie inherent to dealing with anonymous individuals. In turn, this anomie created what has been called a "problem of audience" illustratable in the shift of modern attire. Into the early modern period, there was a ready association between one's attire and one's social class, affording others an ease of identification. Indeed, attempts to outdress or outspeak one's social status would amount to a breach of statutory law. By contrast, paradigmatic modern attire can be described as "neutral," "homogenous," "unremarkable." The egalitarianism of modern dress, which reflects the anonymous character of public culture, is reflected back on modern persons in the theatrical world, where the body is treated as a mannequin to be decorated, adorned, literally made up. Whereas in early modernity one might have good assurances of the status of the person with whom one was interacting, steadily this confidence gave way.[12]

Public forms of speech also have shifted as reflected on stage. Whereas once the verbal back-and-forth between actor and audience in opera and theater was common and commonly bold, increasingly this relationship has weakened into a form of passive entertainment. This shift is reflected in the change of the use of language from *sign* to *symbol*. Before the modern turn, words in and of themselves had been used as *signs* by which to make emotive statements; by contrast, as *symbols*, words came to stand for something else such that, both in the public sphere and on the public stage, modern speech and attire became a "cover" placed over the "real individual"—a symbol. In brief, with the decline of direct language and the rise of egalitarian dress, individuals in modernity were able to keep secret their social positions and keep hidden their real selves, thereby diminishing the prospect of "real" public exchange.

The modern world of work. With the onset of the modern market economy, multiple estrangements have taken place, further stultifying a common public life. First, there was what Marx described as the alienation between the laborer and the product of the laborer: by virtue of a machine, humanity was separated from the product of their labor. Second, there emerged a separation between the *use value* and the *exchange value* of goods, a separation that induced a so-called commodity fetishism whereby goods came to be valued strictly for their exchange value rather than for their utility or intrinsic worth. Third, there arose a distancing between producer and consumer, which brought about a kind of silent shopping, a passive participation in the marketplace.[13] For the first time in history, "window-shopping" became possible.

The passivity and silence of the modern public sphere that have resulted can be illustrated in the shops of nineteenth-century Paris. Merchandise was sold increasingly at a fixed price and less on the basis of open pricing, signifying a disappearance of the roles played by trust and negotiation in economic exchange—dimensions that could only be built on reputation and rapport over time. Goods became purchased, not through a process of interaction with the seller, but through a consumer's inner deliberation with herself. Reflected in and partly reinforced by this silent shopping, deeper forms of social interaction were relegated increasingly to the private sphere, ironically making the public sphere a place of passivity and individuality.

This economic estrangement had taken place not only on the consumer side but also in production. MacIntyre observes, "One of the key moments in the creation of modernity occurs when production moves outside the household." Whereas in antiquity and premodernity the goods of the economy (*oikonomia*) were once produced by and for the household (*koinonia*), in modernity the production of goods became the product of externalized labor, resulting in a means-end separation, or what Weber famously called "instrumental rationality."[14] Furthermore, in modernity social activities of various sorts (the arts, the sciences, and games) have moved to the margins of public life such that only a few individuals perform these activities while the majority have become consumers and spectators. Goods and services have become externalized and commoditized, creating further distance among individuals in the public sphere.

Estrangement and externalization are not the only conditions that beset and reflect a shift in the modern world of work. The modern world also suffers a confused gender-based divide between public work and private religion. Owing to a modernist and distorted dichotomy between the allegedly masculine world of public work and supposedly feminine sphere of private nourishment, other sentimental dimensions of life, such as religion, had been domesticated to the private sphere. The main reason for this domestication is that whereas so-called masculine work moved outside the private realm, religion became sentimentalized and thereby privatized such that it lost its public power and relevance.[15] Silenced consumption, capitalized production, and privatized religion have resulted from and in turn reinforced the modern decline of public life.

Modern social space. The decline of public life and the need for constructing public civility can be seen also in the disappearance of a properly public space, as evidenced in the architectural scheme of modern cities. Here a dual paradox emerges. First, there is the paradox of being isolated amidst social visibility, as exemplified in the rarely used spaces of modern "public" grounds, for example, "public" benches found between large "private" buildings. Such visible but asocial spaces no longer, indeed were never meant to, function as a site for interaction. Second, there is the paradox found in modern workplaces: the more open the space (i.e., fewer walls, fewer cubicles), the less sociability there is, for the barriers that would otherwise protect conversations have been removed; conversely, the more the spaces are closed off, the more sociability there is. There has emerged, as Sennett calls is, "a paradox of sociability in hiding."[16]

Other social critics have made a similar point. Members of a given society often share physical spaces such as concert halls, tourist resorts, and shopping malls without actually engaging in social interaction. The modern public sphere is filled with such nonsocial spaces. Similarly, one critic coined the term *non-places*: where in modern society there are certain spaces that lack a sense of social history and significance—spaces such as airports, motorways, and hotel rooms—"never before in [history] . . . have non-places occupied so much space."[17] Truly shared public space, like modern public life, has become increasingly less available, further constraining the construction of a common public life.

The scene of modern politics. Finally, the emerging scene of modern politics again reflects and reinforces the decline of public life. Private citizens, who increasingly began to rely on politicians to do their job, largely have vacated the modern public sphere, leaving public discourse to the professionals. Sennett illustrates this point in the following way. The advanced modern political scene comprises two types of individuals: "actors," who, having skillfully crafted a public personality, become "skilled performers" (i.e., political professionals); and spectators, who are more comfortable watching someone else's public expression than being active participants in public discourse themselves, merely observing and readily obeying the actors' every move. On stage as on the political platform, the increasingly minimal interaction between performer and audience creates a cast of "public performers," on the one hand, and a host of passive participants, silent spectators, visible voyeurs, on the other. Accordingly, when considering a politician's credentials, what matters is not his credibility or his character but the performance of his personality. For this reason, like the stage performer, the politician is better off moving attention away from the text—specific public policies—and onto himself—his rhetoric and charisma. For, so far as citizens are "moved by him," he has paved the way to do largely as he pleases.[18]

This shift in politics is consistent with the experience of the "public" commoner, that is, the private citizen. The "silence" found in public was particularly conspicuous in the everyday meeting places of pubs, taverns, and cafés where individuals are found "massed together, relaxing, drinking, reading," yet "divided by invisible walls." Ironically, a modern individual would actually leave the private house (the home) to find social shelter in public houses (pubs).[19] Though silent with respect to social interaction, the modern individual found comfort in what we might describe as public privacy. Thus, the modern public sphere became the metaphorical and geographic space of observation, not interaction. Accordingly, as is increasingly apparent, now every modern form of life has its own legitimacy; every person is meant to be left alone and perhaps watched. Hence and very importantly, the modern private individual begins to live in a geographically public space without engaging in the ideological public sphere.

The decline of public life in modernity has resulted from and reinforced the social realities of the egalitarianization of speech and dress; the externalization of labor, arts, academics, and athletics; the emergence of asocial space and "non-places"; and the creation of public personalities and the attendant loss of a veritable politics in the public sphere. In other words, the individualizing ethos that attends religious privatization resulted from and reinforced in many ways certain fundamental shifts in speech, dress, work, use and perception of space, sociality, and politics. The rise of a silent, secular public sphere and the concomitant decline of public life should be, then, unsurprising.

Adam Ferguson noted nearly two centuries ago, "To the ancient Greek . . . the individual was nothing, and the public every thing. To the modern . . . the individual is every thing, and the public nothing."[20] The decline of public life, giving way to pursuits of individualized life plans, has resulted in a loss of social solidarity and public civility. Exacerbating this decline is what I call the *mutual colonization* of the public and private spheres, a discussion to which I now turn.

MODERNITY'S MUTUAL COLONIZATION

As described above, in the classical world there were particular functions deemed proper to different spheres of life. To the private *oikos* belonged economic production and biological reproduction; to the polis belonged deliberations and decisions about the city-state; and to the public sphere of the agora belonged *lexis* and praxis. A good citizen would find himself engaged, indirectly at least, in all spheres of life. By contrast, in modernity, with the public having been subsumed almost entirely by the political, there has resulted a colonization of the public by the private and a colonization of the private by the public. In what follows, I describe this mutual colonization and consider its impact on the prospect of constructing civility, as evidenced in the following phenomena: the rise of *ordinary life*, the spread of individualized freedom, and the birth of the professional sphere. Before turning to these evidences, allow me to explain further precisely what I mean by modernity's mutual colonization and spell out its drastic consequences.

The colonization of the public by the private[21] takes place where private issues are made public—a phenomenon illustrated particularly well in both the increasing loss of moral language and the performative impossibility of verbal offense. I describe below some of the causes and effects of this colonization, and consider implications for the task of public civility. I then analyze the converse, where the private is colonized by the public.

Individuals in modern society have come to share in public their most intimate emotions and actions, thereby making private matters "public" issues. For in modernity there has been a peculiar reversal whereby the private sphere—once characterized by an appropriate sort of secrecy—now claims a "right to publicity." The public sphere has become an arena for airing private matters, and when mass media give their "stamp of public acceptability" to such matters, they move into public consciousness. As the social critic Michael Sandel puts it, no longer does modern public discourse involve "a political agenda that addresses the moral dimension of public questions"; rather, public discussion has become dominated by "the scandalous, the sensational, and the confessional," as seen in talk shows and other media.[22] In these ways, the private colonizes the public.

The first way this colonization can be seen is in a shift in language. This shift can be illustrated by considering the word *seduction*, which has been replaced by the modern word *affair*, a replacement by which sexual relations have come to be construed in radically individualistic terms ("he had an affair") rather than social ones ("he seduced her").[23]

Whereas parents once were considered complicit in the act of rearing a would-be adulterer, the act now is redefined as strictly between two consenting adult selves. An "affair" is merely an act "among freer spirits," whereas "seduction" had to do with immoral social behavior. This example is illustrative of the modern social reality whereby private affairs distort public understanding and thereby deconstruct a collective moral language with individualized iterations. In this way, a framework of interreligious public civility, which the moral dimensions of religious traditions require, is largely undermined.

The colonization of the public by the private may be illustrated in a second particularly telling way: the loss of the possibility of giving offense. At first blush this loss may appear conducive rather than counterproductive to the project of constructing public civility, since offense seems antithetical to civility. But it bears repeating that public civility is not merely about personal etiquette or even social equanimity: public civility is about deep, honest, moral engagement among members of divergent communities whose affirmations, attitudes, and actions may offend (even if only initially) those with whom there is deep disagreement. Thus, giving and taking offense is entirely possible, somewhat expected, when seeking to construct public civility—but not so in a public sphere colonized by the private, for in this sort of sphere there simply is no shared framework of meaning and morality. Thus, within the colonized public sphere, ironically insult loses its power to offend because modernist understandings of morality and meaning differ so drastically from one individual to another.

There is a second reason insult no longer offends: personality has replaced character. Owing to this replacement, the stranger, who would encounter only the personality of another, could never truly offend, or in turn be offended by, the other's real self, that is, character. This social and psychological distance keeps the self safely away from the other, and makes the self unable to give or take verbal attacks, since such attacks cannot hit an invisible target. Ironically, the private self emerged onto the public scene only to diminish the possibility of a common public life.

These two social realities—the demise of moral language and the impossibility of giving offense—reflect and reinforce a secularization of the public sphere that in turn has resulted in part from the colonization of the public by the private. In brief, in advanced modern society, a loss of deep moral engagement—a necessary condition of public civility—stultifies its construction.

Going further, there is not only the colonization of the public by the private but also the colonization of the private by the public—an incisive analysis of which is found in Philippe Ariès's groundbreaking work, *Centuries of Childhood.* Ariès notes that prior to the emergence of the coffeehouses and public houses of the modern era it was the "big house" (the home) that was the site for nearly all of the activities of life, from business transactions to friendships. Functionally, there were "no frontiers between professional and private life," so, for example, "a lawyer's clients were also his friends and both were his debtors." Nearly all of life was lived under one roof: family members, including household servants, would eat, sleep, dance, work, and receive visitors in the same room—a "perpetual community of life."[24]

Gradually, however, the private sphere became distorted in two distinct ways. First, within the modern house individual rooms, now separated by corridors, allowed members of the household to enter and exit the house without ever having to encounter one another. Over time, the patterns of sociality within the private household mimicked those of the public sphere. Second, the public sphere came to dominate the private matters of the household. There emerged what Hannah Arendt called a "nation-wide administration of housekeeping" whereby the state overtook much of the affairs that once belonged to the private realm (as further discussed in the previous chapter). Most notably, the public school and the market economy overtook the functions of home education and domestic economic exchange. Indeed, as Arendt points out, the modern notion of a *political economy* would have been in the classical world "a contradiction in terms."[25] Thus, removed from the modern private sphere (*koinonia*), in contrast to the classical world, is economic production (*oikonomia*). Moreover, robust social interaction, which once belonged to the agora, has been relocated to so-called public houses that were (metaphorically) constructed by invisible social walls. The family, thereby, became constricted to purely "personal" roles, such as childbearing and child rearing. The resultant situation is a colonization of the private by the public, thus completing modernity's mutual colonization.

REVERSAL, INVERSION, AND CREATION

The distortions of the public and private spheres can be seen in areas other than their mutual colonization; namely and importantly in (1) the rise of ordinary life; (2) the spread of an individualized, so-called freedom; and (3) the birth of the professional sphere. These phenomena I refer to respectively as modernity's *reversal*, *inversion*, and *creation*, the causes and implications of which I unpack immediately below.

The rise of ordinary life. The dearth of public life and the near-death of community life, which afflict the modern world, are largely a historical anomaly. A way of understanding this anomalous modern condition may be seen in what Charles Taylor famously calls "the affirmation of ordinary life." Commenting on the social infrastructure of classical Athenian life, Taylor observes a separation between *ordinary life* and *the good life* whereby the former consisted essentially in production and reproduction and the latter in contemplation and political participation. In modernity, however, this distinction has collapsed into a singular "affirmation of the ordinary life," reducing nearly all of life to the mere "making of things needed for life."[26]

Similarly, Arendt observes that there has emerged an unprecedented reversal between the contemplative life (*vita contemplativa*) and the active life (*vita activa*) whereby production and pragmatism (the active life) is prioritized over theoretical contemplation (the contemplative life). Such is a direct reversal of much of earlier history according to which the life of reflection and pondering were prized as worthier and more ideal. Accordingly, a shift has occurred from asking "what" and "why" questions to questions of "'how' [something] came into being" and, now most important, whether it works. In other words, the modern scientific outlook—unconcerned with ethics, aesthetics, and metaphysics—cares not about "belief in objective values"; values do not exist where there are only "motions of material objects."[27] Put simply, modernity favors pragmatics over metaphysics.

The problem multiplies on the level of individuals and turns back on society. In his highly regarded work *Sources of the Self*, Taylor concludes almost prophetically, "Productivity and creativity [have become] the highest ideals and even the idols of the modern age." Why so? Scientific and economic progress, rather than political participation, have become the hallmarks of a successful ordinary life. Accordingly, modern secular society has come to consist largely in an aggregate of "self-fulfillers" whereby individuals' attempts to connect to the political community have become a largely incoherent enterprise: for in a world that prizes the active life over contemplation, the only "officially endorsed norms" are those of "utility." Ironically, the upshot of modern sociality is that "nothing would count as fulfillment in a world in which literally nothing was important but self-fulfillment."[28] And yet self-fulfillment is all that is left.

Even more ironically if tragically, without an objective ontology of the human person and an articulation thereof, there could be no such "fulfillment," let alone communal flourishing and public civility. The idea of fulfillment is coherent only in the context of some good or end (telos) according to which a human person could be said to be fulfilled. As discussed previously, human flourishing is logically dependent on there being an objective human ontology.

In sum, secular modern sociality may be understood as disparate pursuits of substantively divergent forms of life, pursuits based on instrumental rationality. Modern collective life is marked by individual and group identities rather than common interests communicated and negotiated within a given society. In Zygmunt Bauman's words, modern sociality is reduced to the "strategic precept of adult normality": namely, "do not talk to strangers."[29] Secular modernity has made both the good life of a common politics and the construction of public civility performatively nearly impossible. This near-impossibility can be seen further in the lived experience of modern individuals who strive for and possess a particular kind of "freedom."

The spread of "individualized freedom." Bauman has famously described modernity as *liquid*—that is, as being composed of "freely choosing individuals" who themselves are an "infinite collection of possibilities." Tragically, such a world marked by so-called freedom is less secure and thereby less genuinely free than it may seem. For with modernity's "end of totalities"—totalities that once gave an overarching meaning to human life and society—human identity has transmuted from a "given" to a "task" whereby individuals define all things by and for themselves.[30]

In contrast, the premodern public sphere was "the world of the common"—a world lived outside of the private sphere of " 'one's own' (*idion*)." Accordingly, public life was by definition the only one that was not, literally speaking, idiotic. Thus, lost in the modern world is a sense of the pejorative, "privative" quality of privacy— "of being deprived of something"—a tag understood in the classical world.[31] Consequently, the modern individual, in enjoying her private life, fails to recognize the *deprivation* she suffers as she relishes in her modern individualism. One can see how modern, individual, private life, now lived in the visible but not collective public realm, has been deprived of true civic freedom. Individualized freedom is no true freedom.

Going further, modern individuals qua consumers of goods and life plans are faced with myriad options. In this world, such "free" individuals in principle cannot err, for autonomous choice admits of no right or wrong. Ironically, however, neither can they choose with confidence since they remain in constant uncertainty about the options foregone and thereby gone forever. As one historian writes, since the modern self is wholly "indeterminate," it follows that "any self is possible"; yet, contrary to appearances, this phenomenon is not liberating since "the process of self-creation is never finished."[32] A modernist understanding of human identity, in other words, extinguishes any end at which human life can be aimed.

Thus, the unbounded, individualized freedom found in modern sociality suffers a peculiar uncertainty on account of its being detached from a conception of a universal human good. Insofar as there is no objective way of being human, there is no objective standard by which to measure the success or norms of human sociality. The end ought to clarify the means; yet without an objective human good acknowledged or articulated, the prospect of a flourishing human sociality, let alone the construction of public civility, is undermined. Ironically, the spread of individualized freedom came at the expense of security and liberty for society as a whole. So there remains in the advanced modern world "freedom" without a republic, "society" without community, "fulfillment" without flourishing, "publicity" without civility. And much of this state of affairs is owed to there being a human without a good.

In a powerful irony, modern individual freedom is exactly opposed to classical liberty: in the ancient polis only those who had secured the fortunes for cosmic and civic contemplation were considered free, whereas in modern society it is all those who have liberated themselves from the shackles of politics and piety that are alleged to be free. A more promising way forward would be to garner the fruits of Enlightenment political theory (equality for all) while also grounding the human person in the roots of ancient teleology (a nature-bound freedom).

In sum, the affirmation of modern *ordinary life*, along with the spread of individualized freedom, greatly challenges the task of public civility in the secular public sphere. Before turning to various responses to this challenge (responses that I find ultimately inadequate), I consider a final way in which the modern distortions of the public and private spheres constrain the task of public civility: namely, through the creation of what I call the modern professional sphere.

The birth of the professional sphere. A fragmentary sociality, resulting from the forces of modernity as described above, has brought about a chasm between the private sphere of meaningfulness and the public sphere of strangeness. In this chasm has emerged what I call the modern professional sphere, which can be characterized as *the ideological and geographic space wherein individuals are expected to adhere to often unspoken yet powerful codes of conduct which, in globalized modernity, tend to encourage a conformity to an allegedly neutral, secular existence.*

The ethos and logic of this secular conformity can be illustrated by a number of recent legal rulings. In the 2010 case *Eweida v. British Airways*, the English Court of Appeals decided against a Christian woman who at her workplace wore a necklace with a crucifix on the grounds that such was not a requirement of her faith tradition and that the policy set up by the employing company (British Airways) prohibited public expressions of religion. Similarly, since 2004 French courts have made it illegal for public school students to wear "any clothing that clearly indicated [their] religious affiliation." Rulings like these illustrate the ways in which the professionalized nature of modern public life disinvites religious expression and thereby encourages conformity to an alleged neutrality of modern public conduct. This alleged neutrality of the secular professional sphere not only enforces a detachment of personal beliefs and expressions from public life but also mandates actions incompatible with such beliefs. For instance, in 2006 the Boston Catholic Charities in the United States were ordered by a court to provide adoption services to homosexual couples, a practice prohibited by ecclesiastical injunction.[33] As a result, the charity had planned to file a lawsuit against the State of Massachusetts, only deciding later to relinquish the right to provide this service *tout court*.

The modern professional sphere is neither purely private nor strictly public. On the one hand, one's personal (typically religious) beliefs are excluded from the professional sphere precisely because they are considered to be private. On the other hand, the professional sphere does not rise to the level of a legitimate public sphere since its affairs are not exactly political in that, though they affect the collective, they lay strictly speaking outside of political power (e.g., in employment services, educational environments, nongovernmental organizations). Members of this precarious professional sphere, having to adhere to codes and conduct suitable for denuded personalities, are expected to conform to a religiously neutral and secularized existence.

There are, however, counter-instances of the secularization of the professional sphere. For example, the Grand Chamber of the European Court of Human Rights reversed a decision of one of its lower courts in *Lautsi v. Italy*, allowing the display of religious symbols (the crucifix in this case) in public school classrooms. Also, there are countries (e.g., Afghanistan, Palestine, Saudi Arabia) wherein wearing and displaying religious garb and symbols in public space is not only allowed, but legally mandated.[34] In considering these situations, however, one must keep in mind the following: (1) these counter-instances show just how contested the issue is; and (2) countries such as those named above tend to exhibit a more general, thoroughgoing counter-secularization and thereby would fall outside the ambit of liberal democratic societies, in the context of which this exploration of public civility is being considered.

In sum, the social conformity of the professional sphere in secular modernity largely sets the standards of acceptability for modern public life. Thus, modern secular society, in lacking both a transcendent moral order and an objective human teleology, is left without a common vision of natural, social, and human reality. Accordingly, secular modernity, by distorting the public sphere, gives way to a professional sphere premised on alleged neutrality, which in turn induces enclaves of estrangement that lack the resources needed for public civility. Thus, in advanced modernity a shared vision for a common life is largely destroyed, producing a safe if sterile secularized professional sphere. Unless and until a vision of *the human good* is recovered, the task of public civility remains an illusory pursuit.

The three major shifts of secular modernity discussed above—the decline of public life, the distortions of the private and public spheres, and the rise of the professional sphere—bear negatively on the prospect of public civility. Modern society has been compartmentalized largely into a purely private sphere, a depoliticized public sphere, and a secularized professional sphere. One way in which a robust common public life in advanced modernity may be constructed, however, is paradoxically through the very plurality found in modern society. A final insight from Sennett may help to explain this paradox.

Until the modern period, the private sphere was a site where individuals could "check the public" by limiting its reach into their "natural rights." Conversely, the public sphere served as "a corrective to the private realm [where] natural man was an animal [prone to] incivility." For this reason, there is, as Sennett puts it, a need to destroy the "city of ghettoes" such that people would live in "the larger world," a world wherein there exists the necessary and beneficial "jolts" of "face-to-face relationships." In other words, in advanced modernity a common public life and the construction of public civility are most likely to occur paradoxically in a context of robust interaction amidst religious and cultural plurality.[35]

Put differently, in modernizing and globalizing societies the prospect of constructing public civility depends on there being, not a uniform way of life as demanded by the professional sphere, but the presence of and a continual engagement among divergent communities. As one expert on civility writes, the virtue of civility necessarily involves "the collaboration of persons of diverse and often inimical dispositions."[36] I would add that public civility requires that such diversity be not only respected but also resourced; I seek precisely this task of resourcing Catholic and Islamic political theologies in grounding political pluralism and public civility.

Other responses to this fragmented, uncivil public sphere have come from various ideological standpoints: some religious, others secularist. Before turning to such responses given in Catholic and Islamic political theologies (chs. 5–7), in the next chapter I examine the frameworks of multiculturalism and legal pluralism as attempts to ground public civility and lay out the case for my notion of the human good, which I argue must serve as the basis for any viable framework of public civility in plural societies.

CHAPTER 4

A CASE FOR THE HUMAN GOOD

Having considered the tragic decline of public life through the course of modernity, in this chapter I consider two distinct but related attempts at framing a common public life, attempts offered as responses to the deep social fragmentation of the advanced modern world: namely, multiculturalism and legal pluralism. I argue that, given their purportedly nonmoral and thereby morally relativistic character, such frameworks, while useful in some respects, are ultimately inadequate to ground public civility in religiously divided societies.

I then outline my case for the human good, explicating its import and implications, contrasting it with similar terms, and qualifying the concept where necessary. I argue that what is needed beyond multiculturalism and legal pluralism is a more universal basis for constructing a framework, a basis found in the human good. I begin by taking each of the secularist frameworks—multiculturalism and legal pluralism—in turn, beginning with the former.

THE PROSPECT OF MULTICULTURALISM

Increasingly, as one Muslim scholar observes, in various plural societies of which Muslim communities are a substantial part, Muslim citizens are situating themselves in "ethnicized enclaves of parallel societies," which "carry great potential for conflict."[1] My objective here is to evaluate various theories of multiculturalism as prospective models for constructing public civility, especially in multireligious societies. At bottom, I argue that we must seek a framework other than those assumed by these secularist approaches in order to construct a robust public civility.

I begin with the prominent multiculturalist Bhikhu Parekh, who writes, "Almost all societies today are multicultural and likely to remain so for the foreseeable future." Given that in these societies there must be provision simultaneously for cultural difference and social equality, Parekh commends his framework of multiculturalism, which is neither "a political doctrine with a programmatic content [nor] a philosophical theory of man." Rather, his framework represents but "a perspective on human life."[2]

Parekh characterizes his framework as a set of beliefs and practices by which members of a multicultural society could "understand themselves and the world" and also "organize their individual and collective lives." Under his multicultural perspective, no "ideology can represent the full truth of human life." This perspective, he explains, is "dialogically constituted" and presumes certain "preconditions" such as "basic ethical norms, participatory public spaces, equal rights." Most fundamentally, multiculturalism "privileges no particular cultural perspective"—or so Parekh argues. Recognizing that multicultural societies often fail to secure "enthusiastic commitment" to the political community, Parekh's framework engenders a "vibrant cultural life" as well as "social solidarity." It would conduce a society that is "not static and ghettoized, but interactive and dynamic"—one that presupposes "a robust form of social, economic, and political democracy" underpinning it. These are the main features of Parekh's multiculturalism.

To be sure, the conditions and aims of Parekh's multiculturalism seem generally uncontroversial so far as they go. Important questions arise, however. On what basis might such a society become "interactive and dynamic" rather than "static and ghettoized," let alone conflictual? In virtue of what feature(s) of the culturally divergent communities would "social solidarity" emerge? If "no particular cultural perspective" is to be privileged, could there be any universal morality to ground the so-called basic ethical norms? Could there be, in other words, a secularist framework of public civility?

The social and political theorist Will Kymlicka proposes another model of multiculturalism. Kymlicka insightfully points out that, contrary to John Rawls's suggestion, political liberalism—which supposedly proposes "state neutrality"—itself privileges a particular "cultural perspective," namely, political liberalism. Such a position is ultimately incoherent, since liberal states inevitably make particular judgments on various cultural issues (e.g., languages spoken, holidays sanctioned). In doing so, the so-called "liberal [state] unavoidably promotes certain cultural identities, and thereby disadvantages others." Accordingly, Kymlicka suggests rightly that it is imperative that "ethnocultural groups" be protected against majoritarian hegemony—and that his model of multiculturalism provides such protective resources.[3]

A third prominent multiculturalist, Tariq Modood, expanding Kymlicka's argument about cultural minority rights, seeks to include the rights of specifically religious minorities. Modood points to the overlap between the domains of religion, culture, and states, noting that cultures typically are centered on religion and that states are often multireligious.[4] Consequently, Modood argues—and I believe convincingly—that there is no reason not to extend Kymlicka's justification of cultural group rights to religious communities and that to the extent that it does not it is an unjust framework. So if Kymlicka's multiculturalism suffers an antireligious bias, does Modood provide a workable solution?

For Modood, multiculturalism is essentially about the social activity of negotiating differences among divergent expressions of "groupness," a negotiation whose goal is the "remaking of public identities" on the basis of certain rules of social engagement. Central to the aim of such rules is the creation of a polity that is not only liberal but also "pluralist and multilogical"—a polity that would mitigate the dangers of ideological conformism. This multicultural requirement of plurality and multivocality would serve two vital functions. First, it would offer minority groups, Modood argues, an emotional connection with society that would "counterbalance" the strong loyalties often found in such groups and thereby prevent "narrow, selfish communalisms." Simultaneously, the presence of communal identities would serve as "an effective check against monocultural statism." Put briefly, Modood's model of multiculturalism seeks to offset both ethnic-religious communalisms and monological statism. Thus, allegedly, in ways the Enlightenment liberal nation-state could not do, the multicultural "plural state" would stave off the equal and opposite dangers of religious radicalization and secularist statism.[5]

The literature on multiculturalism has provided important theoretical contributions to the task of constructing just and flourishing plural societies in advanced modernity. However, I contend that these leading theories of multiculturalism are fundamentally inadequate to the further task of constructing public civility. Below I offer four reasons why.

THE PROBLEMS OF MULTICULTURALISM

The first fundamental flaw in Parekh's and Modood's models of multiculturalism is that while they offer frameworks that are allegedly noncomprehensive and nonmoral, they in fact are not. Parekh writes, "From the multicultural perspective the good society does not commit itself to a particular political doctrine or vision of the good life," for "no political doctrine or ideology can represent the full truth of human life." Likewise, Modood claims to offer a "non-totalistic" multiculturalist perspective. The problem here is twofold. First, the frameworks put forth are ineluctably totalistic insofar as they seek to discard any and all "ethical and philosophical underpinnings" (see Modood): that is, any de jure nonethical or nonphilosophical framework is itself de facto ethically and philosophically totalistic. Second, in seeking to avoid what Modood calls "moral evaluation," such frameworks end up making evaluations that are necessarily moral in form if not also in function. Thus, on pain of self-referential incoherence, such proposals of multiculturalism are (at best) misinformed.[6]

A second and related problem is that any moral dimension of social analysis, which putatively is excluded from these frameworks, is precisely what is needed for a more philosophically tenable and practicable framework of public civility. That is, whereas Modood contends that "recognition and respect of identities and beliefs" are possible without "moral evaluation" of them, I would argue that the soundness of this contention would depend on the kind of identities and beliefs in question. For surely there are morally repugnant identities (e.g., that of violent religious fundamentalists) and reprehensible beliefs (e.g., racism) that should be neither respected nor recognized in any society, no matter how multicultural. Yet only a distinctly moral dimension of social analysis—the "moral evaluation" that Modood seeks to deny—provides the conceptual resources needed to make his case.

A third problem with multiculturalism is its "identitarian" bent. If, as Modood complains, liberalism dismisses group identities for the sake of the alleged full "legal equality of citizens," then Modood's multiculturalism involves the opposite danger of promoting an "identitarian politics" that it purports to deny. That is, by arguing that groupness is "sociologically real," Modood ends up essentializing group identities; but in doing so, he commits the very error he seeks to avoid: namely, an identitarian politics. Oddly and at the same time, Modood also suggests that identities are "hybridic and fluid," that "groupness" is but another "human product." But if this is so, then Modood's multiculturalism would lack the resources needed to ground the universal social solidarity that it seeks to promote: that is, without an objective set of moral values, one's social solidarity, put bluntly, is another's totalitarianism.[7] Therefore, multiculturalism's identitarianism keeps it from its goal of preventing an identity politics.

My fourth and final objection to the project of multiculturalism has to do with its inherent relativism about moral values. For this point I draw on Charles Taylor's (justifiably) widely cited essay on multiculturalism, "The Politics of Recognition."[8] Taylor argues that central to multiculturalism is a *politics of recognition*. That is, with the decline of traditional hierarchical society, what has come to matter in sociality is an inner "authenticity" in virtue of which an individual comes to forge her unique identity to be respected and recognized by all. Ineluctably, a *politics of difference* has come to dominate the scene of multicultural democratic societies, a politics that demands the recognition of the uniquenesses of this individual or that group. Simultaneously if ironically, a *politics of dignity*, a theme exploited by multiculturalists, also began to emerge, promoting the idea that all cultures are of equal moral worth. Multiculturalists seem to have the best of two worlds: difference and equality.

However, in pointing out the flaws of the so-called politics of dignity, Taylor argues that it makes "no more sense to demand" that a given culture be judged as "great" or "equal" than it does to demand that the earth be judged as "round or flat." For a judgment about the moral worth of a culture entails making a judgment about a fact, namely, a fact about its moral status. Thus, to condone genocide is to make a moral and factual judgment about the status of genocide. Conversely, to condemn certain morally impermissible cultural practices is indeed justified. In sum, the politics of difference that multiculturalists celebrate taken with the politics of dignity that multiculturalists misapply undermines the politics of recognition that multiculturalists most fundamentally seek. So the combination of difference and dignity is as vacuous as it is powerful: for if a politics of dignity demands universal respect, a politics of difference ensures it cannot be given. Hence, the relativistic roots of multiculturalism have borne its fruits.

To summarize, I agree along with multiculturalists that human persons are born into and live in communities that consist of, among other things, their religious and other cultural identities. However, I find the multiculturalist project wanting both in its tendency toward identitarian politics, which leads to a fragmentary sociality, and in its lack of a moral dimension of social analysis, which does not obtain under strictly secularist frameworks. In order to construct a framework of public civility what is needed is a universal and morally objective basis that is found in the notion of *the human good*—the essential attributes of which are shared by every member of any given human community.

In the next section, I consider the prospect of a different but related basis on which some scholars have sought to construct a framework of public civility: legal pluralism. I argue that insofar as legal pluralism entails some kind of multiculturalism, and to this extent and in other respects, legal pluralism too is an untenable framework for grounding public civility.

THE PROSPECT OF LEGAL PLURALISM

The legal structures of many liberal democratic societies make it possible for various minority cultural and religious practices to be given exemptions on the basis of the doctrine of *reasonable accommodation*. Indeed, the models of multiculturalism considered above logically entail some form of legal pluralism since the overarching aim of multiculturalism is to privilege "no particular cultural perspective." I consider below the prospects of legal pluralism and its implications for constructing public civility. I begin by evaluating the merits of the doctrine of reasonable accommodation, then offer a critique of it, and conclude by suggesting a more promising basis for public civility in societies composed of multiple legal schemes.

In his now-classic "What Is Legal Pluralism?" John Griffiths has argued that a theory of legal pluralism rests on the fact that "within any given field, law of various provenances may be operative" and that "legal pluralism is a concomitant" of the now-predominant modern condition, namely, "social pluralism."[9] Other legal scholars, such as Brian Tamanaha, however, argue against legal pluralism, contending that it cannot in principle "locate an agreed definition of 'law,'" since a logical implication of legal pluralism is that necessarily *any* "proffered definition of law" would count as "legitimate."[10] Building on Tamanaha's critique and engaging heavily with Jeremy Waldron's seminal "One Law for All?," I argue below that for the task of constructing public civility, since law reflects a society's moral values, having a legal system that is largely singular in character would be more beneficial than legal pluralism; and that, contra Griffiths, legal pluralism is not a "concomitant" of social pluralism but arguably a detriment to it.

LEGAL PLURALISM OR ONE LAW FOR ALL?

Waldron carefully considers the question of whether a one-law-for-all model is just and operable under the constraints of plural modern societies,[11] that is, whether plural liberal democratic societies require a kind of legal structure characterized by a thoroughgoing and singular rule of law.

Waldron writes, "Our belief in the rule of law commits us to the principle that the law should be the same for everyone: one law for all and no exceptions." For "it would be quite repugnant if there were one law for the rich and another for the poor, one law for black[s] . . . and another for whites." Yet for societies composed of multiple cultures and a diversity of religions, could, or better yet should, there be one law for all?

A common counterproposal to a one-law-for-all approach is *individualized justice*. Under this model, the law is to take into account the specially cultural or religious significance that a given act has for an individual actor and/or those to whom the actor is related in her act, for example, a Sikh carrying a *kirpan*, a priest distributing wine (to underage individuals) in a religious ceremony, and the like. The problem with this counterproposal, Waldron suggests, is that while cultural or religious exemptions tend to promote cultural diversity, they also tend to throw up deeply difficult questions about the limits of such exemptions: "[Are we to] treasure the fact that in our multicultural society there are many responses to spousal adultery, not just one? Some people get upset and go to marriage counseling or ask for a divorce. Others drown their children. Others still set fire to the offending spouse or bludgeon her to death. Do we really want to say that all of this is part of a rich mosaic of diversity . . . ? [And] that our multicultural society would be the poorer if some of these more diverse responses were eliminated?" Clearly not; so, then, what makes one case and not another fall under the remit of "reasonable accommodation"?

The sociologist Grace Davie asks these pertinent and penetrating questions and gestures toward an answer: "Why is it that modern Western societies embrace some aspects of pluralism but not others? Why are we so ready to welcome the [others'] culture, cuisine and artefacts . . . , regarding these as enriching, but we are not ready to welcome their legal systems? Why, in other words, are some aspects of multiculturalism considered more positive than others?"[12] I suggest the reason that legal pluralism is considered generally less acceptable than other forms of pluralism (e.g., social, cultural, culinary) is that it ranges over some of the most fundamental questions that concern human existence, namely, moral questions. While a particular ethnic cuisine may be a welcomed novelty, a pluralistic legal structure would reflect a relativity of moral values.[13] Legal systems, therefore, which reflect (however well or poorly) the moral values of society, matter greatly and gravely to its members. But the problem remains: in plural democratic societies, there are multiple and incompatible moral norms found among divergent communities, so what, if anything, can or should be done?

In his opposition to legal pluralism, Waldron argues also against the libertarian view, according to which any given civil liberty may potentially trump any other—a view found notably in the legal theorists Brian Barry and Ronald Dworkin. As Waldron writes, "There might be something particularly significant about *cultural* resistance [to state law]"—and Waldron includes religious resistance here. The reason for its peculiarity, and thereby its proposed legal exemption, is that there are within a given culture or religion certain "positive regulations" that occasionally depart from state law.[14] There are, in other words, civil liberties within a cultural or religious group that arguably ought to weigh more than generic civil liberties. What Waldron suggests seems right: the right to religious freedom, for example, does and ought to carry more existential weight than civil liberties such as Dworkin's "right" to pornography.[15]

So while there are reasons to maintain largely a one-law-for-all approach, there is also some motivation to invoke simultaneously the legal procedure of cultural accommodation for certain cultural or religious groups. The justification for such exemptions derives from a conviction that a given state law may have a unique kind of impact on one's life, an impact not had on the lives of others. That is, since adherence to a religious tradition typically entails commitment to a particular way of life that is consonant with its respective legal scheme, and given the existential weight that such a scheme places on its adherents, occasional exemptions from state law may be warranted for such religionists. What distinguishes such exemptions from those claimed as a matter of conscience (a la Dworkin) is that those individuals who claim the latter are not under burdens comparable to those faced by religious adherents. Construed within these parameters, then, the doctrine of reasonable accommodation might be seen to escape the relativism of legal pluralism while maintaining the equality of minority groups.

PROBLEMS WITH LEGAL PLURALISM

In most constitutional democratic societies there remains predominantly one law. Indeed, there are many cases in which a particular cultural regulatory scheme is not and should not be given exemption. For example, in the U.S. case *People v. Dong Lu Chen*,[16] Chen was accused of murdering his wife for having had an adulterous relationship. A defense was mounted based on the defendant's cultural background, according to which such a reaction to infidelity is acceptable. The court decided in favor of Chen, maintaining that traditional Chinese values drove him to such violence, and gave him the lightest possible sentence for homicide according to New York state law. Here is a case in which the procedure of cultural accommodation was abused, underscoring the need for a one-law-for-all approach to legal structures within plural societies.

It should be noted that a one-law-for-all approach does not necessarily entail the idea that any one piece of legislation must be determined in exactly one way or other, and by some particular moral fact about the matter. Rather, there is room, indeed need, for the virtue of "juridical prudence,"[17] which at times may require legal flexibility over strict uniformity, for example, in cases of traffic laws and similar statutory matters. Rather, the overall point being made is that with regard to the construction of public civility a predominantly one-law-for-all approach is more promising than legal pluralism, for the latter reflects and reinforces not only a relativized moral ecology but also a moral relativity about legal schemes.

For these reasons, while the practice of reasonable accommodation may be useful and at points necessary in adjudicating contentious matters in plural democratic societies, a thoroughgoing legal pluralism would derail the construction of public civility. What, then, is the way forward? In the ensuing paragraphs, I briefly outline Waldron's way, then conclude with a comment on the need for a nonrelativistic basis for grounding public civility, a basis that Waldron's proposal seems to lack and that I argue can be found in the human good.

For Waldron, crucial to achieving a one-law-for-all approach is robust, continuous social engagement wherein "members of society must *talk to one another* [to] evaluate [a given] proposal," doing their best to "understand what may seem . . . like incommensurable as well as incompatible points of view."[18] That is, in a plural society the effort to create an environment in which law reflects morality involves an ongoing public conversation over contentious matters, a conversation that must be both critical and charitable in order to be effective.

One must wonder, however, whether the doctrine of reasonable accommodation, even if undergirded by such robust, charitable, continuous public deliberation, would suffice as a framework of public civility. Will such "inter-cultural deliberation" succeed in overcoming "cultural [in]comprehensibility" when deciding the legitimacy of legal exemptions? Arguing elsewhere and more recently, Waldron again suggests that judging the reasonableness of the accommodations "is a matter for the people of the broader society (citizens, legislators, judges, etc.)" finally to decide. Such individuals must "make that decision the best way they can, using whatever criteria of justice seem true or right to them."[19]

But surely an approach of "whatever criteria of justice" seem right to a particular society at a given time opens the way for social and moral catastrophes, ones such as have marred the darker side of human history. Rather, there must be found some fixed basis on which to determine what is just for a given matter, a basis that does not fall prey to a relativism that is subject to the flow of time and flux of social preferences. And, of course, the problem with relativism is stated well and famously by W. V. O. Quine: "[The relativist] cannot proclaim . . . relativism without rising above it, and he cannot rise above it without giving it up."[20] In other words, relativism is self-referentially incoherent at best and self-defeating at worst. Rather, a nonrelativistic basis of intercultural deliberation can be found in the notion of the human good, an explication to which I turn in the next section.

Pace Griffiths, if legal pluralism is a "concomitant" of anything, it is of multiculturalism, not social pluralism. For insofar as multiculturalism seeks to "privilege[] no particular cultural perspective," and given that all cultures exemplify some legal structure or other, in any given plural polity a multiculturalist framework would entail some system of legal pluralism. Thus, while social pluralism may be inevitable and indeed paradoxically beneficial in constructing public civility (as argued in the previous chapter), legal pluralism is neither.

In constructing public civility in the deeply fragmented culture of modern plural societies, what is needed are not the relativistic and allegedly morally neutral frameworks of multiculturalism or legal pluralism. Rather, the notion of the human good provides a more conceptually and pragmatically compelling basis.

A CASE FOR THE HUMAN GOOD

Conceptually, the term *the human good* is related to Aristotle's idea of *eudaimonia*—the happiness, flourishing, and well-being that obtains in human persons whose lives are aimed at this "chief good." For Aristotle, politics is the science that investigates the human good in the context of the polis—a science, which together with the other sciences, "strategy, economics, rhetoric," concludes what "the end [of] the human good" is.[21] In what follows, I unpack three features of human personhood that constitute the human good: relationality, purposiveness, and rationality. My main contention is that a recovery of a modified Aristotelian understanding of human teleology is crucial to constructing a framework of public civility; however, because Aristotle (along with many Aristotelians since) grounds his theory of ethics on the basis of human action, his view of the human good does not adequately elucidate the essential human attributes needed for such a framework. That is, in constructing a framework of public civility, what is needed is not only a "theory of moral action," but a consideration of the essential attributes of human personhood on which such a theory is grounded.

According to Aristotle, the end of politics is not governance merely for the protection of human life, but for the promotion of the good life: "A state exists for the sake of a good life, and not for the sake of life only, [for] a state is not a community of living beings only, but a community of equals, aiming at the best life possible."[22] While Aristotle suggests that happiness is "the highest good," he also recognizes that "different men seek after happiness in different ways." This diversity of pursuits of happiness results in "different modes of life and forms of government." In light of the multiplicity of conceptions of the good life and of justice, the notion of a universal human good and its constitutive attributes offers promising resources on the basis of which to construct a framework of public civility in plural societies.

According to Aristotle, to perform a just act one must possess the requisite virtue of *practical rationality* by which one could judge an act's justness. However, as one Aristotle scholar points out, practical rationality is "at odds with our characteristically modern ways of envisaging a rational agent" who, for example, for sheer lack of desire may decide to flout some obligation or other.[23] Under a modernist practical rationality, moral considerations arguably drop out altogether, for post-Hume practical rationality collapses the *is-ought* distinction and thereby disjoins facts—the way things are—from norms—the way they should be.

Contra Hume and in line with Aristotle, there must be some highest point of reference, some "unqualified" or "supreme" good. As argued earlier, an unqualified supreme good depends fundamentally both on what a human being is (metaphysical anthropology) and what human life is for (teleology). Knowing the good one ought to do depends on the kind of being one is: put differently, morality depends on metaphysics. In other words, "Human beings, like the members of all others species, have a specific nature; and that nature is such that they have certain aims and goals, such that they move by nature towards a specific *telos*."[24] Contrary to a modernist mind-set, only such an Aristotelian understanding of human teleology can provide the kind of framework necessary for grounding universal public civility.

Tragically, in traversing from early to advanced modernity there has been a monumental loss of an objective view of human teleology. The conceptual background of metaphysics that once functioned to establish a shared social universe has transmuted into a set of individualized outlooks. Consequently, morality has come to concern itself mainly with right human doing rather than with good human being (so to speak). Yet there remains an essential feature of the human condition, namely, the priority of the good over the right—and this for one simple reason: the right that one is supposed to do depends on the good for which one exists.

In what follows, before turning to consider that in which the human good consists, I describe what the human good is not, doing so by juxtaposing it to two competing but contrasting notions: *human rights* and *human nature*.

HUMAN RIGHTS AND HUMAN NATURE VIS-À-VIS THE HUMAN GOOD

Universal human equality features as a crucial notion in my account of the human good; and one way of grounding universal equality may be found in the discourse of human rights, as articulated notably in the Universal Declaration of Human Rights (1948). Since the UN Declaration, the widespread use of terms such as *civil liberties* and *political rights* highlights the significance of the underlying value of freedom: freedom makes rights and liberty claims intelligible. And discourse about freedom and rights, in turn, arguably requires an essentialist view of human nature. The philosopher Gianni Vattimo writes, "Equality will always be a metaphysical thesis . . . because of its claim to capture a human essence given once for all."[25] (For precisely this reason, Vattimo, a self-proclaimed nihilist, rejects this "essentialistic standpoint.")

It is important to note that human rights are not equivalent to political rights. Since human rights are inherent to the rights-holder (i.e., the human person), they do not depend on political conditions. Thus, human rights ought to be understood as being grounded, not in citizenship, but in human nature. Here, a crucial question arises: Which rights are human? My contention (which I unpack below) is that they are those that conduce to the attaining of the human good, an attainment that results from flourishing according to human nature. This contention can be buttressed by rephrasing the question as follows: What are human rights for? If there were no universal human nature or human good, then every individual human could decide "rightfully" what rights are and what they are for. But surely such a view is not only socially impracticable, but also goes against any attempts to delineate a set of equal rights to which all human persons are entitled (and obligations to which they are bound). So, as I argue below, human rights are for living a properly flourishing human life, and the aims and ends of this life are grounded in and governed by the human good consisting principally in the essential human attributes of rationality, relationality, and purposiveness.

Finally, then, before offering a detailed characterization of these attributes, it is necessary to consider even if briefly the idea of human nature. Parekh observes, "The term human nature refers to those ... universal capacities, desires and dispositions ... that all human beings share by virtue of belonging to a common species." For this reason: "If we encountered a 'human being' who was six inches or six meters tall, immortal, ... spoke a refined language at birth, ... [and never] faced a temptation throughout his or her life, [then naturally] we would feel profoundly disoriented in their presence and would consider that person either an aberrant member of our species or, more likely, that of another."[26] Simply put, that human persons have an essential nature seems beyond dispute.

THE HUMAN GOOD AS A BASIS FOR UNIVERSAL MORALITY AND PUBLIC CIVILITY

I turn now to the more constructive part of this work, which involves providing answers to these questions: What are the essential attributes of the human good? In what ways do they help to construct public civility? To this end, it is helpful to consider a final prior matter: the very possibility of grounding a universal morality. For if, as I argue below, human persons are intrinsically *relational*, then the principles of morality that govern their interaction would constitute an essential dimension of public civility. And if, as I demonstrate, human persons are inherently *purposive*, then conflicts that result from divergent purposes would require a framework to adjudicate between them. And, if human persons are innately *rational*, then it must be the case that both these moral principles and the criteria of adjudication thereof can be known, even if not completely agreed on, by human persons. All of these claims depend on there being some universal morality in light of which relationality, purposiveness, and rationality are made coherent. In this section, I delineate a universal morality based on essential human attributes, attributes that escape problems characteristically found in modern moral theories—those having to do with relativism, the priority of right over good, and loss of human telos.

Since the time of what I describe elsewhere as the scientization of knowledge,[27] modern theories of morality have found minimal or no conceptual space for teleology. The classical world was underpinned by a normativity that the modern world lacks. In response to this shift, the moral philosopher Alan Gewirth offers a monograph-length naturalistic account of universal morality on the basis of "the nature of human action."[28]

Gewirth argues that since morality entails agency, if there is any universal morality at all it must be based on the normativity entailed by human action, and that such normativity is grounded on the twin ideas of human *freedom* and *well-being*. The rationale of Gewirth's moral theory runs as follows. Insofar as talk of rights is coherent in the context of human action, it must consist in at least these two ideas: "the right to freedom . . . so that one's behavior is controlled by one's own unforced choice"; and "the right to well-being . . . so that one has the general abilities and conditions required for maintaining and obtaining what one regards as good." Gewirth universalizes these conditions by arguing that anyone who claims these rights on the grounds that one is a "prospective agent" with purposes to fulfill must also respect the rights to freedom and well-being in all other prospective agents. Thus, freedom and well-being form the basis of Gewirth's *normative moral principle*, which he contends provides the grounding for universal human rights, or what he calls "generic rights."

Gewirth's characterization of universal morality is similar to my account of the human good but differs in one fundamental way: whereas Gewirth seeks to ground a universal principle of morality on the normativity of human action, I contend that it is necessary to consider the essential human attributes on the basis of which such normative human action could be grounded. In other words, the problem is that Gewirth fails to provide an account of what it is that makes freedom and well-being the sine qua non of universal morality, except for his reference to the purposive prospective agency of human persons—an exception that only highlights Gewirth's preference for agency over attributes. Any account of universal morality that lacks consideration of the essential attributes of human personhood is poorer for it, and is thereby less adequate to serve as a basis for public civility.

Similarly and more recently, the philosopher James Griffin grounds his account of universal human rights on what he calls *normative agency*—that is, the "capacity to choose and . . . pursue our conception of a worthwhile life." Nicholas Wolterstorff objects to Griffin's account, much like I do to Gewirth's, by questioning the grounding for the alleged "autonomy" that purportedly guarantees universal rights.[29] Again, though this time in the context of specifically Islamic ethics, Steffen Stelzer similarly maintains that there are "two minimal assumptions" that must be made, namely, "that ethics is a science" and "that the object of this science is human action."[30] What is missing from these accounts is the ontological grounding for universal morality, a grounding that can be located, not in human action, but in the essential attributes of the human good.

The fundamental way, then, that accounts of universal morality based on human action differ from my account is that mine is grounded on the basis of human attributes instead of human action. In this way I depart also from Aristotle himself whose account of political ethics is based centrally on happiness and human action. According to Aristotle, "If there is an end for all that we do, this will be the good achievable by action"; and "happiness . . . is the end of action." Applying his ethics to the political realm, Aristotle holds that "politics [is] the highest of all goods achievable by action."[31] Thus, while making reference to the rational "soul" of human persons, Aristotle ultimately grounds his ethics on the kinds of human actions that allegedly conduce to happiness: hence my aim to recover a "semi"-Aristotelian view of human telos.

In sum, the accounts considered above fail to provide an ontological basis for a purported universal morality. What is needed for bona fide universal morality—which in turn is necessary (though not yet sufficient) for public civility—is the more fundamental basis found in the idea of the human good. The tripartite ground of relationality, purposiveness, and rationality is what makes the construction of public civility in plural societies both possible and necessary. In the next section, I unpack the notion of the human good in terms of its essential attributes to consider its resourcefulness for the task of constructing public civility.

HUMAN GOOD DEFINED

In order both to strip away the strangeness of strangers and to undo the incivility of public life, what is needed is a recovery and reassertion of the essential attributes of the human good, attributes that all human persons share. Put differently, the construction of a framework of public civility among divergent human communities requires a universal basis that consists in human *relationality*, *purposiveness*, and *rationality*. I now delineate each of these essential human attributes and their implications for the task of public civility, beginning with relationality.

Inherent moral relationality. To underscore the attribute of relationality, I build on key insights from Hannah Arendt and Charles Taylor.[32] Arendt observes, "The whole factual world of human affairs depends for its reality and its continued existence upon the presence of others who have seen and heard and will remember." That is, what human society is and that it is depends on "the presence of others"—in a word, relationality. For Arendt to be human is to be relational, to participate in social reality. Thus, in the classical world " 'to cease to be among men' "—that is, to be in exile—was the same as death: "no living creature can endure it for any length of time." Such an understanding makes sense of how Aristotle could say with little controversy that humanity is by nature a "political animal."

According to Arendt, fundamental to humanity's relational nature is the tripartite activity of *speech*, *action*, and *thought*. Speech is essential since humans only experience meaningfulness "because they can talk with and make sense to each other and to themselves." Connected to speech are action, of which speech is but one form, and thought, which is expressible by speech. These three capacities make up *the human condition*. Yet in order for speech, action, and thought to become "worldly things," that is, aspects of social reality, they must undergo a dual process: first, they must be "seen, heard, and remembered" by others—that is, they must be held in common—then, second, they are "reified ... into things." The result is that they become human artifacts (e.g., "sayings of poetry, the written page[,] paintings or sculpture"). In sum, for activities to count as human, they must be iterated in the presence of others. This analysis of human activity helps to illuminate and underscore the inherently relational character of humanity.

But it is not only the activities of action, thought, and speech that underscore humanity's relationality; the very fact of human self-understanding does so as well. As Taylor observes, a "crucial feature of human life is its fundamentally *dialogical* character," as elucidated by the fact that "we define our identity always in dialogue with, sometimes in struggle against, . . . our significant others." Humans learn the various " 'languages' of art, of gesture, of love" always through "exchanges with others," that is, in relationship. Yet such inherent relationality is occluded by modernity's monological bent that privileges the autonomous if isolated individual. Put simply: "Because of . . . the human condition—that we can only define ourselves in exchange with others, those who bring us up, and those whose society we come to see as constitutive of our identity—our self-understanding always places us among others."[33] We must remember that even the autonomous self has dialogical identity.

Connected to this inherent relationality is the ineradicable moral dimension of human life. The principles of morality indeed are needed for the well ordering of society and for public civility; and conversely, our inherent relationality points to the need for principles of morality. In other words, what makes plain the need for public morality is, as Taylor insightfully points out, the fact "that there are human beings in the world, with a certain form of life [who exhibit] certain patterns of caring." The very form of human life presupposes a moral function. "How else," Taylor asks, is one to "determine what is real or objective" other than by seeing the kinds of features that "our best account of things has to invoke?" That is, if the form of life that human persons inhabit intrinsically involves "patterns of caring," then it would seem most reasonable to suppose that morality is essential to relationality.[34] In short, the inherently relational nature of human lives presupposes an ineradicable moral dimension.

Intrinsic purposiveness. It is not enough, however, to say that human lives are inherently relational, or even also that they are thereby inextricably moral. These fundamental attributes merely point out the fact that human persons necessarily interact and do so on some principle of morality. In constructing a framework of public civility, what needs highlighting in addition to the moral-relational character of human life is the fact that human persons are essentially purposive beings, and deserve to be treated as such.

One way to elucidate the intrinsically purposive quality of human lives is by considering the significance of freedom in human sociality. As discussed above, freedom would be neither necessary nor useful were there no distinctively human purposes worth pursuing. Here again Taylor's insight is profoundly helpful: under the "standard Enlightenment view human life seems a matter merely of desire-fulfillment," for this view lacks the dimension of "strong evaluation"—that is, the basis on which to judge goals as "intrinsically *worth* fulfilling," goals that "mak[e] life significant."[35] Thus, without an intrinsic purposiveness, moral evaluation would be a vacuous notion, for there would be no goals for which moral judgment would be required, making freedom strictly useless. But because certain and not other human purposes are valuable, freedom does matter; and insofar as freedom matters, one could see the intrinsic quality of the attribute of purposiveness.

A question arises: Which purposes are intrinsically worthwhile, inherently human? To answer this question, I return to a consideration of the relationship between freedom and rights. Talk of rights makes sense only in a context of freedom. One can only exercise a right that one is free so to exercise. Modernist conceptions of (negative) freedom tend to suggest a priority of *rights* over *freedom*: freedom exists to provide the space in which one can exercise one's self-determined ends. Yet "freedom" construed in these terms is not freedom at all but, literally speaking, anarchy. For if the "right" to determine one's own ends encounters no moral boundaries, what results is an anarchic situation of conflicts over "rights" as well as an emptying of the notion of a right qua right. In this way, "rights" become an avenue for license, not for liberty. As Adam Ferguson put it some two centuries ago, "A right to do wrong . . . is an abuse of language, and a contradiction in terms."[36]

Contrary to modernist views, freedom is logically prior to rights: freedom is that for which rights exist. And what is freedom? To be humanly free is to flourish as a human person, to realize the human good. Or, as one Muslim scholar puts it, "freedom is to act as one's true nature demands."[37] Thus, freedom is not unbounded—as is the case with "freedom" as autonomy. Rather, true freedom is defined by a thing's nature. It is because a human person possesses a given teleology toward which she strives that freedom and rights are necessary, desirable, and coherent at all. In sum, the intrinsic quality of human purposiveness explains why humans pursue freedom at all. Thus, human freedom, which presupposes an intrinsic purposiveness and an objective human teleology more generally, demonstrates that without the essential attribute of human purposiveness there would be no purpose to human freedom—yet surely there is.

Innate rationality. In addition to the attributes of relationality and purposiveness, there is a third attribute of human personhood that must be considered essential—one so fundamental to what it means to be a human person that it risks being left unstated, namely, rationality. One can readily understand the temptation to leave out this essential attribute, especially (but certainly not exclusively) by those whose primary concern is rational inquiry, professional academics. If human persons were not essentially rational, there could be no way to see anything as being true, rendering performatively impossible any line of reasoning or scholarship. So it is understandable that the innately rational nature of human persons would be assumed simply as a given fact. Nevertheless, for purposes of completeness as well as to point out the connection between it and the other essential attributes, I explore this attribute as well.

That rationality is innate, universal, and unique to human persons has been understood and expressed since the intellectual traditions of antiquity. Where Aristotle distinguishes humans from other animals in view of the former's use of "art and reasoning," the Roman orator Cicero suggests, "Reason, which alone raises us above the level of the beasts, is certainly common to us all."[38] These comments are echoed in the religious traditions of Christianity and Islam.

The Christian tradition strongly affirms the innate rationality of human persons. The early Christian thinker Boethius, in commenting on the nature and person of Jesus Christ, characterizes *person* as "the individual substance of a rational nature." For Boethius rationality individuates the human person. Further along the Christian tradition, rationality is connected intricately with another essential attribute of the human good: moral relationality. Thomas Aquinas, for example, echoing Boethius, argues as follows: "Every individual of the rational nature" is considered a person. This rational nature found in human persons inheres in the fact of being made in the image of God. Given, then, the relationality found among the divine persons of the triune God, by analogy human persons who are made *imago Dei*—in the image of God—likewise possess a relational nature like the one found in God.[39] Thus, inherent relationality and innate rationality are inextricably linked in and essential to the human person.

There is also in the Muslim tradition, at least within certain branches of Sunnism (especially those of the Muʿtazilī strand), an intricate connection between humanity's relationality and rationality. As Abdulaziz Sachedina argues, within Islamic ethics there is an "emphasis on a substantial role for human reason to discern moral truth" that is premised on a "thesis about the teleological understanding of nature," including human nature. There is, in other words, an intrinsic connection between rationality and moral relationality owing to an Islamic view of human teleology. Since "ethical necessity is an action that is rationally required," there must be certain knowable moral norms that derive from human nature.[40] In these ways, the attribute of innate rationality, which makes up an essential part of the human good, is entailed by the other essential attributes, an entailment that can be seen to have resonances in both the Christian and Islamic theological traditions.

SOME IMPORTANT QUALIFICATIONS

In sum, human nature (ontology) that exhibits a particular human good (teleology) consists in the essential attributes of relationality, purposiveness, and rationality—attributes that must be recovered, recognized, and respected for the sake of constructing a universal framework of public civility.

Here it is worth pointing out the somewhat heated debate in social theory over essentialism and anti-essentialism, a debate that bears on constructing a specifically universal framework of public civility. Anti-essentialism holds a position that militates against the view that there is some objective human nature in virtue of which human flourishing obtains. For instance, one anti-essentialist argues, "A person [is] a compound of identities. . . . Identities are the basis from which persons are constructed." Similarly, another social constructivist holds that since individuals "are not essences . . . but result from relations and constructions," it follows that "personhood is an acquired characteristic, not a constant truth about human nature."[41] I do not offer here a critique of these accounts of philosophical anthropology in toto but pause only to point out that such views fall prey to self-referential incoherence. Under anti-essentialist views, one would have to presume that these putatively non-essentially formed human authors are writing to non-essentially formed human readers who, on pain of inconsistency, would be non-essentially rational. Indeed, nor are they "essentially" anything else. Consequently, nothing that these authors write could be expected to be comprehended, let alone agreed with, by such non-essentially rational readers. If literary postmodernism ushered in the death of the author, social scientific anti-essentialism has killed the reader.

On the contrary, human persons have essences and essential to human personhood are relationality, purposiveness, and rationality. Without *rationality*, there could be no expectation of making any sense of the discourse about the task of public civility(!). Without moral *relationality*, human persons would have no need to construct public civility. And without an intrinsic *purposiveness*, the task of constructing public civility would become meaningless, for coercion or any other means of establishing social order—or anarchy—would suffice.

It is also worth pointing out here that, despite my emphasis on the sameness of human persons, I recognize along with other social theorists that there are deep differences as well, differences that result from being culturally embedded beings. Indeed, acknowledging difference among persons and cultures is the sine qua non of peacebuilding, and thereby of public civility. Yet what I would like to emphasize is the fact that what unites human persons is greater than what separates them, and what unites them is the human good in which they all share, and which could serve as a universal basis for public civility. Moreover, differences among cultures themselves are only recognizable in a context of sameness. That is, the sameness found among human persons, of which allegedly drastic differences are a part, is only confirmed by the very fact of difference. Differences, in other words, are not only made coherent in a context of sameness; put otherwise, sameness is a necessary condition of difference. One ethicist writes, "We . . . ought to teach each other to perceive that . . . the stranger, and even the enemy, is more like us than s/he is unlike us in morally significant respects."[42]

Here another qualification about the human good is in order. There will always be instances of abuses, aberrations, malfunctions, and dysfunctions of the human good. Yet even in cases where the human good suffers imperfection at the first-order level (through aberrations or dysfunction), the second-order capacity of fully functional human potential remains. That is, there is a capacity in all humans to exhibit full flourishing, even in those who do not presently do so, whether this first-order incapacity is momentary or remains through one's life.[43]

I note a final qualification before concluding this chapter. While I consider these attributes of rationality, relationality, and purposiveness essential (necessary), they are not necessarily sufficient to account for human personhood. One might claim, for example, that human persons are essentially embodied beings, or morally depraved, or reactive, or otherwise. I would not deny such claims (or necessarily affirm them). Rather, I am interested in arguing for attributes that are common, basic, and essential to all human persons, and that help to ground a framework of public civility, especially (though not exclusively) between Catholic and Islamic communities. Accordingly, there may well be other attributes that arguably "constitute human personhood"—emotional experience, language use, interpersonal love, and so forth.[44] These attributes, however, can be analyzed more fundamentally in terms of the three essential attributes of the human good. For example, the fact that all human persons are capable of language use can be analyzed further in terms of the essential attribute of rationality. Similarly, the capacity to experience interpersonal love can be explained more fundamentally in terms of relationality; the same goes for emotional experience and the like. In short, while rationality, relationality, and purposiveness may not be sufficient to account for human personhood, they are no less necessary.

Conversely, others may contend that the attributes I suggest are not even necessary (i.e., essential) for human personhood. They might point out, for example, that a person in a coma still counts as human, even if she lacks the attribute of, say, purposiveness or rationality. This is to miss the point, however. My claim is not that every human person (now or ever) embodies most fully these essential attributes. Rather, my claim is that insofar as a human person is considered to be flourishing she does so by exercising the essential human attributes. Similarly, my claim is not weakened by instances of deficiency or malfunction. For a human person, regardless of her current existential status, is always in possession of a second-order potential to realize the essential human attributes that may not be operational at the first-order level, as I argue above.

The essential human attributes of relationality, purposiveness, and rationality that constitute the human good are those attributes in virtue of which human persons participate in society, and in the realization of which persons and societies function properly. This teleology accounts for what makes human persons the kind of entity they are, and provides the needed resources to ground a universal framework of public civility across divergent communities.

In the next chapter, I consider resources in Christian theology, specifically in Catholic social thought, that provide a conceptual counterpart to the notion of the human good. (The overarching aim of chapter 6 is to do the same with regard to Islamic political thought.) I suggest that there are significant conceptual themes within Catholicism that resonate with my idea of the human good and that provide resources needed to construct a common framework of public civility in plural societies from a Catholic perspective.

CHAPTER 5

THE HUMAN GOOD AND CATHOLIC SOCIAL THOUGHT

Early in the previous chapter, I discussed various problems with constructing a framework of public civility with the nonmoral and relativistic approaches of multiculturalism and legal pluralism. In this chapter, I turn to consider the prospect of securing a basis within Catholic social thought, starting with an examination of the often taken *common good* approach. Engaging with several prominent Catholic moral thinkers and natural law theorists, I argue that such an approach is ultimately either relativistic and thereby not sufficiently universal or conceptually inadequate to ground public civility. For this reason, I explore the notion of the human good as well as concepts within Catholic social thought that resonate with this notion. To this end, I examine several documents from the Second Vatican Council, exploring the Catholic notion of the *imago Dei*, which I commend as a conceptual counterpart to the human good.

NATURAL LAW THEORY AND THE COMMON GOOD TRADITION

The common good tradition has a conceptual history that reaches back notably to the works of Aristotle. In what follows, I evaluate the prospect of constructing public civility on the basis of the common good, considering especially resources within Catholic social thought. (In the next chapter, I evaluate the merits of an Islamic counterpart of the notion of the common good, *maṣlaḥa*.) At bottom, I contend that the common good approach is inadequate to provide a basis for public civility in plural societies given its relativistic character.

The common good tradition, as articulated within Catholic moral theology, has its theoretical roots in Aristotle and has been inflected and informed largely by Aquinas. For Aristotle, the notion of the common good derives from his view that individual parts (citizens) are explained naturally and necessarily by the whole (polis): insofar as citizens live and work toward the common good (or "the common advantage") of the polis, they participate in the good life and thereby experience *eudaimonia*, or happiness. Since we live in what one commentator calls a *web of mutuality*—"families, friendships, firms, neighborhoods, and religious organizations"—justice is and must be the crowning ethical virtue for a prosperous polis, this "association of associations."[1] The common good, thus, is essential to Aristotelian political and ethical theory since the good life is attainable only through citizens' mutual contribution to the good of the polis.

In line with this view, the natural law theorist Germain Grisez characterizes Aristotelian *eudaimonia* as *integral human fulfillment*: "In voluntarily acting for human goods [i.e., basic "reasons for action"] and avoiding what is opposed to them, one ought to choose and [to will] only those possibilities whose willing is compatible with . . . integral human fulfillment." By doing so and only by doing so, human persons aim at happiness. More recently, Grisez has emphasized the need to consider the place of community within which *eudaimonia* is attained: human agents should make a "contribution to integral communal well-being and flourishing."[2] And this communal fulfillment, argues another natural law theorist, results only through an achievement of the common good, which he defines as "the whole ensemble of material and other conditions, including forms of collaboration, that tend to favor, facilitate, and foster the realization by each individual [in the community] of his or her personal development."[3] Thus, the common good is essential to a flourishing society marked (among other things) by public civility—or so it is argued.

Aquinas offers a gloss of *the common good* similar to Aristotle's, although one that is arguably both more "earthly" and "eternal." For Aquinas, the common good not only serves as "the end of [human] law" and is thereby more earthly; it also functions to order the "community of the universe" and is thereby more eternal. As one recent interpreter puts it, Aquinas sought to secure a political foundation on the basis of the natural law given by the "divine Giver"—a foundation that grounds the "edifice [of the] 'cosmopolis.' "[4] In other words, for Aquinas, human law, which is just insofar as it derives from natural law (i.e., God's created order), is "an ordinance of reason for the common good." Thus, human law, deriving from natural law, is "ordained to the common good." In brief, the common good is the goal of human law.

If natural law relates to the common good in this way in politics, what role does it play with respect to Aquinas's ethics? Aquinas answers: Human persons qua rational beings act for some end, doing so under "the aspect of good"; and this fact corroborates what he calls the "first principle of practical reason[, namely,] 'good is that which all things seek after.' " In other words, human persons, when acting rationally, naturally seek (to do) the good. Put differently, "To the natural law belongs everything to which a man is inclined according to his nature." So human persons can be said to function properly (i.e., naturally) when their lives are aimed at their natural (nature's) good. The connection, then, between Aquinas's ethics and the notion of the common good is encapsulated in his contention that "any good or evil done to the member of a society redounds on the whole society." As one Thomistic ethicist puts it, we must consider "the natural social impact of human action."[5] And in doing so we would account for the ways in which all human action bears, whether for good or evil, on the common good—so it is argued.

Similarly, the noted Catholic moral philosopher Jacques Maritain, commenting on the notion of the common good, suggests that political society "lives on the devotion of the human persons and their gift of themselves" to the larger collective. That is, public life is "a concretely and wholly human reality, tending to a concretely and wholly human good—the common good." The common good, thus, "is not only a collection of public commodities and services" such as a sound fiscal policy, a viable military, public highways, and the like; rather, the common good involves also "the sociological integration of all the civic conscience, political virtues and sense of law and freedom, of all the activity, material prosperity and spiritual riches, of unconsciously operating hereditary wisdom, of moral rectitude, justice, friendship, happiness, virtue and heroism in the individual lives of the members of the body politic."[6] All such aspects of the common good, Maritain argues, are unrealizable without the excellences found in the practice and participation of individuals whose good is held in common. Finally, then, this view comports with later Vatican II teaching that states, "The common good [is] the sum of those conditions of social life which allow social groups and their individual members relatively thorough and ready access to their own fulfillment."[7]

In sum, the common good may be construed as an instrumental political good that conduces integral human/communal fulfillment; or as a "collection of public commodities and services" combined with "justice, friendship, happiness, virtue"; or as the "ensemble of material and other conditions [which] favor, facilitate, and foster" aspects of the aforementioned. However construed, the common good is (putatively) essentially that to which all members of the community contribute and in which they all participate, doing so for the sake of human and communal flourishing. On this theoretical ground many Catholic moral and political thinkers have sought to construct a framework for a just society, one within which public civility presumably could be constructed. But does this approach offer such resources? In what follows, I consider the works of several prominent political, legal, and moral theorists who answer affirmatively, doing so in order only to show that each of their views falls prey to a relativism that cannot ground a universal public civility.

THE COMMON GOOD TRADITION AND NEW NATURAL LAW

Before considering prominent contemporary scholars within the common good tradition, scholars who have been called new natural law theorists, I want to sketch the key difference between classical natural law and new natural law theories and then underscore the difference between my notion of the human good and the Catholic tradition of the common good.

As delineated above, the fundamental premise on which the natural law tradition theorizes is that there is some objective human nature according to which human lives are to be lived—a nature that can be seen in the natural law of the cosmos. In recent decades, there has emerged what has been dubbed (by one of its critic) *new natural law theory*, which unlike classical natural law is not premised on human nature but on what is called "the first principle of practical reason."[8]

When new natural law theorists refer to this principle as the foundation of their account of universal morality, they suggest (at least) the following: there are irreducible and noninstrumental *basic human goods* (e.g., knowledge, religion, health) for which a given moral action may be done; the course of action that leads to such goods is picked out (noninferentially) by *practical reason* and done so for the sake of human flourishing; and, because they are so picked out, they are thereby *basic*. For example, if asked why one is endeavoring to stay physically fit, and one responds by saying, "In order to ensure my health," then one is giving an irreducible and noninstrumental reason for performing such activity, an activity that accords with human flourishing; that is, one is pursuing a basic human good. My account of the human good, then, differs from new natural law in that it does not concern the principles or proscriptions of moral action per se but that which grounds the morality of human action: namely, the essential attributes of the human good. In this way, my account aligns itself closer to the classical natural law theory, a theory for which philosophical anthropology plays a more foundational role in its articulation.

But classical natural law theory, argue new natural law theorists (e.g., Grisez, Boyle, and Finnis), is inadequate since the "principles of morality cannot be theoretical truths of . . . philosophical anthropology," lest there be any "illicit inference from facts to norms."[9] That is, given the *is-ought* distinction, classical natural law theory has no ontic grounds (facts) on which to proffer a moral theory that is based merely on human nature (norms). Consequently, rather than ground universal morality on human nature, new natural law theorists seek to ground it in *practical reason*, an analysis of which is given as follows: "The objects of human action are the intelligible goods picked out and directed to by practical reason's first principles. These goods when realized by freely chosen actions . . . make up the flourishing of human beings and their communities."[10] Whereas classical natural law predicates universal morality on the basis of human nature, new natural law theory locates this basis in *practical reason*—the capacity of human reason to reflect on actions appropriate to human flourishing.

Contrary to claims of new natural law theorists, some classical theorists contend that there is no "illicit inference" made at all since classical natural law theory sees moral normativity as inherent to human nature. As Henry Veatch puts it, "The very 'is' of human nature has . . . an 'ought' built into it." Moral norms can be inferred from facts about (human) nature. Simply said: that physically harming innocent persons for pleasure is (normatively) morally wrong is evidenced in (the fact) that bodily integrity is natural and naturally good. Moreover, there is no advantage for new natural law in grounding reasons for action on practical reason: for facts also function as reason; that is, the facts are the "reasons for . . . putting forward certain arguments, for drawing certain conclusions, for holding certain beliefs, and so on."[11] Certain facts about human nature may demand specific moral actions. In short, in moral theory, reasons function no differently than facts: each gives an account for a given moral action.

Thus, the anthropological *essentialism* of classical natural law provides "a secure foundation" that maintains not merely that everything has an essence, but that these essences "are real and knowable."[12] For these reasons and others that I present below, I maintain that metaphysical anthropology has the resources for grounding a universal morality applicable to and accessible by all human persons. In this way, my account of the human good aligns with the classical natural law approach to universal morality. However, it must be noted that my account departs from classical natural law in that I specify further those essential attributes (relationality, purposiveness, and rationality) on the basis of which transcommunal public civility can be constructed. At any rate, my purpose here is not to settle the debate between classical and new natural law theories of morality but to suggest how my account of the human good differs from both natural law's *human nature* and new natural law's *practical reason*.

I turn, then, to consider and ultimately to critique the works of several prominent scholars who continue to ground a Catholic approach to political pluralism (and thereby presumably to public civility) on the basis of the common good.

THE RELATIVITY OF THE COMMON GOOD

For the new natural law theorist John Finnis, "To say that a community has a common good is simply to say that [the] communication and co-operation [which constitute every community have] a point which the members more or less concur in understanding, valuing, and pursuing." In other words, the good ("point") of any common life ("community") is its common good. Finnis distinguishes between two types of common goods: one that pertains to human associations such as friendship, marriage, and religious groups and that is "basic" in nature; another that pertains to political communities and is "inherently instrumental." It is the second of these that Finnis characterizes as the ensemble of conditions that "favor, facilitate, and foster" the realization of human and communal flourishing. And it is the second of these common goods that, if any, is relevant to the task of public civility.[13]

A question arises here: Just how ought the "personal development" of the members of a given polity—or the "intelligible point" of the political community—be determined? Finnis himself asks, "How does a critical political theory go about identifying . . . the various types of intelligible point or common good [of a political] human community?" He answers in characteristically natural law fashion: "It can do so only by going back to first principles. And the first principles of all deliberation, choice, and action are the basic *reasons for action*." Such *reasons for action* are "reasonable" insofar as they derive from "basic human goods"—that is, the so-called basic goods of human life: namely, *knowledge, skillful performance, bodily life, friendship, marriage, inner integrity*, and *harmony with the ultimate source of reality*.[14] Thus, to the extent that a political community's common good is aimed at fulfilling these human goods, it is a "just" society—or so Finnis contends.

The relation between Finnis's approach to the common good, the so-called basic human good, and the natural law is instructive. To be sure, natural law theory rightly highlights the importance of recognizing the various inherent goods necessary for human flourishing. Part of the problem, however, as I argue further below, is that the goods that are considered essential to human flourishing as conceived by the Catholic natural law tradition may be—and in fact are—different from those of another tradition; for my purposes most significantly, those of Islam. For this reason, the prospect of grounding a framework of public civility in plural societies on the basis of the common good is unpromising.

Even in one of Finnis's most recent characterizations of the common good given, this problem of relativity remains. In the introduction to his *Human Rights and Common Good*, Finnis writes, "The common good of a political community . . . includes the upholding of the rights of all its member against threats of injustice from inside and outside the community."[15] As to which rights are those worth protecting, Finnis suggests it is those that accord with human flourishing, those that serve to fulfill the basic human goods (e.g., life, knowledge, friendship). Here, two problems arise. First, as noted immediately above, if the basic goods picked out by natural law differ (as indeed they do) from those, say, of Islamic law, then the "common" good is only nominally common. Second, when it comes to the task of constructing a framework of public civility, what remains missing is the ontic ground of these allegedly basic human goods—that is, that which makes these "goods" inherently goods at all. It is an account of these matters that Finnis's theory of the common good does not offer.

Other notable new natural law theorists such as Germain Grisez and Joseph Boyle at one point offered an articulation of the idea of the common good according to which the "very notion of a *common* good or of a *public* interest suggests . . . a contrasting category of good which [is] *individual* or *private*," stating that in the political realm, "the common good includes goods which the political society as such can *effectively* pursue." While there is in the first part of this statement hardly anything with which to disagree, it also seems trivially true. The second part of the statement, however, while delineating a possible role for the common good—namely, that of a procedural mechanism for ordering political life—fails to offer any substantive content of what the common good is. (It is also worth noting that Grisez and Boyle rescind their view in a later work.)[16]

The articulation of the notion of the common good given by the new natural law theorist Robert George seems promising with respect to clarifying its meaning. For George, the common good consists in the idea that the "interests and well-being" of a given population of a political community are "just as important as the interests and well-being of everybody else." This characterization resembles quite closely that of another of Finnis's, which George references: "a set of conditions which enables the members of a community to attain for themselves reasonable objectives, or to realize reasonably for themselves the value(s), for the sake of which they have reason to collaborate with each other . . . in a community." The objection I have regarding this articulation of the common good (as I have with the ones that follow) is captured in the phrases "to attain for themselves reasonable objectives" and "to realize reasonably for themselves the value(s)": that is, the notion of the common good is ultimately relativistic and thereby inadequate to serve as a basis for a universal framework of public civility. For one group's "reasonable objectives" may well be unreasonable to another; and insofar as these objectives are sought "for themselves," there inevitably would be "goods" in conflict and not in common.[17]

A "PLURALISTIC ENSEMBLE OF GOODS"

The Catholic moral philosopher David Hollenbach also argues that the idea of the common good is essential to the ordering of a just polity, and furthermore that it is fundamental to the enterprise of Christian ethics.

In clear natural law fashion, Hollenbach suggests that for Aristotle "the common good of the community should have primacy in setting direction for the lives of individuals, for it is a higher good than the particular goods of private persons." The good life of an individual is found in the pursuit of not only the individual's own good, but the good of the community of which the individual is an integral part. Hollenbach further observes that Aquinas identifies the common good with no less than God himself, holding that "the supreme good, namely [God], is the [ultimate] common good, since the good of all things depends on [God]."[18] For Aquinas, since any good that exists derives from God, that is, is an aspect of God's eternal law, the common good toward which all human persons are inclined is a function of their being intrinsically related to the good—that is, God—who is the supreme common good. Thus, the good of any human person is common to all human persons insofar as all are naturally and ineluctably attracted to God who is the ground of all good.

There are points in Hollenbach's treatment, especially in his critique of "liberalism's tolerance," that I find helpful for the construction of public civility. Hollenbach notes that the danger of modern political liberalism is that, under its view, a "maximally tolerant society" would amount to one with "a minimum of human interaction"—since according to a so-called liberal tolerance, "the best way to be fully tolerant of others would be never to speak and never to do anything that actually affects other people." Such a fragmented sociality is detrimental for the prospect of a just society marked by public civility. Consequently, Hollenbach recommends a deep "mutual respect," involving a "social give-and-take" characteristic of communal interaction that "enhance[s] the good of all," the result of which he calls *the social good.*

I agree that there are indeed some social "goods" that human interaction requires and promotes, goods such as the promotion of civic virtues; the problem arises, however, when it comes to grounding the social good. Whereas I maintain that social goods are grounded in the human good, Hollenbach commends the common good. What, then, is the common good that purportedly grounds the goods of society? According to Hollenbach, the common good is most simply the "good of a person . . . embedded in the good of the community." The common good fulfills needs that individuals could not fulfill on their own and realizes values that could "only be attained in our life together." If the common good is understood in these terms, there seems to be no reason to deny its import: for the social institutions that humans share in common furnish more than what any individual could achieve on her own; and a life of solitude could not achieve the good that comes only with community. But the question remains: What is it that makes these *social goods* good at all? That is, what is the ontic ground of social goods? Here is where I see Hollenbach's conceptual confusion, a critique to which I now turn.

Hollenbach characterizes the common good as "an ensemble of diverse goods [which] include[s] the good achieved in family relationships, in voluntary associations, in political activity, in economic life, in the church, etc." Yet he further notes that "none of these aspects" is itself "the whole common good," for the latter will "always remain imperfect and fragile." But what, then, makes Hollenbach's view any different from what he describes as the "individualistic alternative to the common good"—that is, Rawls's *overlapping consensus*—an alternative that he explicitly challenges? The problem worsens with Hollenbach's suggestion that in the "globalized world" there is a need to search for "an overlapping set of communities and the overlapping goods [which such communities] make possible." These overlapping goods finally constitute the common good—a "pluralistic ensemble of goods." But a set of overlapping goods, given its pluralistic character, forms a mere aggregate of goods not unlike a Rawlsian overlapping consensus and is thereby inadequate to serve as a framework for social-political public civility.

Furthermore, it would seem that nothing in principle could keep such an "ensemble of goods" from transmuting into an ensemble of evil: one community's good may be another's evil. One way in which Hollenbach seems to counter this potential charge is by suggesting that the common good is specifically "an ensemble of goods that embod[ies] the good of communion, love, and solidarity." But is not Hollenbach's suggestion but one registry of "goods" among others? If so, why prefer his and not another's?

This is the fundamental problem that I see in general with the common good approach as a framework for public civility: the "good" of the "common" is not truly common and thereby only putatively good.

THE "ASSOCIATIVE COMMON GOOD"

Alasdair MacIntyre is another prominent proponent of the common good tradition. MacIntyre argues that there is a deeply "fragmented ethics" present in modern society owed largely to the "compartmentalization" of political philosophy from contemporary politics; and that unless and until the idea of the common good is articulated and maintained within political philosophy and its central role fulfilled within politics there can be no just society,[19] let alone one marked by public civility. What, then, according to MacIntyre, is the concept and role of the common good in political theory?

MacIntyre offers his characterization of the common good as "the ends of a variety of very different types of human association" (e.g., family, schools, professional and voluntary groups)—ends that are common to all their respective members. Under this characterization, MacIntyre distinguishes between several types of common goods. First, there is one that is "no more than the summing of the goods" of the individuals in a given activity (e.g., finances collected in an investment group). Let us call this *the aggregate view* of the common good. A second type results in "the good of association," which cannot be had "antecedently to and independently of" the individuals who make up such an association (e.g., the good of string quartets, of research scientists). This type of common good is "other than and beyond" that which is achievable by individuals alone. Call this *the associative view*. MacIntyre sees the aggregate view as irrelevant with respect to constructing a common political-ethical framework and espouses the associative view. How, then, does the associative common good provide a basis for a shared ethics for a common public life?

MacIntyre's argument runs as follows. In order to achieve excellence in the multifarious activities of one's life, one needs the requisite virtues to offer a proper response to this most fundamental question:

"What place should the goods of each of the practices in which I am engaged have in my life?" Inextricably connected to this question is its communal counterpart: "What place should the goods of each of the practices in which *we* are engaged have in *our* common life?" It is on this basis that MacIntyre argues for the need of "a conception of the common good" in the realm of politics.

MacIntyre continues by warning against an "individualist and minimalist" conception of the common good according to which the state is nothing more than a mechanism to secure a realm within which individuals pursue their own self-chosen ends. This sort of political proceduralism would not conduce to true social flourishing. Rather, MacIntyre suggests the need for a practical rationality that allows and impels members of a community to say to themselves: "I must learn what my good is in different types of situation and I can only achieve that through interaction with others in which I learn from those others and they from me." This more robust form of engagement arguably provides the resources needed to ground the indispensable "communal and individual deliberation" concerning the community's common good. I find this feature of political society (like Hollenbach's "mutual respect" above) a necessary and beneficial dimension for constructing public civility. What I question, however, is whether the conditions needed for this feature are obtainable only or even most plausibly on the basis of the common good; for MacIntyre's proposal of the common good secured by way of "deliberative participation" seems still to suffer the fate of relativism, as I explain immediately below.

While I agree that there might be a "common good" that gives order to associations such as a musical quartet or group of scientists—a good whose realization is possible only insofar as its members collectively and properly engage in the relevant activity—such is not the case for political societies. The reason that the associative view of the common good may be coherent in the context of some human associations while not for a plural political community is elucidated by the characterization of the polis given earlier: an "association of associations."[20] That is, as one political theologian suggests, in plural societies we must consider communities' pursuing "not only their [own] common good but also that of their neighbours."[21] In other words, rather than there being some allegedly singular common good, in plural societies the common good is multiply and sometimes incompatibly conceived and pursued. Thus, because a given plural society comprises an association of people from particular and divergent viewpoints, traditions, and worldviews—in a word, associations—it in principle does not have a singular, shared, common good.

Thus, MacIntyre's conception of the common good falls prey to the same relativist objection I pose above: namely, given the underdetermination of the common good, the "good," which is purportedly "common," may under some views promote evil and under the same views demote good. Given this underdetermination of the common good, there must be found some other theoretical basis on which to ground a transcultural public civility. What is needed is a recovery and reassertion of the fundamental features of humanity that are fixed (by its telos) and thereby free of the perils of relativism. Interestingly, it seems that MacIntyre himself might agree with this point when he writes:

> When philosophers come to evaluate those norms and those conceptions [which constitute the common good], they confront the task of evaluating them as norms for which it is claimed that it would be right and best for all human beings to live by them and as adequate conceptions of the human good, and not of the Greek, or the Indian, or the Chinese good. [That is, they are asking essentially the questions:] What are *the* norms appropriate for human beings as such? What is *the* human good?[22]

Given his clear articulation of *the human good*, it is surprising, if disappointing, that MacIntyre seeks to ground a flourishing society on the common good.

THE NEED FOR A UNIVERSAL HUMAN GOOD

Returning to Aquinas: if human law is "ordained to the common good" and specifically the common good of "peace and justice,"[23] I would ask, Whose justice? And which peace? For while, for example, from a Catholic moral theological perspective, the common good of peace and justice is grounded ultimately on *natural law*, from an Islamic perspective the common good (*maṣlaḥa*) would arguably be based on the purposes of Islamic law (*maqāṣid al-sharīʿa*). So for whose common and for which good is law ordained? And which law? I contend that a more plausible basis for constructing public civility across religious traditions is found not in the elusive, relativistic, and socially constructed common good but in the idea of a universally common human good.

Having considered the conceptual vacuity of the notion of the common good within the natural law tradition, I turn now to consider the resources within Catholic social thought that do indeed resonate with the notion of the human good and which thereby serve as a Catholic conceptual counterpart for universal public civility.

CATHOLIC SOCIAL TEACHING: *IMAGO DEI* AS THE HUMAN GOOD

Here, in order to consider a Catholic counterpart to the idea of the human good, I explore the resources of Catholic moral theology, as found specifically in the Catholic social teaching (CST) of the Second Vatican Council. I argue that the Catholic conceptions of human rights and human dignity, as grounded on the doctrine of the *imago Dei*, approximate an idea essentially similar to my notion of the human good. I explore these concepts by examining two major statements promulgated at the Second Vatican Council that reflect this approximation: *Pacem in terris* (Peace on Earth [1963]) and *Gaudium et spes* (Joy and Hope [1965]).[24]

As I begin my treatment of a possible Catholic construal of the human good, let me clarify what I do not mean. I do not have in mind the human goodness that Karl Rahner's "anonymous Christian" is supposed to exhibit or the good pagan who, as Rahner argues, is (soteriologically) no different from "saved" Catholics.[25] Rather, I am interested in locating a concept within Roman Catholic theology that resonates with the essential human attributes captured in my notion of the human good. I am interested, in other words, in the human good—not the "good human."

Pacem in terris: *Human Rights and the Human Good*

It was only relatively recently that in many places around the world, for example, Eastern Europe, Latin America, and Africa, the Roman Catholic Church emerged as an institution that embraces and encourages robust political and economic rights. As one Catholic theologian writes, the "Roman Catholic church has moved from strong opposition . . . to [becoming] one of the leading institutional advocates for human rights on the world stage."[26] Prior to this point, the Catholic Church disdained modern international politics as premised on universal human rights. One of the clearest expressions of this antagonism is found in Pius IX's Syllabus of Errors (1864).

But since Vatican II, most notably with *Pacem in terris*, there emerged an acceptance, indeed endorsement, of human rights discourse as based on the dignity of the human person who is created in the *imago Dei*: "Any well-regulated and productive association of men in society demands the acceptance of one fundamental principle: that each individual man is truly a person [with] a nature . . . endowed with intelligence and free will. As such he has rights and duties, . . . universal and inviolable, and therefore . . . inalienable" (*PT*, no. 9). These fundamental rights and duties are grounded in the idea of *personal* and *natural dignity* (see also, e.g., nos. 10, 14, 20, 44, 48, 81). Indeed, "those rights . . . derive directly from his dignity as a human person" (no. 145). This understanding provided theological justification for Catholics to build common ground with non-Christians given the premise that one and the same God has created all of humanity. In this way, the idea of inherent human dignity, grounded on the doctrine of the *imago Dei*, provides a basis for the Catholic conception for universal morality, a basis that in turn grounds universal human rights.

It is important to point out that along with a language of rights was a discourse of duties: whereby "in conferring the one [rights]," Catholic thought also "imposes the other [duties]."[27] In this way, a Catholic notion of human rights aligns with the Aristotelian view that promotes a positive freedom and the good life and thereby stands opposed to modernist conceptions of negative freedom as mere noninterference. Nevertheless, there emerges a worry: Which rights and duties are proper to and necessary for human dignity? *Pacem in terris* states that "it is not possible to give a general ruling" on all such rights and duties or "on the most suitable form of government" (no. 67) given "how difficult it is to understand clearly the relation between the objective requirements of justice and concrete situations" (no. 154). Notwithstanding, the document does commend for such judgments a "human standard"—one "[based] on truth, tempered by justice, motivated by mutual love, and holding fast to [freedom]" (no. 149). It is against this *human standard* that acts, whether individual or political, are judged to be proper instances of rights and duties.

Aside from the human standard, there is in *Pacem in terris* (unsurprisingly) another criterion against which rights and duties must be considered: the common good. That is, all human persons make "their own specific contributions to the general welfare" and for this reason "must harmonize their own interests with the needs of others." Given the varying interests within a community, "the sole reason for the existence of civil authorities" is to secure the common good (see nos. 53–54, 55–56). In brief, laws and legislatures, policies and parliaments exist to serve the common good. But, as discussed at length above, the common good is elusive insofar as it is arbitrary: one's good may be another's evil. Thus, the common good as a basis for interreligious public civility remains unpromising.

Yet in *Pacem in terris* the idea of the human good seems to be recognized at least implicitly, despite frequent employment of the common good. For example, the common good is limited to and based on "the inviolable rights of the human person" (nos. 60–61). Also, when discussing "relations between states," the document holds that "a clash of interests among States" ought to be settled "in a truly human way" (no. 93). And most plainly, "the common good . . . cannot be determined without reference to the human person" (no. 139). As a Catholic commentator writes, "Nowhere [is] a collective welfare determinable apart from the individual rights which define, shape, and constitute the common good, the public interest."[28] In this way, resources within

Catholic social thought, especially with respect to the idea of human rights as grounded in *imago Dei*, have resonances with my idea of the human good and serve as a promising basis for public civility from a Catholic perspective.

In the next section, I consider another notion pervasive in CST, namely, human dignity, which also exhibits conceptual resonance with the human good, perhaps even more strongly than the idea of human rights. To this end, I examine *Gaudium et spes*, in which the notion of human dignity, again grounded on the doctrine of the *imago Dei*, is explicated at some length. I begin, however, with a brief history of the term *dignity* as it relates to CST.

Gaudium et spes*: Human Dignity and the* Imago Dei

Ancient Greek and Roman thinkers employed the term *dignity* to denote a distinction between human and nonhuman animals as well as to refer to a sense of elevated status among nonequal human persons. Eventually, in the Middle Ages, *dignitas* was used when referring, not yet to universal human equality, but to the distinction of one's office.[29] A significant use of the term *dignity*, which approaches its contemporary usage, comes at the time of the Enlightenment in the work of Immanuel Kant: "In the kingdom of ends, everything has either a *price* or a *dignity*. What has a price can be replaced by . . . its *equivalent*; what . . . is raised above all price and therefore admits of no equivalent has a dignity." In virtue of its dignity, every human person is to be treated "always . . . *as an end*." What affords humans their dignity is that capacity for "universal practical reason" which is essential to human agency, a capacity that consists in "*the will of every rational being as a will giving universal law* [i.e., autonomy]." Briefly stated, for Kant, human dignity is grounded on autonomous moral reasoning: "humanity insofar as it is capable of morality, is that which alone has dignity."[30]

However, the political theorist Michael Rosen argues that since in the name of dignity courts often override individual autonomy, dignity can be abused.[31] Rosen illustrates with a recent legal case in which dwarf-throwing was outlawed by a French court on the basis that it was "a violation of human dignity," despite the dwarf's willingness to participate in the activity. In the name of "dignity," Rosen argues, the courts overruled individual rights; thus, dignity suffers under an "absolutist resonance" that potentially undercuts the individual's right to autonomy. The problem with Rosen's view, however, is its reliance on a subjectivist view of autonomy, a critique of which I give above. Human freedom, I contend, ought to be construed not as autonomy *tout court* but as that which is in accordance with the human good. For if freedom is simply autonomy, then an arguably irresolvable problem arises: How could one adjudicate among conflicting (autonomous!) rights claims?

Rather than equate autonomy with freedom and freedom with negative rights, Catholic social thought seeks to prioritize positive over negative rights. For example, the positive right of subsistence of those in need overrides the negative right to private property of the less needy. In this way, a Catholic antimodernist view of human dignity gestures toward a register according to which individual rights can be prioritized. After all, universal human rights, which are part of an objective anthropology, derive from human dignity. Rights do not exist for people to pursue their own personal goals; rather, they exist so that human persons achieve the ends proper to a human life well lived. These ends, as suggested in *Gaudium et spes*, involve "bodily concerns" (no. 14), the "intellectual nature of the human person" (no. 15), "fidelity to conscience" (no. 16), "freedom . . . [for] *what is good*" (no. 17; emphasis added), and "communion with God" (no. 18). In sum, goods that promote biological, intellectual, moral, and spiritual flourishing are properly human ones, all of which are grounded in the human dignity (cf. no. 14).

To connect this Catholic view of human dignity and of the *imago Dei* to my notion of the human good, it would be helpful to consider the first section of *Gaudium et spes*.[32] Here, in answer to the question, "What is man?," the document draws on a biblical passage (Gen. 1:27) that "teaches that man was created 'to the image of God,'" and that on this basis humanity is "capable of knowing and loving his Creator." But, it continues, "God did not create man as a solitary, for . . . 'male and female he created them'"; consequently, "by his innermost nature man is a social being, and unless he relates himself to others he can neither live nor develop his potential." A view of inherent human relationality is markedly present; this is one way that the Catholic idea of human dignity can be seen as having conceptual resonance with my notion of the human good.

Furthermore, intrinsic human purposiveness is also underscored: "[Man] was appointed by [God] as master of all earthly creatures that he might subdue them and use them to God's glory." As inherently relational beings (made to know and love God) and endowed with intrinsic purpose (called to tend to creation for God's glory), not only can human persons pursue goods appropriate to human life, but indeed must do so if they are to flourish according to their nature as made in God's image. As one Catholic ethicist observes, the "central motif" in *Gaudium et spes* is the "human person as *Imago Dei*"—a view of the human person which "implies [a particular] ethical ontology."[33] In sum, in CST the ideas of human rights and human dignity, especially as grounded in the doctrine of *imago Dei*, exhibit significant conceptual resonances with the idea of the human good. In sum: "The Catholic view . . . presupposes . . . a philosophical-theological account of the human being as a person endowed with reason [rationality] and free will [purposiveness], intelligible only in a social milieu [relationality]."[34]

HUMAN DIGNITY VIS-À-VIS THE HUMAN GOOD

To be sure, there are differences between my account of the human good and the Catholic conception of human dignity, differences that I highlight by considering a recent exchange between two prominent Catholic legal scholars, Paolo Carozza and Christopher McCrudden. Below is an (albeit brief) engagement with their debate over the question of whether the concept of human dignity is sufficiently robust to ground human rights.[35]

Where McCrudden is pessimistic about the prospect, Carozza seeks to allay any worries. Carozza argues that human dignity holds an "extralegal" status and thereby serves as a discursive and conceptual "mediator" between local political contexts on the one hand and universal moral norms on the other. The notion of human dignity provides resources with which to adjudicate among claims that would otherwise result in irresolvable "conflict between incommensurable values." In other words, legal recourse to human rights norms is justified because in the idea of human dignity there is some "meaningfully intelligible commonality" of value. Were it otherwise, "the transnational circulation of human rights norms" would amount to no more than an "idiosyncratic preference of a judge for some norm over some other one." Without human dignity, in short, human rights discourse would be ineluctably relativistic.

How, then, does my account of the human good differ from that of Carozza's view of human dignity? To answer this question, it may help to consider a further one: What is it about the notion of human dignity—construed differently by divergent communities—that allows it to escape the perils of relativism? For Carozza, the answer is a society's commitment to "*dia-logos*"—that is, "a sharing of reason with one another [about] the meaning of human flourishing [and of] the common good." Precisely here is where my account differs. As argued above, the common good remains either conceptually vacuous or unhelpfully vague without some fuller conception of the good of the human person to ground it.

Cognizant of the potential perils of relativism, Carozza stipulates further, "Transnational dialogue [about the common good] . . . is a provocation to reflect more deeply, collectively, and comparatively on the breadth of human experience and the fulfilment of elemental human needs and desires." Here Carozza appreciates the importance of the role played by human teleology: but, in order truly to escape relativism, such dialogue about human "needs and desires" would need to be construed in terms of a more fundamental and fixed basis than what is provided by the "transnational" reflections thereof, for even such reflections are subject to the relativity of persons, places, and times, as argued above. What is needed, instead, is the universal basis of the human good, expressible in terms of relationality, purposiveness, and rationality.

A RESPONSE TO A CRITIQUE OF NATURAL LAW

An objection often raised against natural law theory is worth considering here, given its potential charge against my account of the human good. Walzer argues that "human or natural [rights] do not follow from our common humanity; they follow from shared conceptions of social goods; they are local and particular in character." Similarly, there is a sort of multiculturalist objection that challenges the idea of there being a universal human nature and therefore human good. Amartya Sen writes, "Muslims, like all other people in the world, have many different pursuits, and not all of their priorities and values need be placed within their singular identity of being Muslim." For, after all, human identities consist over a range of categories such as "citizenship, residence, geographic origin, gender, class, politics, profession": thus, human persons are "divided selves" with a variety of "interests," "identities," and "ideals."[36]

While these thinkers put forward theses at slight variance from one another, the thrust of the objections is largely the same: that is, that human persons cannot be conceived in essentialist terms and that therefore ideas of the good and of justice are necessarily differently and sometimes conflictingly conceived across individual/communal boundaries. In what follows, I focus primarily on Walzer's works as they represent a more direct attack against natural law theory, an attack that if successful would undermine my proposal that the human good serves as a basis for universal public civility.

Walzer suggests that there are "thick" local, particular moralities (plural) and a "thin" universal morality (singular); and that the "thick" moral terms in a given community do not go beyond its moral walls so as to merit synonymous readings in other communities. Since there exists "no neutral ... moral language," any attempt to adjudicate on public matters must be carried out "in terms of one or another thick morality." In other words, since the principles of morality are "reiterated in different times and places," the terms by which one community articulates such principles can be only locally apprehended and applied.[37] Thus, conceptions of justice and of the good do not reach across communal boundaries to make up some elusive universal morality. So argues Walzer.

On the contrary, I suggest, pace Walzer, that there is a basis that grounds a universal morality on which a framework of public civility can be constructed: the human good. I note several reasons why Walzer's account (along with others such as Sen's) is wrongheaded.[38] First, Walzer's account seems to collapse ineluctably into ethical relativism. Walzer argues, "Justice is a human construction [and] the principles of justice are themselves pluralistic in form; [consequently,] social goods ought to be distributed for different reasons, in accordance with different procedures, . . . [and] all these differences derive from different understandings of the social goods themselves." This ensemble of differences, he goes on to argue, is "the inevitable product of historical and cultural particularism." Since there is no "*good* simply," it is necessarily the case that "justice is relative to social meaning." However, I would argue that if justice is in fact nothing but a human construction and if there is no goodness as such, then an ethical relativism across cultures is entailed necessarily. For who is to say that the account of justice given in one "sphere" is or is not sound in another? So if each human community has an exclusive right to adjudge what is just or unjust, how does ethical relativism not follow? And if relativism follows, the conception of "justice" that one community has is not true justice but mere pragmatic social efficiency.

Second, on Walzer's account, there seems to emerge a problem having to do with the "size" of spheres. For if each sphere were indeed a product of particularism, what would keep the spheres themselves from subdividing into smaller spheres whereby each subsphere would be its own particularism? How small could one human community be and still count as its own "sphere of justice"? Could there be a community of one? If so, would there not follow an ethical relativism among individuals? Conversely, could there not emerge, at least in principle, a global sphere wherein a single understanding of justice would supervene? Walzer is silent.

Third and last, in proposing his "value pluralism" thesis, Walzer seems committed implicitly, if ironically, to a universal account of morality. According to Walzer, justice is humanly constructed, localized, and relative to communities. However, this view is itself a metaethical theory about justice: namely, that every form of justice is constructed and confined to cultures—which itself is a universal truth claim. Put differently, Walzer's claim that there is no "list of basic goods" for which "the philosopher" is always in search is itself a claim about the list: Walzer ostensibly has found and formulated in toto this list(!). Furthermore, at one point Walzer writes explicitly in favor of the idea that a universal justice prevails in the realm of politics.[39] By maintaining a universality of scope with regard to political values (e.g., equal citizenship, prohibition of coercion, and the importance of persuasion), Walzer insists on a universal standard of justice that he in turn presumes is shared by his readers, many of whom would undoubtedly occupy "spheres" other than his own. Yet precisely this universality is what Walzer impugns. Apparently, the alleged barriers to establishing a universal view of justice across communal boundaries do not apply to Walzer; or if they do, then his objection against a shared humanity loses its logical force.

In this chapter I argue three main points: (1) that the common good approach of the Catholic theological tradition is either relativistic or otherwise inadequate to ground a universal framework of public civility; (2) that the universality of the human good, constituted by moral relationality, purposiveness, and rationality, offers a more promising basis for such a framework; and (3) that the resources of Catholic social teaching, especially when considering the doctrine of *imago Dei*, offer a conceptual counterpart to my notion of the human good. Finally, I consider and critique objections lodged against natural law theory, objections that would otherwise undermine my proposal of the human good.

Having considered within Catholic social thought resonances with my notion of the human good, in the next chapter I consider such resonances within Islamic theological ethics. My goal is to construct an Islamic political theology that is consonant with the human good and amenable to the construction of public civility in plural societies.

CHAPTER 6

THE HUMAN GOOD WITHIN ISLAMIC POLITICAL ETHICS

Having looked at a conceptual counterpart to the notion of the human good within Catholic social thought, the aim of this chapter is to investigate an Islamic equivalent amenable to the construction of public civility in plural societies. The overarching argument is that while the resources of Islamic jurisprudence are important and integral to the centuries-old tradition of Islam, on their own they are inadequate to ground public civility; and that the discourse of Islamic theological ethics serves as a more promising avenue for this task. Central to this tradition of ethics is the Islamic notion of *fiṭra*, or original human disposition—a notion that underscores Islamic ethics' rightful reliance on human teleology.

The respective aims of this chapter and the next are (1) to show the conceptual resonance that *fiṭra* has with my notion of the human good and by implication also with the Catholic doctrine of the *imago Dei*; and (2) to construct a pluralistic Islamic political theology on this basis. The chapter proceeds in two main stages: first, I consider certain key concepts within Islamic jurisprudence along with their potential for and shortcomings in grounding public civility; and second, I explore, as an alternative to the resources of Islamic jurisprudence, the conceptual fecundity found in the Islamic notion of *fiṭra* along with its conceptual resonance with my notion of the human good. I conclude by offering some general comments on conceptual resonance and by prefacing the next chapter, whose aim is to construct a pluralistic Islamic political theology on the basis of *fiṭra*.

Before moving ahead, it is important to note briefly the distinction between Islam and Islamism, made pointedly by Bassam Tibi. For most Muslims, Islam is not a political enterprise per se but a "cultural system that determines their worldview and way of life." By contrast, Islamists seek the total "remaking of the existing political order in pursuit of the Islamic shariʿa state," having in mind an undying—and arguably un-Islamic—vision of "din-wa-dawla," the unity of state and religion.[1] My aim is to consider the resources of Islamic theological ethics, as distinct from, indeed contrary to, Islamist political ideology.

To note further, my concern is not with the compatibility between Islam and democracy per se; rather, it is to seek a basis for public civility between Muslim and non-Muslim communities in the plural societies of advanced modernity. In light of this point, I begin with a comment about the need for what I call a *secular imperative* in liberal democratic societies.

PUBLIC CIVILITY AND THE SECULAR IMPERATIVE

Both non-Muslim scholars of Islam and Muslim scholars themselves have suggested that certain key political values of modernity—for example, religious tolerance, universal citizenship, gender equality—have problematized the experiences of Muslim communities in public life. For there is a supposed requirement of "religious and metaphysical neutrality" to which members of modern democratic societies are expected to adhere.[2] Muslims have responded to this so-called requirement of neutrality in diverse ways. While some have sought to establish Islamic law (*sharīʿa*) through the vehicle of the state, others have sought noninterference from the state in the lives of Muslim citizens, tending toward social-political withdrawal. In either case, what is sought is not some allegedly neutral political structure to which Islamic law must conform but a social space in which Muslims can live out their lives in authenticity and freedom.

When considering the viability of various political structures in advanced modernity, we must note that there is no political given, no universally neutral political structure. As Thomas Nagel points out, every political "arrangement has to be justified by comparison with every other real possibility."[3] While I have described at length the negative impact that both secularism and secularization have on the prospect of constructing public civility, there is an important sense in which the political order of a given plural society ought to remain "secular" with respect to religious traditions. There is a need for what I call the *secular imperative*, which befits democratic plural societies.

There is a premodern, indeed Augustinian, sense of the term *secular* that I have in mind with respect to my notion of the secular imperative, which means, not "profane" or "vulgar," but simply "plural." This sense of *secular* is clearly different from that of secularization theorists such as Marx, Durkheim, and Weber who contend that through the course of time and progress, religion would diminish and modern society would find itself eventually thoroughly "secular." By contrast, Augustine uses the term *secular* to refer to the *saeculum* where the city of God and the city of man "are entangled together in this world [*saeculum*]"—as a plural society—until the final judgment at the *eschaton*.[4] In this sense, the secular is not the same as the profane—the latter referring to the antithesis of religion, the former simply to temporality. To confuse one with the other would be to commit a category mistake: the religious and the secular do comingle. It is in this sense that I suggest the need for a secular imperative in plural democratic societies.

One key reason we must secure such secularity (plurality) is for the signature civic purposes of liberty and equality. Here we must distinguish political *secularity*, which serves to procure religious liberty and civic equality, from a dogmatic *secularism*, according to which the state would wrongly endorse religious privatization. In other words, political secularity, or the idea of the *secular imperative*, undergirds a religiously plural polity in which authentic public expressions of religion are not only allowed, but in fact encouraged.

There are other important reasons that motivate us to seek such secular (plural) polities. With respect to the political life of liberal democratic societies, it is helpful to keep in mind that a people's voting conscience is necessarily informed by a set of beliefs, including religious ones. And such beliefs are not, indeed must not be, dismissed when voting or otherwise voicing political commitments. After all, democracy does not demand a moral neutrality: for it is "rule by the people," not moral relativism. As one Muslim scholar notes, any dogmatically secularist (antireligious) political arrangement would be "undemocratic," since it would not reflect the will of the *demos* who regularly, naturally, and rightfully seek to express their religious convictions within the political realm.[5] The secular imperative is needed for the sake of both religious and democratic authenticity, which in turn are needed for public civility.

With the secular imperative in mind, the question must be asked, Are Islamic ideals amenable to being integrated into the world of plural modernity? As noted in chapter 1, the Global Terrorism Database indicates that in recent years Muslim terrorist groups account for an overwhelming majority of attacks around the world. So are there resources within Islamic political ethics that would serve as a basis for constructing universal public civility?

Arguably, from even rather liberal views, while Islam may comport with a separation of religion and politics, it tends not to permit a separation of religion and law. More traditionally, in the famed words of Ḥasan al-Bannā', "Politics is part of religion. . . . Caesar and what belongs to Caesar is for God Almighty alone." According to a recent interpreter of al-Bannā', "To impose upon Islam the Christian separation of loyalties is to deny it its essential meaning and very existence."[6] Clearly, the encounter of Islam with secular modernity is of crucial importance for constructing a framework of public civility.

In light of this crucial importance, in what follows I consider the possibility of locating a basis of public civility specifically within the resources of Islamic jurisprudence, arguing ultimately that, in view of its internalizing legalistic tendency, such a basis of universal public civility must be located elsewhere: namely, in the theological-ethical resources of Islamic political thought.

THE PROSPECT OF PUBLIC CIVILITY WITHIN ISLAMIC JURISPRUDENCE

In the context of Islamic jurisprudence, if there were to be found a basis of public civility, it arguably would have to be rooted most fundamentally in the Qurʾān, particularly in regard to its view on religious diversity. Some Muslim scholars distinguish between a "de facto plurality" and "de jure pluralism," arguing that the Islamic corpus might admit of a de facto plurality, which requires only a "recognition" of religious diversity but does not allow for any "advocation" of religious pluralism.[7] That is, while the Qurʾān might accept plurality as a social fact about humanity, an outright pluralism is not necessarily supported.

Yet scholars such as Abdulaziz Sachedina hold that the Qurʾān permits, indeed promotes, a view of pluralism, suggesting that scripture is consonant with, and even offers theological grounds for, a "civic pluralism." Similarly, other Muslim scholars argue that there are historical and Quranic resources that would motivate Muslims not only to live peaceably within modern democratic societies but also to engage in the common life thereof.[8]

Slightly more reservedly, Bhikhu Parekh suggests that under certain characterizations Islam could be considered compatible with civic pluralism.[9] Following Parekh, I suggest that the prospect of an Islamic basis of public civility depends on the kind of Islam in question. Immediately below, I explore various "Islams" along with key concepts within Islamic jurisprudence relevant to the task of constructing public civility: namely, those of *uṣūl al-fiqh* (Islamic legal theory), *sharīʿa* (Islamic "law"), *ijtihād* (juridical prudence), and *maṣlaḥa* (common good). I take each idea in turn.

THE CONTEXTUALIZABILITY OF *SHARĪʿA*

After the death of the Prophet Muḥammad and over the course of subsequent generations, there emerged multiple and competing understandings of so-called Islamic law (*sharīʿa*), understandings situated within the larger framework of Islamic legal theory (*uṣūl al-fiqh*). It is worth noting here at the outset that *law* in Islam is not the same as *law* in the modern sense, as the former and not the latter includes regulations on diet, pilgrimage, ritual cleansing, and so on.[10] For Sunnī Muslim communities, interpretations of *sharīʿa* had come to be based initially on the decisions of the four rightly guided caliphs (*al-khulafāʾ al-rāshidūn*), who assumed the role of Islamic leadership after the Prophet's death. By contrast, within the Shīʿi tradition, devotion to the ways of ʿAlī (the Prophet's nearest of kin) was essential to understanding the content of *sharīʿa*.

In time, in an attempt to overcome the variety of interpretations, different schools of law (*madhāhib*) codified *sharīʿa* within different legal frameworks (*fiqh*). The four major schools in the Sunnī majoritarian tradition are Ḥanafī, Mālikī, Shāfiʿī, and Ḥanbalī.[11] In what follows, I shall limit my discussion mainly to the Sunnī tradition for two reasons: first, it makes up nearly 90 percent of the Muslim population in the world today; and second, the Sunnī schools of law—specifically Shāfiʿī—make up nearly all of the Muslim population in Mindanao. That said, I will consider carefully and build heavily on the Shīʿi tradition, especially its conceptionalization of a teleological ethics, the resources of which I find crucial for the construction of public civility within Islamic political thought. It is this minority tradition that possesses the conceptual resources to ground such civility; so we must recover Islamic teleological ethics over against the legalistic enterprising of Islamic jurisprudence.

Within Sunnism it is generally accepted that there are four main sources of jurisprudence, two textual and two extratextual: (1) the Qurʾān, which represents the divine revelation given to Muḥammad; (2) the Sunna, reports of the sayings of or about the Prophet; (3) *ijmāʿ*, consensus among either or both the *ʿumma* (community) and *ʿulamāʾ* (religious scholars); and (4) *qiyās*, analogical legal reasoning that involves various interpretive tools to determine the "correct" opinion of a given legal matter.[12]

While many traditionalist Muslim scholars maintain that *sharīʿa* is unalterable given its divine origin, reformist scholars tend to point to its interpretation and application as being context-dependent. An example of the latter is Tariq Ramadan, who holds that while *sharīʿa* expresses core principles of Islam it is more fundamentally about "faithfulness to the divine will," a faithfulness that at points requires "active and creative" reasoning in order to establish the norms for a given social-historical context. In other words, *sharīʿa* is a "framework" that helps to "actualiz[e]" eternal principles within history. Consequently, a Muslim's attempt to discern what Islamic fidelity requires in a given situation involves both the texts (i.e., Qurʾān and Sunna) and an "understanding of the context" (i.e., *ijmāʿ* and *qiyās*). Accordingly, Ramadan distinguishes the "way to the source" that is *sharīʿa* from "the Source" who is God: whereas the latter gives "the absolute and the universal," *sharīʿa* must be considered "in time . . . immersed in the reality of humankind."[13]

Similarly, the Emory University scholar Abdullahi Ahmed An-Naʿim notes that while *sharīʿa* is the "whole Duty of Mankind [involving] all aspects of public and private law," he highlights elsewhere its contextualizability, suggesting that interpretation of it is necessarily "a historically-conditioned *human* interpretation." Again elsewhere, he writes, "There is nothing to prevent the formation of a fresh consensus around new interpretative techniques . . . of the Qurʾan and Sunna, which would become part of Shariʿa."[14] Social-historical context can and often does demand a fresh reading of *sharīʿa*.

Of course, not all scholars are sympathetic to the idea of contextualizability. With the rise of Western geopolitical dominance, for example, in Mindanao as well as in many Muslim majority countries, the various principles that make up *sharīʿa* were split largely into two sets: (1) the ritualistic aspects (*ʿibādāt*); and (2) those aspects that deal with civic norms (*muʿāmalāt*). Historically, while certain of the ritualistic aspects were allowed to persist—though relegated to the private sphere—the civic aspects of *sharīʿa*—with occasional exceptions made for family and personal law—were replaced by Western constitutional norms. Interestingly, this proposal may seem prima facie a promising way of enhancing the prospect of public civility between Muslims and non-Muslims; for by granting significant measures of religious expression without condoning a wholesale "*shariʿa* politics," a given political order might appear promising in maintaining the secular imperative. Yet such an arrangement has delegitimizing effects on authentic public life for Muslims, who then are confined to a delimited adherence to *sharīʿa*—not to mention the fatal effects resulting from modern-day Islamist movements as violent reactions to it.[15]

Here it is important to discuss how any given interpretation of *sharīʿa* is formulated necessarily within the framework of Islamic legal theory—the juristic methodology developed in an effort to establish what is considered as decreed by God. This fact suggests that divine commandment—or *sharīʿa*—is one thing; human jurisprudence about *Islamic law*, another. This distinction between divine law and human jurisprudence underscores the deeply constructive character of Islamic law. On this basis, any interpretation of *sharīʿa* can be seen to be necessarily a product of Islamic jurisprudence, a fact that renders Islamic law as necessarily contextualized, to some extent or another, along some criteria or other. (In the next chapter, I return to a discussion of the contextualized nature of *sharīʿa* as I argue for the need to recover an ethics-based view of Islamic law in contrast to the overly juristic view of traditionalist scholars, the latter of which tends to seek an implementation of *sharīʿa* within state law—a move that violates the secular imperative.)

Nevertheless, given either the contextualizability of *sharīʿa* or, even more conservatively, the constructed character of *fiqh* (Islamic jurisprudence), formal implementation of *sharīʿa* would entail a legal pluralism that would not only jeopardize the secular imperative but also gravely diminish the prospect of a common public life. At the end of the next section I discuss further the problems with legal pluralism. Next, however, I consider another major resource within Islamic jurisprudence that some scholars suggest is adequate for securing a basis for public civility.

IJTIHĀD AS "INDEPENDENT REASONING"

While literally *ijtihād* means the "exertion of mental energy," it may be characterized more usefully as a juridical methodology used in determining the applicability of a legal opinion in a context different from the one in which the original textual sources of Islamic law (i.e., the Qur'ān and *ḥadīth*) were given. The practice of *ijtihād* is, for some scholars, a promising basis for public civility.[16] But is it?

Put simply, the practice of *ijtihād* is juridical reasoning about *sharīʿa*—a characterization in view of which An-Naʿim suggests that "any understanding of Shariʿa is always the product of *ijtihad*."[17] Of course, not all scholars would agree with this view, as *ijtihād* represents a methodology in Islamic legal thought that is under significant contestation. In what follows, I discuss a central aspect of this contestation that bears on its viability (or inadequacy) for constructing public civility.

On the one hand, there are scholars who argue that in early Islamic legal history there had been a "closing of the gate of *ijtihād*" and that therefore *sharīʿa* is now a matter of taking *as given* what is found in the textual sources. If this position holds, then all legal reasoning would be confined to Islamic doctrine as given "once and for all"—that is, it would necessitate *taqlīd*, or "the unquestioning acceptance of the doctrines [as] established [by the] schools and authorities" prior to the closing of the gate (ca. ninth century).[18] Thus, it would seem that in societies that are majority Sunnī (such as in Mindanao) where *taqlīd* is favored, the prospects of public civility would be less promising since the practice of *ijtihād* would be invalidated.

On the other hand, for many if not most Muslims scholars, including those in the Sunnī tradition, the gate of *ijtihād* is considered not to have been closed. Rather, the principles of *ijtihād* are recognized by jurists to be used for the purpose of Islamic legal theory (*uṣūl al-fiqh*). A widely recognized authority on Islamic law, Mohammad Hashim Kamali, argues that the practice of *ijtihād*, which is used to harmonize reason and revelation, is "the most important source of Islamic law next to the Qur'an and the *Sunnah*." He explains, "Justice is the supreme goal and objective in Islam"—for which reason any aspects of Islamic jurisprudence that are now deemed unjust must be considered not to "belong to the *sharīʿah*" and should "be revised through *ijtihād*."[19] Accordingly, scholars will want to argue that there are indeed significant resources within Islamic jurisprudence for a basis of public civility given the practice of *ijtihād*. But even with the resources of *ijtihād*, there remain points of plausibly irresolvable tension between Islamic law and the social-political norms of liberal democratic societies, a discussion to which I now turn.

The renowned scholar of Islamic law Rudolph Peters delineates various crucial aspects of *sharīʿa* that may undermine the prospects of securing an Islamic basis of public civility in plural societies by way of the practices of *ijtihād*. As examples of intractable tension between "Shariʿa criminal law" and international human rights norms, Peters points to issues such as "inhuman punishment," the principle of equality "before the law," religious freedom and "freedom of expression," and the right of children "not to be subject to the death penalty." Similarly, the legal theorist Erich Kolig contends that the "laws, norms, values, practices, and customary conventions" of liberal societies stand "in direct conflict" with those of Muslim societies, even "to the point of total incompatibility." Whether or not the incompatibility is "total," unquestionably there are significant "contradictions at many levels" and "a noticeable degree of incompatibility" between *sharīʿa* and non-Muslim legal systems. At bottom, should certain central aspects of *sharīʿa* be implemented in the legal structures of liberal societies, such societies "would be in danger of negotiating away [certain] fundamental liberties" such as "exercising religious choice," "freedom of expression," and the like.[20]

Denis MacEoin, a scholar of Islamic jurisprudence, likewise points out that since *sharīʿa* encompasses a "full range of human behaviour" there inevitably would be significant challenges to certain modern liberal rights—unless special legal status were given to communities that would arguably unjustly place them "above the law to which we are all bound." *Sharīʿa* legal codes range from criminal matters and business affairs to ritual practices and dietary regulations and even to matters concerning international law. Given this wide range of aspects within private and public life to which *sharīʿa* applies, any "dichotomous legal system" in plural societies would create obvious and intractable points of tension. In the United Kingdom (about which MacEoin is concerned directly) as well as in other plural societies, such as Mindanao, legal pluralism would result in irresolvable legal quagmires. Consider an example from family law: "Marriage in itself invites rulings on whether the bride may be underage or not; whether the husband may have sex with his wife even if she is underage; whether a husband may marry more than one wife; . . . and whether the bride's consent is needed in what is regarded as a civil contract between her male guardian . . . and the groom."[21] Thus, with respect to criminal law as well as personal and family law, the problems of legal pluralism illustrated here would undermine gravely the task of constructing public civility. The question remains, then, What resources if any might provide an Islamic basis of public civility?

MAṢLAḤA AS "THE COMMON GOOD"

Within Islamic jurisprudence there is a notion of the common good, captured in the term *maṣlaḥa*, that also has been used in attempts to construct public civility. However, as I argue below, there are problems with attempts to ground a framework of public civility on this basis, problems that in many ways mirror those considered in the previous chapter with respect to the Catholic common good tradition. I discuss now the notion of *maṣlaḥa* in order to consider its (in)adequacy as a ground for public civility, arguing that it fails to serve as a universal basis since it necessarily pertains only to Muslim communities.

Maṣlaḥa literally means "a source or cause of well-being and good" and can be translated as "public interest" or "social good." While *maṣlaḥa* may be understood as "the common good," it is more precisely a legal criterion by which the common good is to be realized.[22] The following comments about the history of the idea and the use of *maṣlaḥa* as a juristic practice may help both to illuminate its meaning and to elucidate the problems it poses with respect to its serving as a basis for a universal framework of public civility.

The juristic practice of *maṣlaḥa* can be traced to the eighth century, and the first mention of it is found in Mālikī jurisprudence in the tenth century. Essentially related to *maṣlaḥa* is the notion of *maqāṣid al-sharīʿa*—the objectives of Islamic law—developed by al-Ghazālī (d. 1111): "What we mean by *maslahah* is preserving the objective of the Law that consists in five ordered things: religion, life, reason, progeny, and property." For al-Ghazālī, *maṣlaḥa* is fundamentally about preserving the *maqāṣid*—that is, the goals of *sharīʿa*. Similarly, the fourteenth-century Muslim scholar al-Shāṭibī (d. 1388) contends that a jurist is expected to consider *maṣlaḥa* in order to secure the *maqāṣid*.[23] In short, in an effort to maintain the *maqāṣid* through historical change by applying them to modernizing contexts, various schools of jurisprudence began to understand *maṣlaḥa* as one of the key juristic tools by which to address the accompanying and inevitable legal change. In other words, *maṣlaḥa* became a juristic tool by which to implement and ensure the goals of Islamic law—the *maqāṣid*—in novel contexts.

Here the central problem arises in trying to construct a framework of public civility on the basis of *maṣlaḥa*: the so-called common good is informed necessarily by the *maqāṣid*, or the objectives of Islamic law. Thus, even if *maṣlaḥa* is taken into account when securing the *maqāṣid*, still the *maqāṣid* is given for the good of a Muslim qua Muslim. As Muhammad Qasim Zaman puts it, "The good in *maṣlaḥa* [is] defined by *sharīʿa*" (or, more exactly, *maqāṣid al-sharīʿa*); so while "the *sharīʿa*'s good is meant for the people," and in this sense might be said to be concerned with the common good (*maṣlaḥa*), "it is not the people who determine [the good of *maṣlaḥa*]" but the *maqāṣid* that do so. Put simply, the *maqāṣid* ground and govern *maṣlaḥa*. Qasim Zaman continues, "The importance of the common good in . . . the *sharīʿa* is recognized and indeed stressed, but any such idea only holds inasmuch as it is grounded in the *sharīʿa*" (or again, more exactly, the *maqāṣid al-sharīʿa*).[24] The same problem, then, that challenges the Catholic view of the common good—the relativistic character of the good that is only putatively common—besets the Islamic conception of *maṣlaḥa* as well. As one scholar of Islam writes, "The shariʿa may be functionalized for uncivil ends."[25]

However, many Muslim scholars, for example, Hashim Kamali and Mashood Baderin, continue to argue for the viability of the common good approach, pointing to the contextualizability of the *maqāṣid*, especially in light of the resources of *maṣlaḥa* and *ijtihād*. Hashim Kamali recommends the resources of *ijtihād* to bridge "the gap between the Shari'ah and modern conditions" in order to ensure the aim of Islamic law (*maqāṣid*). Baderin takes an even stronger view, arguing that *maṣlaḥa* concerns not only the "welfare of the Muslim community" but also the protection of "the rights and welfare of individuals" qua human individuals. Other Muslim scholars such as the famed Yūsuf al-Qaraḍāwī and his disciple Ṭāhā Jābir Fayyāḍ ʿAlwānī consider the *maqāṣid* a suitable "framework of argumentation" or a "framework of reference" within which Muslims could pursue "the common good."[26] In short, it is argued that given the scope and flexibility of *maṣlaḥa*, the *maqāṣid* do not preclude but rather promote the common good as a basis for constructing public civility across divergent communities.

However, the problem with such attempts to construe the *maqāṣid* (again, the purposes of Islamic law) as an ever-adaptable framework can be seen when one considers the fact that the contextualizability of the *maqāṣid* does not imply their being contentless. That is, while *maṣlaḥa* and *ijtihād* are useful in determining how and which aspects of *sharīʿa* are to be implemented, they do not empty the *maqāṣid* of their specific content. Put positively, the *maqāṣid* set the parameters of *maṣlaḥa*, making *maṣlaḥa* mainly about human and communal flourishing as construed from a specifically Muslim perspective. Thus, though it is argued that the purpose of *sharīʿa* is to attain "the well-being (*maṣlaḥa*) of humanity," *maṣlaḥa* is ultimately "synonymous with God's purpose in revealing His law":[27] that is, a Muslim God (Allāh) revealing Islamic law (*sharīʿa*) to Muslim believers (*ʿumma*). For these reasons, a so-called Islamic common good approach (*maṣlaḥa*) is an unpromising basis on which to construct public civility in plural societies.[28]

As a final comment, it is instructive to note that many scholars of Islam have suggested that Islam emerged in large part "to embrace mankind in a truly universal *umma* [community]," one that would "supersed[e] all sectarian splits and tribal particularisms," especially those of Christianity and Judaism. As such, it is argued, Islam could be considered the true "carrier of the common good."[29] Yet, to be sure, many Catholic scholars would claim as much for their own tradition. Consider, for example, the words of David Hollenbach, who writes on the Catholic Church, "[In our pluralistic age] we might learn something from the largest NGO on the globe today that has also been the principal bearer of the common good tradition."[30] Further still, a scholar of Islam claims that, given democratic ideals separating church and state, "it is secularism that articulates the common good."[31] In short, it is plain to see that a central problem for plural polities is the presence of multiple, sometime conflicting, and inevitably incompatible notions of "*the* common good." Instead, then, of a *common good* approach, crucial to the task of constructing public civility in plural societies is a recovery and a reassertion of the notion of *the human good*, along with an articulation and an acknowledgment of this notion within the respective traditions of a given plural society.

In sum, attempts to ground public civility on the basis of the common good are subject to either a relativism whereby the good is defined insularly and is thereby not truly common (as in the case of *maṣlaḥa*) or a conceptual incoherence owing to the fact that there are multiple and conflicting "common goods" within an "association of associations" that is the plural polity (as in the case of the Catholic common good approach). To note finally, the common good approach bears a further fatal flaw. The political theologian Mark Chapman writes, "The obvious problem with common good language is this: where a majority defines the common good, the minority can easily lose its voice."[32] And it is precisely this problem faced by Muslim communities in non-Muslim majority societies, and conversely by non-Muslims in Muslim-majority contexts. A universal and thereby more promising basis for intercommunal public civility is found in the notion of the human good, the essential attributes of which inhere in everyone regardless of one's tradition. In the next section, therefore, I consider the conceptual resonances between the human good and the Islamic notion of *fiṭra*, or original human disposition.

In the preceding sections, I considered the question of whether there is within the resources of Islamic jurisprudence a promising basis on which to construct a framework of public civility between divergent communities. In doing so, I discussed the notions of Islamic legal theory (*uṣūl al-fiqh*) and Islamic law (*sharīʿa*) along with the juristic tools of *ijtihād* (independent legal reasoning) and *maṣlaḥa* (common good). I argued that unless some other basis could be found, what remains is an inadequate framework of public civility.

The inadequacy notwithstanding, I note along with Hashim Kamali that "the invaluable contribution of the great *ʿulamāʾ* [scholars] of the past to the legal and intellectual heritage of Islam is undeniable and never to be taken lightly."[33] The points I make remain, however: (1) that, rather than within the resources of jurisprudence, an Islamic basis for public civility is more promisingly located within the dimension of *sharīʿa* having to do with morality (*akhlāq*); and (2) that this dimension provides the resources needed for public civility especially when considering the Islamic counterpart to the notion of the human good, *fiṭra*.

The purpose of the next section, then, is to consider whether this notion of *fiṭra* could indeed serve as a conceptual counterpart to the idea of the human good. I proceed by examining the essential attributes of the human good—relationality, purposiveness, and rationality—in the context of the Islamic scriptural corpus, especially the Qurʾān. My contention here is modest: namely, that within classical and contemporary Islamic scholarship there is a legitimate way of reading the Islamic corpus that resonates with my notion of the human good. In the section that follows thereafter, I build on this material to consider resources within Islamic theological ethics in order to construct an Islamic political theology of public civility based on the notion of *fiṭra*.

AN ISLAMIC CONCEPTION OF THE HUMAN GOOD

The reading of *fiṭra* that follows admittedly goes against the grain of contemporary mainstream understandings. In seeking to construct a framework for public civility in plural societies, however, this alternative reading is to be preferred; it is one that incidentally finds resonances in many of the works of not only contemporary reformist Muslim thinkers but also classical Muslim scholars. It is worth noting here, as one scholar points out, that "the existing secondary literature on *fiṭra* [is] not very extensive" and also that, aside from its use by one Muslim scholar—namely, Sachedina—to my knowledge the notion of *fiṭra* has not been used to frame a pluralistic Islamic political theology.[34] Rather, as we have seen, approaches to constructing an Islamic political theology in plural societies typically is framed on the basis of *maṣlaḥa* (the common good).

Having discussed the conceptual resonance between the notions of the human good and *imago Dei* in the previous chapter, below I show

how the notion of *fiṭra* (original human disposition) serves as a promising Islamic counterpart to the human good and thereby as a basis for public civility. First, I build on several Muslim scholars and key Quranic passages to make this case. Then I respond to charges that *fiṭra* does not comport with the view of universal human flourishing that I present but instead connotes the idea of flourishing specifically as a Muslim; that is, *fiṭra* is inextricably tied to what it means to be a "good Muslim." Here I engage with both contemporary and classical thinkers on either side of the issue. I close this discussion with remarks about the possibility of there being conceptual resonance at all between the notions of the human good and *fiṭra* (and, by implication, that of *imago Dei*).

The aim of this discussion is to set the theoretical groundwork for an Islamic political theology amenable to the construction of public civility in plural societies. An outworking of such a political theology makes up the next chapter, where I employ the basis of *fiṭra* in constructing this ethics-based political theology.

FIṬRA AS THE HUMAN GOOD

Key texts in the Qur'ān recognize the diverse communities in which humanity is situated: "If your Lord had pleased, He would have made all people a single community, but they continue to have their differences" (11:118; cf. 5:48).[35] Yet there are also passages that indicate the commonalities of all human persons in virtue of their humanity. For example, *sūra* 91:7–10 speaks of a morality common to every human person in virtue of each having a soul created by God; 7:172 suggests a common spirituality in which all human persons participate, having descended as "Children of Adam" with the same "Lord"; and passages such as 3:104–15 and 9:71 describe a common human rationality. In brief, there are many Quranic passages that point to the moral, spiritual, and rational attributes common and intrinsic to all human persons.

Furthermore, the Qur'ān emphasizes the dignity of human persons in passages such as 17:70 that teach, as one Muslim scholar notes, that every human being has a "spiritual compass" and thus is "granted dignity by God." Some scholars even have argued that the grounds of human rights may be given a Quranic basis.[36] Not all scholars agree. At any rate, my contention is that this idea of a God-given universal human dignity with its attendant rights can be captured in the term *fiṭra*, which provides an Islamic basis for universal public civility.

There are recent and varied explorations of the theme of *fiṭra*. One Muslim scholar notes that while *fiṭra* "linguistically means an inborn natural disposition" it may more accurately be characterized as humanity's "common spiritual essence." Another defines it as "innate human nature," connecting it to the notion of *khalīfa*—that is, humanity's role as God's viceregent.[37] My account of *fiṭra* builds on the first account ("common spiritual essence") but differs from the second ("God's viceregent") in that I focus on what it means for a human person to flourish qua human person—not in terms of a function that a human person is supposed to perform.

Sachedina gives an account of *fiṭra* that resonates strongly with my notion of the human good. In his *Islam and the Challenge of Human Rights*, Sachedina offers an extensive treatment of Islamic theological ethics in an attempt to provide an Islamic grounding for human rights.[38] For Sachedina, human rights, human dignity, and *ḥisbah* (i.e., the fundamental call for all Muslims to "order what is right, forbid what is wrong") are intricately connected; and the notion of *fiṭra* undergirds this connection. In this landmark work, Sachedina's goal is "to reach a consensus about human agency [as] linked to human dignity" and to argue that human dignity, which is the "special mark of humanness," entails a set of "inalienable human rights." In brief, a robust notion of both human rights and human dignity is necessary to ensure that Muslims fulfill their *ḥisbah*: "to create a just public order." However, going further than the action-based approach of human agency, Sachedina argues that grounding an authentically Islamic political ethics in plural societies must ultimately be based on human dignity, which makes such action possible. For Sachedina, the Islamic conception of human dignity is captured in the term *fiṭra*.

There are central features of Sachedina's characterization of *fiṭra* that resonate with my idea of the human good. For example, with respect to the attribute of rationality, human persons possess a "universal moral worth" in view of the "intuitive reason" inherent in *fiṭra*: for intrinsic to *fiṭra* is "a substantial role for human reason to discern moral truth." Furthermore, regarding the attribute of relationality, human persons in virtue of their *fiṭra* are understood to be "essentially social," having an "existential sacredness" as "beings in God's image." Sachedina's characterization of *fiṭra* illustrates well, then, the connection between *fiṭra* and the attributes of rationality and relationality found in the human good.

With respect to *fiṭra* and purposiveness, the connection may be illustrated in the discourse of religious freedom. Many Muslim scholars seek to limit seriously the exercise of religious freedom, doing so largely by condemning dissent and criminalizing it as a form of apostasy. However, noted scholars such as Abdullah Saeed argue that the so-called apostasy laws, as allegedly derived from classical Islamic law (*fiqh*), ultimately and tragically depart from long-standing Quranic principles that in fact promote "tolerance and freedom of religion." Also, Hashim Kamali points out that apostasy does not even fall within "the purview of *ḥudūd* [i.e., prescribed punishment]" since the Qur'ān does not specify any punishment for such an act.[39] Furthermore, based on various Quranic passages (17:15, 6:104, 18:29, 29:46, etc.), Saeed argues that religion is to be understood as "a human good" and that as such it cannot be coerced: human persons have been created with "intellect and free will" (rationality and purposiveness) and should be free to abandon religion if they choose to do so.[40] In this way, religious freedom, grounded on *fiṭra*, can be seen to presuppose the essential human attribute of purposiveness.

In sum, an Islamic view of human dignity captured in the term *fiṭra*—expressible in terms of human rationality, relationality, and purposiveness—provides a promising counterpart to the notion of the human good. For Sachedina, *fiṭra* signifies the "native, innate, original . . . property with which humans are created by God"—the very "humanness of humanity." In short, humanity's rationality ("intuitive reason"), which exists for the sake of relationality ("a just public order"), both of which presuppose and respect human purposiveness ("a human good"), is captured and undergirded by the Islamic notion of *fiṭra*.[41]

FIṬRA: FLOURISHING AS A MUSLIM HUMAN?

To be sure, there are other arguably more mainstream ways of understanding the notion of *fiṭra*. Here I first consider a more traditionalist understanding of *fiṭra* that seems to be in tension with the one I present above. By building on several notable classical and contemporary Muslim scholars, I suggest a way to hold to my admittedly more idiosyncratic gloss of the term—one that nevertheless lies within the purview of classical Islamic thought.

The so-called *fiṭra* tradition—that is, the *ḥadīth* in the context of which the idea of *fiṭra* is most often discussed—originates from the following saying of the Prophet reported by his contemporary and companion Abū Hurayra: "Every child is born with the *fiṭra*; it is his parents who make him a Jew or a Christian or Majūs [i.e., Zoroastrian]." That is, according to this tradition, all of humanity is born Muslim; it is the education they receive from their environment that "leads them astray" to other faiths.[42]

It is important to note that in the context of this *ḥadīth*, the notion of *fiṭra* is connected typically to certain Quranic passages that deal with the creation of humanity:

> So [Prophet] as a man of pure faith, stand firm and true in your devotion to the religion. This is the natural disposition [*fiṭra*] God instilled in mankind—there is no altering God's creation—and this is the right religion, though most people do not realize it. (30:30)

> When your Lord took out the offspring from the loins of the Children of Adam and made them bear witness about themselves, He said, "Am I not your Lord?" and they replied, "Yes, we bear witness." (7:172)

In the first passage, *fiṭra* forms an Islamic view of humanity according to which Muslims are inherently made for devotion to Islam; that is, *fiṭra* points to the natural disposition that underscores humanity's innate knowledge of religious reality. Thus, it appears that *fiṭra* is connected intricately with the religion of Islam. Much the same is the case regarding the second passage about which the Islamicist Livnat Holtzman writes, "Although the term *fiṭra* is not explicitly used, this verse [7:172] suggests that the monotheistic faith [of Islam] is the primordial state of humankind."[43] In other words, the innate constitution of humanity (*fiṭra*) is such that each human person is created to recognize that Allāh is Lord. In both passages, then, it seems that *fiṭra* is tied inescapably to the identity of human persons as Muslim believers.

But is this the only possible or even most appropriate reading of *fiṭra* as found in the *ḥadīth* and Quranic passages? In order to answer this question, it is helpful to consider a related Islamic notion, "right guidance and going astray" (*al-hudā wa-al-ḍalāl*), that appears in various Quranic passages (e.g., 2:26, 6:125, 20:123, 34:50). This notion of *al-hudā wa-al-ḍalāl* lies at the heart of debates over divine predetermination and human free will. The second caliph, ʿUmar Ibn al-Khaṭāb (d. 644), who favored the predetermination view, held that passages such as 7:172 (referenced above) suggest that at the time of the creation of humanity God predetermined the fate of all the offspring of Adam, designating some for Paradise and the others for Hell. Likewise, the noted Ḥanbalī scholar Abū Yaʿlā (d. 1066) argued that human obedience results from God's having placed in believers the right faith; and that disobedience results from the apostasy predeterministically created in those who disobey. Similarly, Abū Hurayra (d. 681; reporter of the *ḥadīth* in question) favored a determinist view: "There is no changing God's creation with which He created all the children of Adam, that is, apostasy and faith, recognition [of "the existence of God"] and denial."[44] The point is that if God is the one who guides and leads astray, then the nature of *fiṭra* is delimited in its original disposition of either being rightly guided or not, leaving no room for human choice.

By contrast, several famed medieval Muslim scholars such as Ibn Sīnā (d. 1037) and Ibn Taymiyya (d. 1328) argued that human free will does play a role, an indispensable one, with respect to "right guidance and going astray," and, most important, that one's exercise of free will crucially depends on one's *fiṭra*. Below I consider the thought of Ibn Sīnā and Ibn Taymiyya (among others) in explicating an understanding of *fiṭra* that comports with a more universalistic view contrary to the deterministic offerings of Abū Hurayra, ʿUmar, and Abū Yaʿlā.

To begin, it should be noted that certain theological problems arise under the determinist view of *fiṭra*. For one, it would be difficult to say which religion an anachronistically labeled "Muslim" would embrace, were her *fiṭra* supposed to be "Islamic."[45] For before Islam came onto the world scene, on the assumption that *fiṭra* is innately Islamic, how could anyone properly be called a Muslim? To be sure, a solution to this problem has been put forward that exploits the notion of *ḥanīf*, "a way of being created." In *sūra* 6:75–79, for example, Abraham is called a *ḥanīfan musliman*, that is, one whose *ḥanīf* is submitted to Allāh. Thus, the argument goes, monotheists who lived before the inception of the religion of Islam are said to have been guided rightly by *fiṭra* in virtue of their being created as a true believer. But this response seems to result in a further problem: if *fiṭra* were sufficient to guide, why, then, would there have been any need for revelation as found in the Qurʾān? The answer that Ibn Sīnā gives to this question is that while one's *fiṭra* helps one to understand matters like "grammar [for] speech and metric rules [for] poetry," when it comes to something cognitively more demanding ("*rawiyya*") as well as to moral judgments, one's *fiṭra* must be "assisted by God Exalted." That said, elsewhere Ibn Sīnā contends that *fiṭra* delivers knowledge that is common to all humanity, calling such deliverances "commonly accepted judgments [*al-mashhūrāt*]"—a view that comports with the universalistic conception of *fiṭra* that I present above. (Other "jurist-philosophers" such as al-Shāṭibī as well as Ibn Tufayl make a similar point about common rationality.)[46]

Another classical Muslim thinker whose ideas support a nondeterminist view of *fiṭra* is Ibn Taymiyya. In keeping with a traditionalist understanding, Ibn Taymiyya conceded that a child of non-Muslim parents typically follows in the religious way of his parents, since he "must have someone who educates him." But, as he writes in his "The Dispute about the *Fiṭra*," over time every human being has the ability "to accept the faith that God has ordered" as well as "to abandon unbelief."[47] In arguing against divine predetermination, Ibn Taymiyya concluded that *fiṭra* does not close off the future exercise of free will.

What, then, does he do with the passage in 30:30 that declares that "the natural disposition [*fiṭra*]" can suffer "no altering"? Here Ibn Taymiyya distinguishes between God's *normative will*, expressed in terms of absolute "commands and prohibitions," and God's *creative will*, which human persons qua "created beings" may choose to disobey. Arguing that the passage in question uses the latter notion, Ibn Taymiyya contends that *fiṭra* is innately Muslim yet potentially other (e.g., Jewish or Christian or Zoroastrian), though ultimately reconvertible to an Islamic nature. In support of this view, the famed Ibn Kathīr (d. 1373), in explicating the relevant *ḥadīth*, argues that the creation of the offspring of Adam is not a once and for all event but one that takes place "a generation after a generation"; so the eternal destiny of each human creature is not predetermined but dependent on human obedience based on the free will inherent in *fiṭra*.[48]

In sum, if one holds to the Taymiyya-Kathīr view, one could argue that a given person's *fiṭra*, while non-Islamic at birth, possesses a second-order capacity to take on an Islamic nature. Conversely, by implication, given human choice and the religious "flexibility" of *fiṭra*, one also could argue that a *fiṭra*, which is Islamic at birth, could take on a non-Islamic one later in life. Indeed, it is precisely this conclusion that Holtzman draws, emphasizing the capacity of *fiṭra* to "journey from unbelief to faith and vice versa."[49] In this way, *fiṭra* can be seen to exhibit significant conceptual latitude that overlaps with the notions of the human good and *imago Dei*. Thus, while Ibn Taymiyya's view stands in tension with the interpretation of the *fiṭra* tradition by early generations, it remains an important way of construing this tradition, one that is compatible with that of other classical mainstream Muslim thinkers.

Much more would need to be said before a case could be made that an Islamic political theology, grounded on the basis of *fiṭra*, provides the resources needed for constructing public civility. I return to such a discussion about this connection between *fiṭra* and Islamic political theology in the next chapter. For now, I would like to offer some further crucial comments with respect to the suggested conceptual resonance between the notions of the human good and of *fiṭra*, and by implication of *imago Dei*.

COMMENTS ON CONCEPTUAL RESONANCE

Here I would like to consider more directly the matter of conceptual resonance as captured in this question from the natural law theorist Joseph Boyle: "Why should it be impossible that the same proposition or prescription can be expressed in different languages or arrived at with very different starting points and presuppositions?" Indeed, for Boyle, conceptual latitude isn't impossible. Many propositions, though expressed in different languages, carry essentially similar meaning. Consider mathematical propositions or very simple ones such as *eggplants are a kind of thing different from elephants*—as expressed in different languages or from divergent perspectives. The legal theorist Raymond Plant offers a helpful comment on this matter: "Words and networks of words are undoubtedly learned in specific contexts . . . , but this does not, of itself, entail that the subsequent use of words has to be tied in an internal way to these contexts." Meanings of various moral terms may be apprehended across traditions. From "different narrative contexts" there can emerge "a common set of values" on which is constructed "a moral framework" that extends beyond the "boundaries of particular narratives."[50] The terms *fiṭra* and *imago Dei*, though originating in different contexts, can, and as I have shown do, share significant conceptual overlap with the idea of the human good and thereby with each other.

Thus, while an Islamic conception of the human good might be justified by way of the Qurʾān, a Catholic one might be justified given the resources of the doctrine of the *imago Dei*. To be sure, there are parallel examples of differing yet conceptually resonant ideas within the Christian and Islamic traditions, particularly and unsurprisingly where they draw on Aristotelian thought. In other words, what is crucial with respect to the idea of the human good as a basis for public civility is not identifying some singular justification or vocabulary of it; rather, its fecundity derives precisely from having resonance within divergent traditions.

A telling example of such resonance can be seen in the comparison of the fundamental Muslim duty of *ḥisbah*—"order what is right, forbid what is wrong"—and Catholicism's first precept of natural law—"good is to be done and pursued, and evil is to be avoided."[51] While the Islamic version is a commandment and the Christian one a precept, that they serve as respective conceptual foundations for ethical theorizing within the respective traditions is worth noting.

That said, there may be concerns as to whether the notions of *fiṭra* and *imago Dei* are substantially theologically disparate so as not to warrant an essentially similar gloss. Thus might go the argument: The notion of *fiṭra* comports with a distinctly positive view of the human condition, that what is needed for a flourishing human life is mainly, or merely, legal guidance; whereas the notion of *imago Dei*, especially when considered under an Augustinian view of original sin—whereby humans are marred by the deeply deleterious effects of sin—would tend toward a much more negative view.[52] More concretely, one might argue that the universalistic conception of *fiṭra* that I put forward does not cohere well with the determinism of the majoritarian (Ashʿarī) theological traditions in Islam; and conversely, within at least a Protestant theological tradition, a rather pessimistic view of *imago Dei* would not resemble the more positive understanding of the human good as found in the idea of *fiṭra*.

I offer several comments that should allay such concerns. First, as I argue in the next chapter, there are compelling reasons to reject Ashʿarī theology in favor of the Muʿtazilī tradition, the latter of which conceives of human persons as robustly moral, rational, free-willed beings. And the Muʿtazilī theological tradition would be amenable to a more universalistic understanding of *fiṭra*, and thereby more conducive to the construction of public civility in plural societies. Second, while a Protestant conception of the *imago Dei* may tend toward more pessimistic views of the human condition, a Catholic conception, with which my project is concerned, is generally optimistic. Catholic social teaching consists in, if anything, "optimistic statements about humanity," offering a view of the human person that comports well with the attributes of the human good.[53] Indeed, from the earliest centuries of the Christian theological tradition, there have been thinkers such as Lactantius whose commentary on the idea of the *imago Dei* resembles quite closely that given by many Muslim scholars on the idea of *fiṭra*: "So much for what is due to God. Now I shall say what is due to man—though whatever you grant to man, you also grant to God, since man is the likeness of God. . . . The greatest bond between people is their [shared] humanity; . . . If we all spring from the one man whom God made, then we are certainly linked by blood."[54] For these reasons, I maintain that certain key themes within the traditions of Islam and Christianity, namely, *fiṭra* and *imago Dei*, exhibit deep conceptual resonances with the notion of the human good and thereby represent promising grounds on which to construct public civility in plural societies. Thus, though situated and articulated differently within the traditions of Christianity and Islam, the notion of the human good coheres with and draws on the ideas found within these traditions.

What is presented above is an investigation into the grounds for a universal moral framework that protects and promotes a common life marked by public civility in plural societies, a framework that may help to overcome the inadequacies of the commonly taken common good/*maṣlaḥa* approach. I also argue that the prospect of locating a basis for a framework of public civility with the resources of Islamic jurisprudence is ultimately unpromising given the specifically Muslim purposes of Islamic law (*maqāṣid al-sharīʿa*). And as argued above and in the previous chapter, a promising basis for grounding an Islamic framework of public civility is found in the notion of *fiṭra*. The overarching contention in this chapter and the previous one is that approaches to grounding public civility found within both Catholic and Islamic political theologies—the common good/*maṣlaḥa*—must be reframed on the basis of the human good; and that fundamental to this reframing are the notions of *imago Dei* and *fiṭra*, respectively.

In the next chapter, I turn to the task of articulating an Islamic political theology grounded on this notion of *fiṭra*, a theology arguably amenable to a framework of universal public civility. I do so by drawing on the resources of Islamic theological ethics rather than on those of Islamic jurisprudence, having considered above the shortcomings of the latter. By way of introduction, I first analyze more generally the notion of political theology and the crucial role it plays in plural societies.

CHAPTER 7

PUBLIC CIVILITY AND ISLAMIC POLITICAL THEOLOGY

Having looked from an Islamic perspective at the notion of *fiṭra* to ground a framework for universal public civility, in this chapter I seek to construct an Islamic political theology that would provide the conceptual structure of this framework. I build on the work of key contemporary Muslim scholars, arguing for a crucial need to recover a teleological ethics premised on a shared human nature (*fiṭra*) rather than on Islamic law (*sharīʿa*). I conclude the chapter with a comment on a more appropriate place for Islamic law within plural societies. Before doing so, however, immediately below I analyze the notion of political theology *simpliciter* and the crucial role it plays for Islamic communities in plural societies.

William Cavanaugh and Peter Scott offer this succinct and helpful characterization of political theology: "Theology is broadly understood as discourse about God, and human persons as they relate to God. The political is broadly understood as the use of structural power to organize a society. . . . Political theology is, then, the analysis and criticism of political arrangements . . . from the perspective of differing interpretations of God's ways with the world."[1] Following Cavanaugh and

Scott, I use the term *political theology* to refer to those aspects of theology that bear on questions of politics: Should the adherents of a given theological/religious community engage the political? What is the relationship between religion and politics? How, if at all, do and ought the ethical dimensions of a given theological tradition bear on social-political order? Put roughly, political theology concerns the theology of politics.

Is, then, political theology inherent to the Islamic tradition? One Islamicist writes, "Islam had its own political theology in that, on the one hand, (almost) all its rulers sought the legitimization of their power in religion, and, on the other hand, God is held to be the main source of legislation and power." Similarly, the classical jurist al-Māwardī (d. 1058) suggests, "The Imamate [religious-political leadership] is prescribed to succeed prophethood as a means of [both] protecting religion and managing the affairs of this world."[2] A theology of politics seems undeniably a part of the Islamic intellectual tradition.

In what follows, I seek to commend an Islamic political theology that is conducive to, indeed crucial for, the construction of public civility, drawing centrally on a contention shared by many Muslim scholars, namely, that there is a deep need to return to the so-called original Islamic vision that seeks to prioritize ethics (*akhlāq*) over law (*aḥkām*). Such an Islamic political theology would offer a promising framework for intercommunal—Muslim and non-Muslim—public civility in plural societies.

A FRAMEWORK FOR NEGOTIATION

Abdullahi Ahmed An-Naʿim offers a robust Islamic political theology based on his analysis of the Islamic corpus and on the historical-social reality found especially at the time of the Prophet Muḥammad. The core of An-Naʿim's political theology consists in the dual contention that the early history of Islam permits, indeed prescribes, a separation of the religious and political spheres of authority; and any authentically Islamic political theology must presuppose a *secular state*. In the following sections, I unpack An-Naʿim's ideas, highlight several implications of his proposal, and offer an appreciative critique of both. I begin with a brief historical sketch of the early political history of Islam.

Separation of the Spheres of Authority

In the early history of Islam—during Umayyad rule (ca. 661–750) and the ʿAbbāsid monarchies (ca. 750–850)—Muslim rulers began to see themselves as not only successors of the Prophet, but as "deputies of God" or caliphs (Ar. *khalīfa*), thereby essentially enmeshing religion and political rule. During this period, alongside caliphate rule, there emerged significant juridical enterprising, which took up the all-important role of establishing the principles of Islamic law. Over time and through the classical period (from the tenth to the fourteenth century), the so-called three circles, *religion*, *state*, and *society*—which initially were one and the same circle—began to pull apart. More precisely, as the renowned scholar of Islam Patricia Crone observes, while state and religion no longer overlapped, society was "still organized on a religious basis"—that is, as a nomocracy, a social order based on religious law.[3]

Other scholars are quick to point out, however, that even the overlap between religion and politics originally was not meant to be so complete: even though Islam as a religion was constituted within the political organization "almost from the start,"[4] the original Islamic vision in Mecca was one whereby politics and religion were not enmeshed. In the Meccan period—when the very idea of *sharīʿa* was revealed to the Prophet (see *sūra* 45:18)—a normative political structure did not feature at all. Again it was in Mecca that 85 of a total 114 *sūra*s of the Qurʾān were given; and these passages largely concerned ethics and ritual regulations. Moreover, even in the time following the original caliphate of the Prophet's Medina, there was a distinct separation between state administration and divine guidance, a sort of "double administration." In short, the supposed complete identity of religion and politics existed neither in Mecca nor throughout most of the classical and medieval periods after the Medinan polity. Accordingly, the contemporary fundamentalists' "cry [of] 'religion and state'" does not fit well the history of Islam.[5] What was normative was the separation of religion and politics. Such an understanding makes Crone's claim that the political embodiment of Islam existed "almost from the start" just that: almost. I turn now to consider further arguments for this view.

In a recent work, An-Naʿim maintains the need for a *secular state*, which he argues best accommodates, indeed ensures, an authentic Muslim way of life.[6] According to An-Naʿim, wherever Islam and the state are enmeshed, Muslims are subject to coercion by the state. This subjugation inevitably promotes *nifaq*, or hypocrisy, which is "categorically and repeatedly condemned by the Qurʾan." For this reason, only a religiously plural (i.e., secular) state guarantees the possibility of Islam being practiced as it should be: freely. Therefore, a secular state is necessary for Islam.

Here An-Naʿim notes an important distinction between *Islam-and-state* and *religion-and-politics*. A failure to separate Islam and the state would be to contravene certain fundamental tenets of Islam (e.g., the exercise of free worship, complete submission to Allāh), whereas to separate religion and politics is neither beneficial to democratic society nor even possible on the basis of the internal logic of Islam. The rationale runs as follows. The *state* is meant to implement the deliverances of a given society's political processes, whereas *politics*—the activity of political actors vying for their "competing visions of the public good"—means to contribute to the discourse and well-being of a liberal democratic society. So while it is arguably necessary and beneficial that Islam, or perhaps better, Muslims, remain connected to politics, it ought to remain distinct from the state as such. A primary role of the state, then, is to provide a "framework for negotiating ethical differences among citizens." Only a functionally secular state could grant this kind of political equality among its divergent communities.

Furthermore, not only is a secular state necessary for Islam, but the internal logic of Islam itself makes a so-called Islamic state impossible, for the simple fact that a secular state is incompatible with Islamic theocracy.[7] Consequently, An-Naʿim writes plainly, "the claim of some Muslims to [a right] to enforce Shariʿa through state institutions must be forcefully blocked because it constitutes an immediate repudiation of the right of all citizens to believe in Islam or another religion or opinion." For Islam to flourish it must be adhered to freely. Thus, given its "essentially religious nature," *sharīʿa* cannot undergo political implementation lest it yield both an untenable liberal political theory and an inauthentic Islamic polity. Furthermore, historically considered, *sharīʿa* would not have been enforced by the state because the state did not have the authority to enact it; this authority lay with the religious scholars (*ʿulamāʾ*). Thus, while Islamists see the so-called state of Medina as the ideal Islamic polity, An-Naʿim argues that "unless there is another prophet (and Muslims do not accept that possibility), that first polity of state cannot be replicated anywhere." Simply put, "the state has always been a political, not religious, institution." Therefore, a functionally secular state is not only most conducive to constructing public civility, but it is theologically normative in Islamic political thought ("because no other human being can enjoy the Prophet's combination of religious and political authority").

Implications and Critique

There are three important implications of An-Naʿim's work that I find relevant for constructing an Islamic political theology of public civility. I spell these out before turning to a more general, appreciative critique.

The first implication is that the separation of the religious and political spheres does not entail the strict *dogmatic secularism* described above. Simultaneously and paradoxically, religion does require a *political secularity* in order to "mediate relations among different communities" who occupy a common space. In this way, An-Naʿim's Islamic political theology not only accommodates but also positively requires religion's crucial if careful involvement in the political. The second implication is that conceptual justifications of the *secular imperative* (described above), as given by divergent traditions, need not be identical to be valid. Different religious and nonreligious traditions may ground differently their justifications for a secular state; indeed, it is precisely because they would so ground them that the secular imperative is necessary. The third and final implication is that, as An-Naʿim himself writes, his political-theological "framework does not preclude the application of some principles of Shariʿa through state institutions," provided that such application is (1) grounded in "civic reasons"; (2) subject to the safeguards of "constitutional and human rights"; and (3) in harmony with "the rights of others."[8] This last point brings me to an appreciative critique of An-Naʿim's overall project and its implications. As to the three implications delineated above, I offer empirical evidence in favor of the first, a critical comment on the second, and a challenge regarding the third.

Regarding the first implication, I agree with An-Naʿim that separation of Islam and the state does not entail a dogmatic secularism, and also affirm that the separate spheres of politics and religion stand to benefit mutually from one another. In fact, there is a critical distance between the activities of religion and politics that must carefully be maintained in order for public civility to flourish. Political scientists like Toft, Philpott, and Shah have investigated hundreds of cases of religious terrorism in the past century on the one hand and several dozen cases of democratization on the other. In summarizing their findings in cases where religion either had a positive effect on democratization or was a nonfactor with regard to terrorism, they conclude that (1) the society in question was characterized by neither religious-political *integration* nor religious-political *isolation* but a careful balance between these extremes; and (2) a carefully articulated political theology delineated this proper distance from both integration and isolation. In cases of religious violence, an integrationist political theology is to be avoided: "Religious actors who seek integration . . . are the chief cause of religious terrorism. . . . [I]f a religious actor that is *not* privileged by the state holds a political theology that runs counter to the interests of the state, then that religious actor will likely seek a change in the status quo. If the political theology of that actor supports the use of violence, the state is likely to face a higher risk of religious terrorism." And in cases of religion and democratization, an isolationist political theology is unworkable: "Religious actors are far more likely to be prodemocratic when they enjoy some [but not complete] institutional independence from the state . . . , and when they have a democratic political theology. Where religious actors lack either or both of these qualities—one institutional and the other ideological—they are likely to fall well short of prodemocratic activities." In sum, for the sake of both procuring democratic freedom and deterring religious terrorism, neither a secular suppression of religion (isolation) nor a religious-political regime (integration) is beneficial, and the political theologies of the religious communities largely help to determine the relevant outcome. In this way, recent evidence from political science corroborates An-Naʿim's Islamic political theology.[9]

As to the second implication of An-Naʿim's proposal—that different traditions ground their justifications for a secular state differently—this argument runs parallel to my account of the human good with respect to the *imago Dei* and *fiṭra*. The advantage, however, in grounding a political theology on the basis of the human good over against An-Naʿim's proposal is that the former provides more specific content (i.e., the essential human attributes) to help adjudicate on contentious matters among divergent communities. That is, by considering the common humanity shared by members of various communities, there is a large and robust set of resources common to all human traditions from which to draw in constructing public civility.

Third, An-Naʿim suggests that, provided certain conditions of constitutionality, citizenship, and equality, his framework does not disbar the application of at least "some" principles of *sharīʿa* through state institutions. Aside from giving these rather general prescriptions, however, An-Naʿim is conspicuously silent. Questions naturally arise: Which aspect of the principles of *sharīʿa* would be allowed? And by what criteria would decisions about this allowance be made? Even given these three criteria, however, there could just as easily and unfortunately be "shariʿatized" constitutions as well as differing Islamic views on the equality between, say, men and women and between Muslims and non-Muslims.[10] Moreover, substantive elements of criminal and family law in *sharīʿa* do not comport with the legal systems that befit liberal democratic societies. A more promising way forward is to ground an Islamic political theology on the basis of *fiṭra*—a notion located specifically in the ethical dimensions of *sharīʿa*. (I discuss this approach in the next section in dialogue particularly with Abdulaziz Sachedina.)

By way of a final comment on An-Naʿim's work, I note the following. Realizing that his view—a political theology that proscribes the conflation of Islam and the state—is not prevalent, let alone popular, among a majority of contemporary Muslim scholars, An-Naʿim suggests that this fact "does not by itself mean that it is wrong." Indeed, "the deep crisis Muslims . . . are experiencing regarding the relationship of Islam to the state . . . indicates the need for a fresh reading" of Islamic political thought, a radical "Islamic reform."[11] In other words, an originally more authentic (i.e., Meccan) and historically more faithful (i.e., pluralistic) Islamic political theology is needed in order to navigate the terrain of plural democratic societies.

This call for a "fresh reading" of Islamic political ethics is admittedly and by definition reformist. The merit, therefore, to this recovery is not in its being currently mainstream but precisely in its not being mainstream as well as "radical" in the truest sense of the term: going back to the root.

"INCLUSIVE POLITICAL THEOLOGY"

Sachedina is another Muslim scholar who recognizes the need and argues for a radical recovery of a more pluralist Islamic political theology (*al-kalām al-siyāsī*):[12] "The most critical challenge facing the traditional leadership [*ʿulamāʾ*] is to search for an inclusive political theology that no longer discriminates by faith to determine an individual's rights and duties. . . . [For this challenge to be met, a] major shift has to occur from a juridical to a theological-ontological status of human personhood." Sachedina's overarching contention is that in order for Muslim communities to articulate a pluralistic Islamic political theology, what needs recovering is the original ethical Quranic vision that acknowledges the universal and equal dignity of human persons qua human persons; and that prerequisite to this recovery is a radical reevaluation of the juridical tradition that has eclipsed this more fundamental moral Islamic vision. In what follows, building on Sachedina's work, I consider several crucial ideas essential to overcoming what Sachedina refers to as "the restrictive provisions of the Islamic juridical heritage"—that is, crucial ways in which the juridical tradition has undermined the prospect of a pluralistic political theology. Central to this discussion are considerations of (1) the historical displacement of the more rationalist Muʿtazilī theological ethics by the revelationist Ashʿarī tradition; and (2) the subsequent need for a recovery of a robust view of human teleology in Islamic ethics. This reappraisal of Islamic theological ethics is needed in order to articulate a pluralistic political theology, which in turn is needed for the task of constructing public civility in Islamic contexts.

The Juridical Closure of Pluralistic Islamic Political Theology

The Muʿtazilī and Ashʿarī traditions grew out of the debate over the question of free will and predestination, a debate that originated in the Umayyad period. This debate stirred great political controversy among the early Muslims—second only to that of the Imamate, which entailed the succession of rulership following the death of Muḥammad. The controversy had centrally to do with the Jabarites, who used the doctrine of predestination (*jabr*) to justify their existing political rulership over against the Qadarites (*qadar* refers to human free will), who opposed both the former's predestinarian doctrine and their claim to caliphate legitimacy. The Qadarites made a rather powerful argument. Whereas the Jabarites, given their predestinarian bent, grounded justice in revelation (Qurʾān), the Qadarites viewed the notion of justice as something that people would have known before the Quranic revelation was given. Hence, contra Jabarite theology, when it comes to determining the requirements of justice, human knowledge and free-willed choice fulfills a more crucial role than what revelation on its own can determine.[13]

Over time, where Jabarite predestinarianism was taken up in Ashʿarī theology, Qadarite views continued in the tradition of Muʿtazilī theology. Here Sachedina offers a helpful characterization of these subsequent traditions that explains well their main differences with regard to Islamic theological ethics.[14] Whereas Ashʿarī theology denies human reason "any ability to understand the [morality] of an act" apart from divine revelation, within the Muʿtazilī tradition reason is "God's gift to humanity to develop their moral consciousness." And the latter view better supports the justice of God: "God's justice requires God to guide humanity to attain the goal for which it was created, namely, to establish justice on earth. . . . [Accordingly, h]umanity's endowment with innate moral cognition and volition to carry out intimations is part of God's justice." Thus, in their search for what Sachedina calls "a common foundation upon which to construct a universal morality," Muʿtazilī theologians constructed what may be termed an Islamic "natural theology" based on a rational-moral human nature (*fiṭra*); and on this basis Muslims are expected and able to "institute the good and prevent the evil" (*ḥisbah*).

Prior to this juridical enterprising during the classical period, along with its attendant Ashʿarī theology, stands an earlier history that allowed for political pluralism. Yet the majoritarian Ashʿarī theology had tended to close off the prospect of a pluralistic political theology. In view of this historical displacement—what I call *the juridical closure of pluralistic Islamic political theology*—Sachedina (among others)[15] argues for the need to recover a specifically teleological, that is, *fiṭra*-based, Islamic ethics; and such a mode of ethical reasoning is found in the Muʿtazilī tradition within which Sachedina constructs his political theology, grounding it on the basis of *fiṭra*.

Sachedina observes, with a reserved hope, that although currently forming a minority tradition in Islamic thought, the Muʿtazilī view has resurfaced among many well-respected Sunnī Muslim jurists, such as Fahmī Jadʿān and Naṣr Ḥāmid Abū Zayd. Other scholars also have pointed to similar signs of change in this regard.[16] Such hopeful signs are promising for the construction of an Islamic political theology of public civility.

Before moving to consider several issues relevant to the recovery of a more teleological Islamic ethics and concomitantly of a pluralist Islamic political theology, I note several seminal points that lend support to Sachedina's project. First, there was a considerably long period between the compilation of the Qurʾān and the establishment of Islamic jurisprudence (*fiqh*), making *fiqh* both chronologically and logically secondary to the ethical admonitions found in the Qurʾān. The time at which Islamic law contained its major components was around AD 950 or at most about a century earlier—in either case, nearly two to three hundred years after the compilation of the Qurʾān. This fact suggests *sharīʿa* would have been based more on the ethical principles found in the Qurʾān than on the juridical enterprising thereof. Second, it is mistaken to think, as many Muslim jurists do, that there exists a uniform history of Islamic legal thought. The nonmonolithic character of Islamic jurisprudence is evidenced not only by the emergence of (initially at least) hundreds of schools of law (*madhāhib*) but also by the fact that even the Sunna itself was a product of the competing and often conflicting views of the companions of the Prophet. Third, against a view that sacralizes Islamic jurisprudence, it must be recalled that Islamic legal theories were formed against the backdrop of a particular social reality, as demonstrated by the presence of multiple *madhāhib* and the attendant social contexts against which legal judgments were made. Moreover, throughout the medieval period there were many influences on the *madhāhib* from neighboring models of law and justice. Fourth and last, in addition to the diversity of legal opinions among the *madhāhib* there was the application of law codes in diverse ways by Muslim laypersons.[17] In sum, it is important to underscore the originally established ethical dimensions of *sharīʿa* now undercut by a *fiqh* jurisprudence that, it should be noted, is less integrated and less purely "Islamic" than jurists tend to concede; and this eclipse of the more malleable Muʿtazilī ethics by an Ashʿarī revelationism has worked to close off a more promising pluralistic political theology.

Thus, the reestablishment of a Muʿtazilī theological ethics, which stands over against the nonmonolithic juristic enterprising tradition of Ashʿarī theology, would help to recover not only the original Islamic vision of a just public order but also an Islamic political theology amenable to public civility.

Recovering a Teleological Islamic Ethics

The recovery of a teleologically based Islamic ethics will require a recovery of the importance of the role of human reason in ethical judgment—as opposed to an Ashʿarī "fideism" whereby a given act is deemed good or evil simply because "God so wills." Under Ashʿarī theology, there is no "natural system of ethics," whereas a Muʿtazilī theological ethics, in allowing a role for human reason to "discern moral truth," underscores and presupposes a "teleological understanding of nature." Thus, under the Muʿtazilī view, human moral reasoning, in addition to making use of divine revelation, is guided by and grounded in human teleology. As the Muslim scholar Sohail Hashmi puts it, the truth of God's laws as presented in the Qur'ān is "accessible through human contemplation of nature," including human nature.[18]

In regard to constructing a pluralistic Islamic political theology, then, we must note that, in contrast to contemporary expressions of *din-wa-dawla*—unity of religion and state—there was in Islam's early history a functional secularity that accommodated a religious diversity amidst a "multicultural social reality."[19] Essential to reestablishing such functional secularity is a recovery and reassertion of the human good in Islamic political theology. Sachedina writes, "[The original] Islamic political theology . . . had laid the doctrinal groundwork for the Muslim community to work toward reaching a consensus about the need for peaceful and just relationships with other faith communities on the basis of a common humanity." Yet, given the current predominance of Ashʿarī theology, two ideological obstacles lay in the way for such a recovery. First, the Ashʿarī theological voluntarism has eclipsed a Muʿtazilī view of justice, undermining the universal morality needed to ground public civility. Second, the two forms of guidance, God-human (*ʿibādāt*) and interhuman (*muʿāmalāt*), which rely on a distinction between the ethical aspects of Islamic law (*akhlāq*) and legal ones (*aḥkām*), have collapsed into a conflated one: *sharīʿa*-for-all. This conflation has worked to undermine the "tolerance-generating principle" found in the Qur'ān (cf. 109:6 and 2:256) that would otherwise engender a more pluralistic political theology. The solution, for Sachedina, is "to go to the foundational sources of Islamic doctrines in the Qur'an . . . to demonstrate . . . that it shares the universal language of morality and human agency."

In this way, Sachedina's "Islamic notion of natural law" would serve to provide Muslim jurists with a "teleological justification" to improve on the traditionalist solutions to "interhuman and international relations."[20] In this way, a specifically teleological conception of the human person, captured in the notion of *fiṭra*, can supplement an Islamic political theology with the resources needed to ground a common moral discursive universe. Yet in order for this radical recovery to take place, Muslim scholars must deal with Islamic theology rather than Islamic law, as the former and not the latter provides the basis for a teleological view of the human person. More specifically, as I argue below, *akhlāq*—that is, the ethical dimensions of *sharīʿa*—is the more appropriate (and promising) site on which to construct an Islamic theology of public civility.

ISLAMIC POLITICAL THEOLOGY VERSUS ISLAMISM

It must be noted that modern-day Islamists such as Ḥasan al-Bannāʾ and Sayyid Quṭb have also (and eerily) suggested that the solution to the problems of modernity is "to look back, before the development of the 'religious sciences' in which the scholars [*ʿulamāʾ*] specialized, straight to the great and inspiring source: the Qurʾan itself." Troublingly, then, this Islamist argument seems similar, in form at least, to the political theology that I commend above. Indeed, Sachedina himself notes how extensively Quṭb used the notion of *fiṭra* in his political theology(!). The problem, however, with the Islamist project has to do neither with their desire to return to the original Islamic vision nor with their reliance on the notion of *fiṭra*. Rather, the problem has to do with, first, their conceiving of the political state and the universal message of Islam as necessarily intertwined; and second, their call to *tatbiq al-shariʿa*, or the implementation of *sharīʿa* as a totalistic "governing law."[21] This is not to mention the main, obvious difference: Islamists' approval and appropriation of violence within their ideology.

Consequently, when Islamists call for a restoration of *sharīʿa*, they do not do so in accordance with the classical Islamic law or through the deliverances of the religious scholars (*ʿulamāʾ*); rather, they do so under the aegis of the legal codes of the modern state, and such efforts yield an innovative "set of Islamized constitutional arrangements." The political theorist and Muslim scholar Nazih Ayubi summarizes succinctly, "The juridic theory of the Islamic state, trying as it did to incorporate the State into the shariʿa, was based on fiction (since there is very little in the Quran and Sunna about politics and the State). The theory of the 'Islamic state' is little more than an elaborate fiqh presented as though it were pure shariʿa."[22]

To illustrate this point, consider the words of the famed Yūsuf al-Qaraḍāwī: "[When] Western crusader colonialism invaded the abode of Islam [it] changed its way of life[, and] shariʿa receded to a personal law"; therefore, the Islamic solution aims to restore the *shariʿa*.[23] It is worth pointing out here that of the over 6,200 verses in the Qurʾān, only approximately 350 of them have to do with legal rulings as such, making Islamic law somewhat peripheral to its theology and morality.[24] After all, the central concern of *sharīʿa* has always been to enjoin good and forbid evil (*ḥisbah*). The modern-day Islamist project of the "shariʿatization of politics," then, is a recent invention. As one Muslim scholar comments, there is a crucial and overdue need of a "reformed shariʿa . . . restricted to ethics."[25] We must indeed stop pretending that what some consider to be "pure *sharīʿa*" isn't more than "elaborate *fiqh*."

Yet again scholars like Crone disagree, arguing that since at least the medieval period Muslims did not see religion as "above politics" but as a "prescription for [its] regulation," fusing the religious and the political, "truth and power." But as the early twentieth-century Muslim scholar ʿAli ʿAbd al-Raziq argued famously, even if truth and power comingled to an extent, Muḥammad's rule in Medina was not ultimately a "leadership of kings" but a "leadership of the Message," and "there is much distance" between religious and political leadership in Islam. Drawing on myriad Quranic passages and *ḥadīth*, al-Raziq goes on to contend that the Prophet was commissioned by God, not to establish a theocratic state, but to deliver a moral message from God to humanity. Even Crone takes note of the "absence of the state" in the Umayyad and ʿAbbāsid eras as well as the observations of famed scholars such as al-Ghazālī and al-Rāzī who held to a distinction between "secular government and society," state and *ʿumma*.[26]

One contemporary Muslim scholar points out that despite the lack of any Quranic "blueprint" for politics, classical jurists became overly concerned with the "minutiae" of legal-political arrangements—even though the Qurʾān is concerned fundamentally with "broad moral guidelines," rather than "specific legal rulings."[27] It is against this long historical backdrop of juridical enterprising that I commend the recovery of the original Islamic vision of social-political pluralism.

REVISITING THE ROLE OF *SHARĪʿA*

What, then, is the proper role of *sharīʿa* in religiously plural and liberal societies? To conclude this chapter, I return to a discussion of the secular imperative and the role of *sharīʿa*. First, we must note that there is conceptual ambiguity about what *sharīʿa* is. While taken by some as unequivocally "God's law," we must remember that *sharīʿa* has been "developed through human agency," being based on "exegesis, interpretations, analogies, [etc.]." Hence, the noted scholar of Islam Wael Hallaq gives this succinct characterization of *sharīʿa*: "a non-state, community-based, bottom-up jural system."[28] As such, *sharīʿa* has come to take on divergent forms and to be expressed in multiple and often conflicting sets of regulations. Accordingly, *sharīʿa*, while sacred, is conceptually suffused and thereby in principle unable to serve as state law in a given liberal democratic society.

Second, when it comes to the task of constructing public civility, what is in view are the ethical dimensions (*akhlāq*) of *sharīʿa* rather than its legalistic injunctions (*aḥkām*). Emerging initially within the arguably less mainstream, philosophical tradition of Islamic thought, the notion of *akhlāq* became a part of common juristic practice during the classical period. Given that *sharīʿa* is concerned fundamentally about the morality of Muslims' lives, situating an Islamic political theology of public civility in this context (*akhlāq*) is not only acceptable, but indeed most appropriate. As the noted Muslim scholar Fazlur Rahmam observes, the Qurʾān, from which *sharīʿa* is derived, is "a work of moral admonition through and through"; thus, in seeking to maintain the Qurʾān's message, "one must start with [its] theology and ethics ... and only then approach the realm of law."[29] Thus, while the *aḥkām* of *sharīʿa* is "law" in the sense of providing normative moral guidance for Muslims to live out authentically Islamic lives, it is suitable to neither the making of legislation in plural democratic societies nor the construction of public civility therein.

Third, the term *sharīʿa*—which literally means "a way to the watering place"—appears only once in the Qurʾān, in *sūra* 45:18, in the context of which it has more to do with belief in Allāh and moral obedience than with the legalism of classical Islamic law. This contention about the morality of *sharīʿa* is buttressed by two facts regarding the passage in question: (1) this verse was given in Mecca at a time when no form of Islamic law or governance featured in the Qurʾān; and (2) in this verse the term *sharīʿa* is used in contradistinction to *ḥawā*, the "whimsical desire" of the Meccan idolaters, which underscores the fundamentally moral, not legalistic, nature of *sharīʿa*. In other words, Muslims were called to follow the moral *sharīʿa* specifically in order to avoid disobedience and idolatry. This understanding fits well the words of the Prophet himself, who stated clearly his markedly moral mission: "I have been sent to accomplish the virtues of morality."[30]

It is clear that since *sharīʿa* is most fundamentally about morality, its *akhlāq* dimensions—Islamic theological ethics—are the most appropriate resources with which to construct an Islamic political theology amenable to public civility. For this reason, a recovery of the original ethical Islamic vision of Mecca is needed, a vision that relies on the Muʿtazilī view of justice and that is grounded on the Islamic notion of *fiṭra*.

On a final note, there have been recent moves in various Muslim majority countries to implement what is known as "*sharīʿa*-oriented policy" (*siyāsa al-sharīʿa*)[31] as part of their legal-political framework. One might argue that this way of implementing *sharīʿa*—albeit somewhat qualified by the use of legal tools such as *ijtihād* (independent reasoning), *maqāṣid* (purposes of the law), and the like—may be amenable, even in its juridical manifestation (*fiqh*), to the construction of public civility. The worry in pursuing this more legalistic route, however, is that it would resemble, if not degenerate into, an Islamist state insofar as it seeks to integrate the principles of *sharīʿa* into the legal-political structure of the state. And this worry is not merely academic. An example of the danger of this "shariʿatization" of the state can be seen in Malaysia, where "*fatwā* making" recently has become bureaucratized into the remit of the state; such "etatization" has resulted not only in a semi-state-controlled Islam but also in a calcification of Islamic law. Or consider Saudi Arabia, where government "in accordance with the shariʿa" (*siyāsa al-sharīʿa*) means that *sharīʿa* is the state constitution. For these reasons, in constructing public civility in plural societies I suggest not *sharīʿa*-oriented policy (*siyāsa al-sharīʿa*) but an Islamic political theology (*al-kalām al-siyāsī*) based on an "ethicalized" *sharīʿa*. Such a political theology would be premised on the relationality, purposiveness, and rationality that is inherent in the notion of *fiṭra* and that stands opposed to the "scholastic fanaticism" that looms large over the long legal history of Sunnism.[32]

To reiterate, this call for an ethicalized *sharīʿa* is admittedly not currently mainstream; but it is precisely in its being "out of fashion" that we find its potency to undo the legalistic enterprising and to provide a robust basis on which to construct a plural political theology.

This chapter has three main objectives: (1) to point out the political-religious secularity within early Islam; (2) to consider theological and political-scientific reasons for constructing a pluralist Islamic political theology; and (3) to construct such a political theology on the basis of *fiṭra*, which in turn is based on the resources of Muʿtazilī teleological ethics. In doing so, I have commended the historical precedence and Quranic justification for the *secular imperative*; a pluralistic Islamic political theology based on the moral-rational nature of *fiṭra*; and an ethics-oriented view of *sharīʿa*.

In the next chapter I illustrate my critique of modernity (chs. 2 and 3) and my constructions of Catholic and Islamic political theologies (chs. 5 and 6) with the findings from my field interviews in Mindanao, Philippines—a modernizing, secularizing, religiously conflicted plural polity.

CHAPTER 8

THE PROSPECTS OF PUBLIC CIVILITY

This chapter applies the framework for public civility in the specific context of Mindanao, Philippines, and considers the global scope of the framework as based on the notion of the human good. I begin by offering a historical sketch of the Mindanaoan struggle in order to lay the groundwork for discussing the content from interviews I conducted with key religious and political leaders who have been involved in the Mindanao peace process. This discussion represents a worked illustration of the various critiques and constructions thus far presented. I close this chapter with two key conclusions: that interreligious dialogue, especially when grounded on the human good, contributes positively and significantly to the construction of public civility; and that certain political theologies of Muslim communities continue to pose a challenge to achieving sustained public civility.

A SPECIAL STUDY: MINDANAO, PHILIPPINES

The forty-year span from 1968 to 2008 constitutes the time period of my case study. The geographic area is the Autonomous Region of

Muslim Mindanao (ARMM), whose population includes both Muslims and Roman Catholics. During this period, conflict between Muslim communities and the Armed Forces of the Philippines (AFP) resulted in over 160,000 deaths and 2 million displaced persons. The ARMM consisted of approximately 4 million people; and Muslims, while accounting for only approximately 5 percent of the total Philippines population of 88 million, made up an overwhelming majority. In what follows, I offer a historical sketch of the major events that mark significant attempts (and failures) at peacebuilding and civility construction in Mindanao since the start of the interreligious conflict.

A BRIEF HISTORICAL BACKGROUND, 1200s–1960s

As early as the thirteenth century, Muslim merchants had settled in the Philippines, beginning in the southernmost islands of Sulu. Through the course of the next few hundred years much of the islands served as a trade center for Muslims from India and the Middle East. In 1565, during the reign of Philip II (after whom the country has since been named), the Spanish led by Legazpi conquered and colonized the northern, central, and southern parts of the Philippines, leaving only the Sulu islands under Muslim dominance. In 1898 the Spanish-American War resulted in U.S. control over the whole of the islands. In the next year the Bates Treaty, which allowed for local Muslim governance, was signed in Sulu; however, in 1902 it was rescinded, thereby bringing all "Moro" (Muslim) provinces under the control of the colonial government based in Manila, which was monitored closely by the United States.[1]

Throughout the early 1900s, on the basis of a number of legislative acts, the colonial government reappropriated a majority of the Mindanaoan islands, privatizing them for use by business corporations and non-Muslim Filipinos from Luzon (northern Philippines). By 1946, when the Philippines gained its independence from the United States, the southern Philippines comprised three main communities—Catholics, Muslims, and Lumads (indigenous communities). By the 1960s, with the further migration of Catholic Filipinos from the northern and central Philippines, the Muslims and Lumads had become minority communities throughout the south, though in several provinces Muslim communities still made up a majority of the population.

In addition to land appropriation, other Muslim grievances, such as the abolition of Muslim systems of trade and the breakdown of Islamic social structure more generally, contributed to animosity and resentment, which eventually erupted in the Jabidah Massacre of 1968. Under the direction of the AFP, Muslims in Mindanao had been forced to engender sentiments in their coreligionists to annex parts of nearby northern Malaysia. The massacre resulted when the Mindanaoan Muslims refused to follow AFP orders and were executed for their alleged mutiny. Immediately following this fatal incident, the Muslim Independence Movement (MIM) emerged, whose expressed goal was full political sovereignty.

PEACE AGREEMENTS: ATTEMPTS AND FAILURES, 1970s–1990s

On December 23, 1976, the Organisation of the Islamic Conference (OIC) mediated the first major peace agreement—the Tripoli Agreement—which was signed by the National Philippine Government and the Moro National Liberation Front (MNLF) represented by its founder, Nur Misuari. The overall aim of the agreement was "a just and peaceful political solution to the problem of the Muslims in the South of the Philippines."[2] The agreement's main points of resolution were (1) an autonomous region for the Muslim communities in Mindanao; (2) the autonomous region's being given certain rights that included the establishment of Muslim Courts based on *sharīʿa*, Islamic schools and universities, and an Islamic financial system; and (3) a cease-fire. To be sure, much would remain under the jurisdiction of the national government, such as mineral resources and a "reasonable percentage" of the revenues from them. Also, it was made explicit that, though being granted a measure of autonomy, the region in question would remain a part of the "sovereignty and territorial integrity of the Republic of the Philippines." Yet, while later concessions such as the

1977 Code of Muslim Personal Laws offered even further autonomy, interreligious hostility continued to mount.

In 1989, soon after the historic People Power movement, which resulted in the ousting of President Ferdinand Marcos and the installation of Corazon Aquino, the Aquino government established the Autonomous Region in Muslim Mindanao in keeping with the 1976 Tripoli Agreement. However, following a plebiscite vote, among the original thirteen provinces that were enumerated as part of the ARMM, nine of them, having a large number of Catholics by then, chose to opt out.

The unresolved conflict persisted under President Fidel Ramos, even after the hopeful 1996 Peace Agreement, which was viewed as a failure for its ineffectiveness to secure long-term peace. By this time, the breakaway and the (then) comparatively more militant group, the Moro Islamic Liberation Front (MILF; founded in 1984 by Hashim Salamat), gained greater membership and momentum. The MILF was adamantly opposed to any negotiations that would not result in both full independence and the creation of an Islamic state. (This is an interesting fact given that, as I discuss below, the MILF recently has become the principal negotiating partner with the Philippine government.) Until the late 1990s, the MNLF and MILF, which consisted respectively of some 15,000 and 12,000 soldiers, contributed to deep social unrest as they continued to seek full independence.

POLITICS, PEACEBUILDING, AND CIVIL SOCIETY, 2000s–2008

On April 30, 2000, President Joseph Estrada declared an "all-out war" against the MILF, which responded with an "all-out war [against] the Philippines government"—a war marked by intermittent and ultimately unsuccessful peace talks over the next eight years. Also in 2000, a much more radicalized Islamist group in Mindanao, the Abu Sayyaf, "Bearer of the Sword," stultified the prospects of peace with its terrorist actions that even the MNLF and MILF decried. By the mid-2000s, hundreds of thousands of war deaths, widespread poverty, and over half a million displaced persons set the grim background of Mindanao.

Finally, on October 14, 2008, in an eight-to-seven vote, the Supreme Court of the Philippines declared unconstitutional the Memorandum of Agreement on the Ancestral Domain (MOA-AD), an initiative to honor all ancestral land claims made by Muslim communities. The MOA-AD would have put into effect certain terms of the 2001 Tripoli Agreement of Peace, which had detailed the stipulations of the original 1976 Tripoli Agreement. Unsurprisingly, the Memorandum was viewed generally favorably by the Bangsamoro, the Muslim communities of Mindanao. The two most significant resolutions of the MOA-AD would have been (1) establishment of a Bangsamoro Homeland that would extend the Moros' geographic region; and (2) establishment of the Bangsamoro Juridical Entity (BJE), which would be given "authority and jurisdiction over the Ancestral Domain and Ancestral lands."[3] But the MOA-AD was ruled unconstitutional. The prospect of peace in Mindanao became an increasingly political matter.

Yet not all are convinced of the prospect of a political solution. Many scholars give greater weight to civil society actors, such as the Bishops-Ulama Conference (BUC; founded in 1996), which is composed of Catholic, Protestant, and Muslim religious leaders engaged in interreligious peace talks and collaborative efforts. Here it is worth pointing out the divergent modes of conflict resolution efforts used in Mindanao. The largely legal approach of Muslim communities, based on traditional Islamic law, is highly relational, localized, and largely subordinate to *sharīʿa*, whereas the Government of the Philippines (GPH) favors a positive law approach. Thus, while the GPH opposed the MOA-AD in view of its (un)constitutionality, Muslim communities argued in favor of it on the specifically moral basis that "past injustice" must be served. Given these divergent methods of conflict resolution, some scholars suggest the need to draw on third party mediation, one without which peace and political reform would be impossible. In the words of one analyst, "There have emerged two culturally separate societies existing under the same roof of national statehood but adhering to two widely differing notions of belief, culture and loyalty[: namely,] Christian traditions shared by the majority of Filipinos [and] the Moro historical tradition [which] stems from the traditional Malay sultanates."[4] While scholars point to a number of factors crucial to peacebuilding in Mindanao—from land interests and Muslims' being treated as second-class citizens to the government's inability to address past economic injustice and the Lumads[5]—it is sensible to conclude, among other things, that any prospect of peacebuilding would need to involve religious actors and their political theologies.

The forty-year period that begins with the Jabidah Massacre of 1968 and ends with the MOA-AD debacle in 2008 represents one of the most politically charged and hostile periods in Mindanao's history. During this time a plethora of civil society organizations was founded and a number of significant national and international peace talks took place. It was also through this period that the issues discussed in the previous chapters—such as those relating to legal pluralism, social separatism, the decline of public life, and the role of *sharīʿa*—became especially pertinent to the prospect of constructing public civility in Mindanao.

In his analysis of the sources and nature of the Mindanaoan struggle, the Philippines expert Steven Rood concludes that the drive toward "Muslim separatism [represents] the main challenge to peace and development."[6] As Rood suggests, and I argue below, what is needed for peace is not separatism but deep interreligious civility.

THE MINDANAOAN STRUGGLE

In order to consider an application of my framework of public civility, I draw on relevant academic literature, key arguments from previous chapters, and the findings from my interviews in Mindanao. From my interviews I draw two broad conclusions. The first is that those who were most effective in contributing to the successes of the peace process were neither political actors nor grassroots groups per se but civil society organizations whose work was focused most specifically on interreligious dialogue and peace education. This is not to say that the political leaders and community organizers had no positive impact: without official state apparatus, no formal peace agreements would ever have been put forth; and without local efforts, there would have been no support for such agreements. However, what kept political actors responsive and community organizers active was the persistent and particular work of interreligious dialogue forums.[7] The second major conclusion I draw is that the prospect of constructing public civility in religiously divided societies such as Mindanao depends crucially on the political theologies of the communities involved.

The overarching aim in this discussion is twofold: to illustrate the way in which the notion of the human good may serve as a basis both to ground theoretically the work of interreligious dialogue and to create spaces for a common public life; and to demonstrate the crucial role of political theologies in constructing public civility. In order to situate my interviews, I make a final comment on the history of the Mindanaoan struggle with particular regard to the issue of Muslim representation in official peace negotiations.

Since the 1968 Jabidah Massacre and until the 2000 "all-out war," a number of hopeful yet ultimately unsuccessful peace negotiations took place between the GPH and MNLF. Owing eventually to seemingly insurmountable barriers to resolution with the MNLF, in 2002 the GPH replaced the MNLF with the MILF as the main negotiating partner in the Mindanaon struggle. The question of legitimate representation of the Muslim communities is illustrative of the history of the peace process itself, a question complicated by several factors. First, there is the Lumad community, who have felt that their concerns have been underrepresented or not represented at all, because of which many violent reactions have resulted. Second, throughout the negotiations, the "aboveground" MILF representatives have been working with an "underground ulama" who are considered by some scholars as seeking to engender separatist sentiments.[8] Third, there is the historical tension between the relatively recently introduced group of Muslim religious scholars (*ʿulamāʾ*, or *ustadzes* as they are called in Mindanao) and the *datus*, who represent long-standing local Islamic authorities. According to the *datus*, the *ustadzes* were unduly influenced by the Islamist movements in the Middle East. This intrareligious struggle has exacerbated the matter of representational legitimacy. At any rate, over the course of four decades the *ustadzes*, initially represented by the MNLF and then by the MILF, have become the official negotiators recognized by the GPH.

Given the inclusion of the *ustadzes*, there has been in Mindanao, as one Muslim scholar observes, "a greater emphasis on Islamic rather than nationalist identity," which underscores the fundamentally religious nature of the Mindanaoan struggle. This point is confirmed by one of my interviewees, Albert Alejo, who points out plainly that the *I* for "Islamic" in MILF indicates that their struggle is unmistakably religious.[9] If the work of constructing public civility is to succeed, one must arguably consider two crucial factors: the political theology of Muslim communities and the interreligious work between Muslim communities and their neighbors.

It is a discussion of these and related themes to which I now turn as I summarize the findings from my interviews. I note that this discussion is limited in nature, given the specific context of Mindanao from which it is drawn, but it is one that nevertheless may have relevance to similarly situated societies marked by religious divisiveness.

POLITICAL THEOLOGY AND INTERRELIGIOUS ENGAGEMENT

The interreligious relations scholar Michael Barnes contends that crucial to reconciliation in religiously divided societies in general is the need to "negotiate the common space" of a given locale.[10] Accordingly, in Mindanao one particularly problematic if not fatal point of contention in negotiating such common space has to do with the role of *sharīʿa*.

The crucial issue of *sharīʿa* in the Mindanao peace process is evident in view of the failure of the four major peace proposals—the 1976 Tripoli Agreement, the 1989 Organic Act, the 1996 Peace Agreement, and the 2008 MOA-AD—since the Jabidah Massacre.[11] Every attempt to implement various aspects of *sharīʿa* in these agreements has failed: the political theology of the Muslim communities is unquestionably a most fundamental matter. Yet, notwithstanding the grave concerns regarding the implementation of legal pluralism, some scholars commend certain legal resources (*ijtihād*, *maṣlaḥa*, etc.) by which to contextualize *sharīʿa* in an effort to harmonize it with existing constitutional laws found in democratic liberal societies (discussed in chs. 6 and 7).

However, since the majority of the Muslim communities in Mindanao follow mainly the Shāfiʿī school of law, which makes minimal allowances for legal flexibility, *sharīʿa* remains for these communities "the ticklish issue" (put euphemistically).[12] Given that Muslims in Mindanao favor the idea of instituting *sharīʿa* to a large if not complete extent, how might public civility be constructed?

In an effort to consider this question and to learn more generally about the peace process in Mindanao, I met eight prominent leaders from both Muslim and Catholic communities who have been actively involved in the peace process over the past several decades. I conducted semistructured interviews with these individuals, who are widely regarded as key contributors to the peace process. I discuss my findings from the interviews below, drawing out content specific to the political theologies of and interreligious efforts in Mindanao.

FINDINGS FROM FIELD INTERVIEWS

Since the Jabidah Massacre there has been within Catholic communities a significant and concerted effort to think and work toward an enduring peace. Angel Calvo, a Catholic bishop, has worked as a peace advocate in Mindanao for over four decades.[13] In light of his experience and research, Calvo suggests that dialogue is never the end goal, for dialogue for the sake of "mutual enrichment," while "attractive" in itself, "is still too narrow." Rather, dialogue must be thought of as a means to a "common commitment to the sacred peace." Accordingly, dialogue must not remain merely theological but must engage "social, political, and economic realities." Such "dialogical education" is the goal of his organization, Peace Advocates Zamboanga (PAZ; founded in 1994). One of the main projects of PAZ is the Interreligious Solidarity Movement for Peace, which hosts the annual Mindanao Week of Peace. Peace is achieved largely through working in solidarity on issues of "poverty, socioeconomic discrimination, marginalization." Notwithstanding his emphasis of the "on-the-ground realities," Calvo offers a theoretical basis for his work: the "common ground" of belief in God and of universal peace that is the will of God. It is on this basis that "Interreligious Solidarity" could count as a "Movement for Peace."

For Calvo, to build peace is to "walk with," "feel the insecurity of," and "build something with" the other. Peacebuilding is about being able at once to maintain one's identity and hold that the other possesses a truth that is crucial for "the future of humanity." Of course, the truth that another holds may be a threat to one's power, especially for those in political leadership. Consequently, Calvo suggests that activists in civil society, who do not suffer the same "institutional risks" as politicians, have been the more effective actors in the "real work" of peace. While political symbols are necessary to remind local communities of the achievements of peace, symbols alone "cannot solve the crisis."

Another organization that has had immense impact is the Silsilah Dialogue Movement founded by Sebastiano D'Ambra.[14] Having arrived in Mindanao in 1977, D'Ambra served as one of the key negotiators in the 1996 Peace Agreement. For D'Ambra, a major though often overlooked obstacle to peace is *cultural factors*. Especially within the Muslim communities, what has stalled the prospects of peace is the long history of *rido*, defined by Amado Picardal (a colleague of D'Ambra's) as "the cycle of violence or vendetta killings between feuding families and clans."[15] Another example of such an obstacle has to do with the norms of governance that have tended to favor local tribal customs over against a system of national democracy, as discussed above. A third example is the emergence of overseas Filipino workers (approximately 11 million to 12 million individuals), which has divided a multitude of Filipino families. D'Ambra refers to this phenomenon as a kind of "secularization" that tears apart traditional family structures: children raised without the necessary psychological support often go on to participate in political leadership with corrupt characters, which leads to a corrupt politics. For this reason, "formation is critical."

For nearly thirty years Silsilah has had dialogue forums in over eighteen major cities in the Philippines with thousands of participants. Regarding its success, D'Ambra points to the basis of his approach. The term *silsilah* comes from the Sūfī Muslim tradition, referring to a "link" between God and humanity. D'Ambra adopted the term and applied it horizontally to highlight the "link which binds humanity." Yet Silsilah is not merely a "social strategy"; it is theological in that it is primarily about dialogue that "starts from God and brings people back to God." In commenting on my idea of the human good, D'Ambra suggests it is already a part of the group's approach: a *culture of dialogue* grounded in the idea of a "linked" humanity is "the path to peace."

The social anthropologist Albert Alejo underscores the importance as well of the "vertical [dimension of] peace communication" that connects politics with the people.[16] For Alejo, a main reason that official negotiations have not brought about enduring peace has to do with their failure to involve the "communities and peace constituencies." To be sure, we must balance the *confidentiality of peace talks* with the *confidence of the communities*: "Too many cooks spoil the broth," he quipped. At the same time, we cannot "leave behind those who have to ratify" the peace process—and far too "little is being done" in this area of vertical "peace communication."[17] That said, Alejo does not dismiss the importance of interreligious dialogue. Indeed, when asked about whether my notion of the human good might help to bridge the distance between religious communities, he responded, "There have been attempts ... even at our university [Ateneo de Zamboanga University] to provide some meta-platform—for example, by way of Lévinas's [] *commonality of humanity, ... ideal speech situation, et cetera*." Alejo went on to point out the need for discussions about common humanity: "There is a lot of room [to discuss this idea] for practitioners who are into action[, and] who want to reflect before heading back into the field. This [forum] is a very good place for this [idea]."

For Alejo, the Moro struggle, however, is not exclusively religious. To say either that the history of conflict is simply a matter of religion or that it is not truly religious at all: "both are reductionistic." The struggle is "not just religious; it is political and economic [and concerns] the loss of land. The combination was fatal." For Muslims, the issue is essentially two-pronged: political, insofar as there is a need to recognize "identity" and "self-governance"; and "land related." That said, Alejo also noted that the struggle is becoming increasingly religious. For while MNLF negotiated the 1996 Peace Agreement, which "was more secular" in tone, in the 2008 MOA-AD the MILF had in mind a "religious basis" for "an Islamic State." It is worth noting also that throughout the history of conflict both Christians and Muslims forged armed groups in the name of religion.[18] Furthermore, a crucial point of contention throughout the negotiations has concerned the implementation of a religious *sharīʿa*. Alejo concluded by saying that if there is any "meta-thinking" to be done in constructing a framework for peace, then respective religious communities must "discover from within [their] own resources the capacity, not just to draw boundaries, but to build bridges."

Fernando Capalla, cofounder of the Bishops-Ulama Conference, shares this view of religion's role in the construction of peace.[19] The BUC was established in 1996 by government mandate to help in the implementation of the peace process. The efforts and aim of the BUC were "to be guided by Islamic and Christian values," for which reason it is composed of Catholic bishops, Muslim *ʿulamāʾ*, and Protestant pastors. Since its beginnings, the BUC has introduced a series of seminars focused on teaching the values of peace and development from within respective religious scriptures—an idea that Capalla adopted from Calvo's PAZ group. Capalla confessed that when he began to work in the area of interreligious dialogue he thought peace was simply a matter of having in place "the right kind of politics." Now he believes that one of "the main obstacles to peace is ignorance" about the relationship between faith and peace. Most people, Capalla intoned, have been educated to consider peace in terms of the Greek idea of *eirene*—"the absence of war"—or of the Roman idea of *pax*—"peace accord on paper." Instead, Capalla suggests, "as Christians, what we need to do is look at peace from the Hebrew culture [where] *shalom* means wholeness, harmony, integrity in individuals and community." Interestingly, the Arabic term for peace (*salaam*) is that from which the term *Islam* derives. Capalla also emphasized the need to establish "deep friendships," the most effective basis for "real dialogue." He explained, "We had to rid [the sentiments found in] slogans such as 'A good Moro is a dead Moro' and 'You could never trust a Christian.'" Capalla recalled one afternoon, during a meeting with all the leaders present, when he suggested that rather than hold the seminar indoors they should head down to the beach to continue the conversation there. According to Capalla, this one afternoon did more for the work at BUC than many previous months combined: friendship is indispensable to interreligious peace.[20]

Capalla outlined what he sees as the three factors crucial to achieving peace through interreligious dialogue. First, more than the need "to be experts in conflict resolution," an "openness to friendship" is essential to interreligious engagement, for when "we first build the root of friendship, then we can discuss all the possibilities of peacebuilding [in a context of] trust and patience." Second, we need "community support," that is, civil society organizations "on the ground" that can support the work of religious leaders. Third, "we need funds": not only "human resources, [but] material resources." In concluding our conversation and commenting on the idea of the human good, Capalla mentioned that "the idea of the human person is the basic philosophy of Pope John Paul II" for whom "to dialogue is to be human." (Here Capalla seems to have in mind the following: "There is a *moral logic* which is built into human life and which makes possible dialogue between individuals and peoples. . . . The universal moral law written on the human heart is precisely that kind of 'grammar' . . . needed [for an enduring peace].")[21] After all, we share "a common origin and destiny"; and as Christians "we believe we are created in [God's] image" with a particular shared nature. Capalla suggests that ultimately there is "no other way to solve human problems except through respectful and patient dialogue" on the basis of commonality.

In addition to the work of interreligious dialogue groups is the indispensable work being done by international nongovernmental organizations (NGOs) such as Catholic Relief Services (CRS), the Mindanao branch of which is headed by Myla Leguro.[22] Like those of the BUC, the programs of CRS began as an initiative mandated by the 1996 Peace Agreement "to bring together Muslims, Christians, and indigenous people." The holistic approach taken up by CRS consists in five dimensions: (1) interfaith dialogue, (2) peace education, (3) grassroots efforts, (4) structural transformation, and (5) personal relationships. First, interfaith dialogue represents "a safe space where diverse communities could come together [to] understand the roots of the struggle," to "listen to the experiences of the supposed 'enemy,'" and to "teach and enhance capacities for conflict resolution." Dialogue is "dreaming for the communities in collaboration"; more concretely, it is "used as a problem-solving process [for] analyzing the conflict, exploring perspectives and positions, and envisioning a [common] future." Second (and in consonance with Alejo's idea of vertical peace communication), CRS "helps schools to implement [the] government mandate to integrate peace education into the curriculum." Third, at the grassroots level, "we work with communities which have declared themselves 'zones of peace'—safe communities which were previously war zones." Fourth, CRS is keen on structural transformation, as it "actively negotiate[s] with both government forces [and Muslim] armed groups to respect zones of peace." Fifth, critical to building and maintaining a lasting peace is the development of personal relationships both in the private sphere and across civil society organizations. In sum, CRS's *conflict transformation paradigm*, which involves these *personal*, *relational*, *structural*, *cultural*, and *spiritual* dimensions, is used in workshops and "dialogues processes" with an eye to address the more "systemic issues" of peace and conflict.

On a final note, Leguro points out that with respect to the "basis for Muslim-Christian engagement," when CRS began its work in Mindanao its *theory of change* was based on the idea of a *dialogue of commonality*, much like that of the BUC. However, the deep inequalities, land issues, and more required a dialogical "maturity" that comes only with a *dialogue of difference*. For example, only after Christian groups have had an *internal dialogue* about the need to understand Muslims' desire for self-governance would there emerge a "maturity to accept" differences and act generously; this maturity "to take in the contentious issues" can only come by way of a dialogue of difference. According to Leguro, "We need to be exclusive to be inclusive. Be exclusive first within each group [to] prepare that group to actually deeply practice solidarity with other groups." Without this internal dialogue, "how can we move forward" on contentious issues? Or, as Alejo put it, we need "*intrafaith discussions* in the service of *interfaith dialogue*."

CRS's conflict transformation paradigm offers a successful and time-tested approach to peacebuilding in Mindanao. This shift from a dialogue of commonality to one of difference, however, has been criticized by many groups as "regressive." While I agree with Leguro's notion of internal dialogue for the sake of "interreligious maturity," I would argue that such intragroup dialogue is coherent only insofar as it is considered in the larger intergroup context. For interreligious dialogue—the end goal of internal dialogue—presupposes a common humanity, which makes intergroup communication possible, and without which internal dialogue would be unnecessary. Thus, not only is intergroup dialogue the "goal of [internal] dialogue"; the former grounds the latter. The human good makes both possible and necessary *internal* as well as interreligious dialogue.

Others who find the idea of the human good attractive, particularly as applied to dialogue among religious leaders, are Amina Rasul and Moner Bajunaid, whom I interviewed concurrently at the Philippine Center for Islam and Democracy (PCID) which is located at the University of Philippines, Diliman, in Manila.[23] It is unsurprising, given their academic background and bent (Rasul did postgraduate work at Harvard; Bajunaid received degrees from Al-Azhar), that they would find this idea appealing. The outlook at PCID, however, is not simply academic. Rasul and Bajunaid, along with their staff, have been active in conducting "programs and activities [to] explain to our [Muslim] people the meaning of democratic processes which involve human rights issues, governance, peace and development[, etc.]" Also, they are involved directly with the *ʿulamāʾ* through two major organizations: the National Ulama Conference of the Philippines (NUCP), a federation of some 160 member organizations, and the women's sector of *ʿulamāʾ* (known as *aleemat*) as represented by Noorus Salam, "Light of Peace." "Furthermore," they said, "we have been involved in the early stages of the negotiations of MILF with the government."

PCID's goal is "to advocate peace and democratic principles along Islamic lines" since, as Bajunaid suggests, "education is the key" for peacebuilding and development. Bajunaid insists that Islam and democracy are indeed compatible since, given the principle of *shūrā* (consultation), the ideals of Islam arguably promote "governance, participation, liberties." That said, both Bajunaid and Rasul recognize the rather difficult issue of *sharīʿa*. Yet, for Bajunaid, "*sharīʿa* belongs to the Muslims, and only the Muslims can decide [to] what extent [and how] it should be implemented, [since] after all it is applicable only to the Muslims, not [to] other people." But surely, such a *sharīʿa* poses significant if not insurmountable challenges to a liberal democratic society like Mindanao. If *sharīʿa* is "only for Muslims" and yet non-Muslims share the same space where *sharīʿa* is upheld, then there inevitably would be major legal conflicts. (In fact, at the time of this writing, the minimum needed for provinces in Mindanao to opt into the proposed Bangsamoro [Muslim nation] is only a 10 percent Muslim population.) In this way, legal pluralism, as discussed previously, would pose intractable if not irresolvable problems that would stultify democratic processes.

As an alternative solution, Bajunaid suggests the idea of *maṣlaḥa*, or common good: "There can be a *maṣlaḥa* which is universal, [and one which is] particular to a people. [Thus,] *maṣlaḥa* may be [used] to determine the aspects of *sharīʿa* which apply to particular people and those which apply to all. [That said,] wherever you go, there are human rights, consensus, consultation, education: in short, universal values and concerns. [In looking back, we now can] say that this is the *maṣlaḥa*, the general welfare for humanity." Bajunaid's distinction between *maṣlaḥa*-as-the-common-good-of-Muslims and *maṣlaḥa*-as-the-general-welfare-of-humanity confirms what I argued in chapter 6.[24] That is, with respect to the first type, *maṣlaḥa* is "common" only to Muslim communities since it originates in and is shaped from a specifically Islamic perspective; in regard to the second type, it too fails to secure a truly universal common ground given its contingent character: for, on its own terms, it is historically accidental that "human rights, consensus, consultation, education" are part of it (even by Bajunaid's own admission). For this reason, it is subject to a relativism of values, making this allegedly universalistic *maṣlaḥa* in fact context-dependent and thereby inadequate to frame a universal public civility. Indeed, when asked what grounds the universal values of the second type of *maṣlaḥa*, Bajunaid conceded that it is "based on the Qurʾān and *ḥadīth*." Thus, what is needed is an Islamic political theology grounded on the notion of the universal human good rather than a "common good" that is in fact not common.

Finally, from my interview with Mohagher Iqbal, the MILF peace panel chair and principal negotiator for Muslim communities, it is clear that *sharīʿa* plays a crucial role in the Mindanao peace process.[25] For

Iqbal, religion is strictly speaking not an explicit factor in the peace process: "It's not a part of the agenda of the two groups." Yet he concedes that, insofar as "Islam is part of the communities which MILF represents," there are religious aspects to be considered. In agreement with Bajunaid, Iqbal says that *sharīʿa* is "internal to Muslims and not to Christian and IPs [indigenous peoples]"; at the same time, it remains "the ticklish issue." That is, given the judicial "supremacy of the Supreme Court" of the Philippines and the Muslim conviction that "*sharīʿa* is supreme," there are "two immovable things." What may be needed, for the sake of peace, is a temporary "constructive ambiguity" to allow parties to discuss details at a later time.

In light of this comment, I asked him about his view of peace, to which he responded, "Peace is . . . not just the absence of war or conflict between people. [Peace] transcends people. . . . [There must be] peace within oneself, one's family, one's community, the whole population in Mindanao. [It is] not just forgiving and forgetting—it has to do with justice. Peace with justice is the ultimate meaning of peace." Yet throughout the history of Mindanao peace has been lacking as "religion has divided people": "When wars broke out [in Mindanao], hundreds of thousands of people died. As for MILF, our guidelines [for] Muslim and Christian communities are very clear: all people of religion think their religion is right; Islam fully respects the religion of other people [since there is] no compulsion in religion; [and we consider] Christians [the] most fortunate friends of Muslims." (Here Iqbal seemed to be alluding to *sūras* 2:256, which states, "There is no compulsion in religion," and 5:82, according to which Muslims "are sure to find that the closest in affection . . . are those who say, 'We are Christians.'") Further to this comment, Iqbal suggested that "there is only one God who has created all persons; so there is no reason to quarrel over religion." Concluding his thoughts, Iqbal observed, "Islam promotes respect. [It is] on the basis of mutual respect that we could live together in a peaceful society." Religion is a resource for peace insofar as it encourages mutual respect. Iqbal's political theology, experience, and role as the chief Muslim negotiator are highly instructive for the prospect of peace and public civility in Mindanao. His point about the need to draw out from divergent religious traditions a deep mutual respect for a common public life underscores the importance and advantage of constructing public civility on the basis of the universal notion of the human good.

What Iqbal refers to as "the ticklish issue"—the role of *sharīʿa*—is the most crucial one about which Muslim and Catholic communities in Mindanao will need to engage in dialogue before an enduring peace and public civility can be constructed. And the political theologies of Catholic and Muslim communities play an indispensable role in determining the role of "the ticklish issue" in Mindanao (and other plural societies similarly situated).

KEY CONCLUSIONS OF THE FIELD STUDY

Two key findings from my interviews are (1) that over the course of the four decades of deep social unrest and civil war, interreligious dialogue and engagement have played a pivotal and positive role in the peace process, especially when grounded on the basis of the human good, as the success of the many interreligious dialogues forums demonstrates well; and (2) that the political theology of Muslim communities continues to pose a challenge for resolving the peace process and thereby for constructing public civility.

With respect to the first point, the peace studies expert John Paul Lederach corroborates the results of my field research that the work of peacebuilding is done typically most effectively by the so-called middle sector—the academy, civil society, religious groups, and the like.[26] With respect to the second point, one Muslim scholar observes that Muslim communities in liberal democratic societies are faced with (1) two conflicting legal traditions, legislative democracy and authoritarian law; and (2) the fact that, despite recent attempts to politicize *sharīʿa*, throughout Islamic history in the absence of a Muslim ruler *sharīʿa* was never given legal sanction.[27] And according to the secular imperative, in liberal democratic societies the absence of a Muslim ruler is precisely what must be the case.

Since the 1970s the GPH has adopted various forms of legal exemptions for Muslim communities in Mindanao.[28] The legal scholar Michael Mastura—who, following the Tripoli Agreement (1976), participated in drafting the Code of Muslim Personal Laws (1977)—notes that only those aspects of *sharīʿa* that were "fundamentally personal" (i.e., those "relating to personal status, marriage and divorce," etc.) were codified in the legal system. The central criteria used for the legalization of these codes were the *maqāṣid al-sharīʿa* (the purposes of Islamic law).[29] This procedural requirement shows how central a role the *maqāṣid* play for Muslim scholars in Mindanao when arbitrating what they consider to be authentic Islamic law. But such proposals not only suffer the pitfalls of legal pluralism, as argued in chapter 6, but also have worked to undermine the prospect of past peace agreements, as shown above. Thus, a legal pluralism that results in a state-backed *sharīʿa* society is unpromising with regard to the task of public civility, for it would render impossible the establishment of a unified body of law. Instead, what is needed for peacebuilding is what one Philippines expert, Rocco Viviano, calls a "dialogue of common action," the grammar of which is found in the universal human good.[30]

This chapter comprises an illustration of my framework for public civility as applied to the context of Mindanao, where interreligious dialogue based on the notion of the human good and the political theology of the Muslim communities about the role of *sharīʿa* fulfill crucial roles with respect to construction of public civility.

I turn finally to consider whether this framework could justifiably be applied elsewhere. I move from the particular case to the general principles under discussion. In the next chapter, then, I argue not only that such an application may be justified but also that no less than a global application of this framework is morally required. In other words, I consider the scope of a framework for public civility as based specifically on the idea of the universal human good.

CHAPTER 9

THE HUMAN GOOD AND THE SCOPE OF PUBLIC CIVILITY

Having looked at the prospect of constructing public civility in the second-longest internal religious conflict in history, in this final chapter I consider a crucial implication of my framework for public civility as based on the human good, namely, that the scope of moral responsibility entailed is no less than global. Thus, I have not only tested my theory in a particular geographic context but also extended my framework along a cosmopolitan dimension. In doing so, I offer an argument for what I call *moral cosmopolitanism* and explore the resources within both Christian and Islamic theological traditions that commend this global outlook. I conclude this chapter with a consideration of the virtues of gratitude and friendship as dimensions crucial to the construction of public civility in plural societies.

My overarching aim is to show that a framework based on the notion of the human good—given that every human person possesses an essential anthropology marked by rationality, relationality, and purposiveness—both justifies and demands a global scope of public civility. I make the argument in three main stages: first, by specifying the kind of cosmopolitanism that I have in mind, namely, moral cosmopolitanism; second, by offering philosophical and prudential reasons for accepting a moral cosmopolitan stance and subsequently by responding to critiques of cosmopolitan theory; and third, by considering theological justifications of moral cosmopolitanism specifically within the Christian and Muslim traditions.

MORAL COSMOPOLITANISM DEFINED

Recent literature on cosmopolitanism includes the works of political and social theorists such as Charles Beitz, who argues that the essential human capacities—consisting in the right to effect justice and to "pursue a conception of the good"—necessitate cosmopolitanism. Michael Walzer, who takes the view that the limits of justice are bounded by historical, cultural, and geographic contingencies, argues otherwise. Famously, Joseph Carens has applied the discussion of universal morality and global justice to questions of immigration and citizenship, making a cosmopolitan case for "open borders." More recently, proponents of cosmopolitanism such as Charles Jones and Thomas Pogge and detractors such as David Miller and Onora O'Neill have weighed in. Martha Nussbaum's essay in *For Love of Country*, which spawned criticisms from notable scholars such as Amartya Sen and Kwame Anthony Appiah, has made a significant contribution to the debate as well.[1]

The cosmopolitanism that I propose is similar to but also significantly different from ones put forward by other contemporary theorists: I call it *moral cosmopolitanism*. It is different from most other formulations in at least two fundamental ways. It is unlike many other models of cosmopolitanism in that it is not connected (in any necessary way) to a Rawlsian *political liberalism*, nor is it, strictly speaking, a form of *political* cosmopolitanism. Rather, moral cosmopolitanism is a proposal about the obligations that human persons of one polity have toward those of another, irrespective of the political memberships of either; it is about the extent of moral care that humans ought to have toward one another qua "citizens of the world" (to borrow a term from the ancient cosmopolitan Diogenes of Sinope).

MORAL COSMOPOLITANISM DEFENDED

The first justification for moral cosmopolitanism is based on the fact that like all associations and identities nationalities too are humanly constructed and therefore have a morally ambivalent status. While it is true, as Sen observes, that individuals and groups will always possess and find themselves beholden to a set of "plural affiliations,"[2] these loyalties are historically contingent and thereby strictly speaking inessential to humanness. By contrast, moral cosmopolitanism maintains that human persons owe a moral obligation of public civility to all other human persons throughout the world in virtue of their instantiating (whether actually or potentially) the human good of relationality, purposiveness, and rationality.

To make this point further, consider Walzer's view, which stands in contrast to moral cosmopolitanism.[3] Walzer contends that given that each community has a unique set of moral terms articulated against a background of peculiar "social meanings," we need "protected spaces" that match the varying needs of "the different tribes" in question: in short, an ensemble of "parochialisms." Walzer's thesis is based on the idea that the only true commonality of humanity is "particularism," for "we participate, all of us, in thick cultures that are our own." To the contrary, I argue, Walzer's "thick" conception of community-based morality makes problematic the identitarian thesis of theorists—like Walzer himself!—who suggest identities are multiple and overlapping. For if identities overlap, then determining which communities and which "social meanings" pertain to a given individual would be difficult if not impossible. So how would thinkers like Walzer, who favor this hybridic view of identities, begin to suggest a way in which to demarcate these alleged islands of identities? No answer seems forthcoming.

Related to this point is Martha Nussbaum's comment on the historically contingent and thereby morally ambivalent character of national identities.[4] She offers the following (counter)example. On a noncosmopolitan view, those who emigrate from China to the United States would be considered "fellows," whereas those who remain in their country of origin would be considered "foreigners." Nussbaum asks, "What is it about the national boundary that magically converts people toward whom we are both incurious and indifferent [foreigners] into people to whom we have duties of mutual respect [fellows]?" Arguably, there is nothing magical (or nonmagical) that would justify such a noncosmopolitan outlook.

To be sure, for Nussbaum as for myself, cosmopolitanism does not necessitate that an individual must give proportionally equal moral care to all human persons. One may justifiably give one's own nearest national association "a special degree of concern"—after all, the politics of a common life would be "poorly done" if everyone "thinks herself equally responsible for all." In this way, moral cosmopolitanism is compatible with having "particular loves" for family, religious or ethnic communities, or even country. Rather, the issue of the legitimacy of moral cosmopolitanism has to do with the "respect" that ought to be given to "humanity as such." Thus, moral cosmopolitanism, while not requiring proportionally equal moral responsibility, does entail a universal respect and global concern that ought to motivate individuals to attend to deep human needs that in turn may sometimes demand utter unconcern for national boundaries and identities.

A second reason that moral cosmopolitanism should be adopted is that it comports with an intuition about universal moral obligation articulated since antiquity, an intuition that ought to be considered even more compelling given modern globalization. An early use of the term *cosmopolitan* is found in the fourth century BC when Diogenes the Cynic, in answer to the question about where he is from, stated that he is a *kosmopolitēs*—a "citizen of the world"—suggesting that he saw the concerns of humanity outweighing local ones. Likewise, the ancient historian Plutarch of Chaeronea, commenting on the work of Zeno the Stoic, writes, "Indeed, the much-admired 'Republic' [by Zeno] is all directed towards this one summary point: that we ought not to dwell in cities or in districts, dividing ourselves up into local systems of justice, but instead come to think of all human beings as fellow citizens of the . . . single cosmos, . . . ruled in common by a common law."[5]

Relating these ancient views to the point at hand—that moral cosmopolitanism coheres with the long-held intuition of global moral obligation—consider again the insights of Hannah Arendt, who, drawing on the classical tradition, points out, "The *polis*, properly speaking, is not the city-state in its physical location; it is the organization of the people as it arises out of acting and speaking together, and its true space lies between people living together for this purpose, no matter where they happen to be."[6] The nonphysical space of human interaction is the polis. From this classical perspective, and given the increase of instant communication and of the concomitant globally shared spaces of "acting and speaking" that characterize contemporary society, a moral cosmopolitanism is a fortiori more relevant, that is, more possible and more necessary, in our world today. In brief, the increasingly global dimension of human relationality demands moral cosmopolitanism.

This discussion brings me to a third reason for moral cosmopolitanism: with awareness comes moral responsibility, and the gravely morally unjust situations around the world make obligatory a moral cosmopolitan stance. Nussbaum illustrates:[7] awareness of the thousands of orphans dying from malnutrition in China demands "action as a world citizen," action that may include financially supporting Human Rights Watch, advocating for children and women on their behalf, and so forth. Even if the nation-state remains the "fundamental political unit," this fact ought not keep one from recognizing the "astonishing degree [of] luck of being born in a particular country." Nussbaum goes on to consider life expectancy in places like Sweden (78.2 years) and Sierra Leone (39.0 years) and concludes, "This is not just, and we had better think about it. Not just think, do." To consider another example: owing to instant information, there is a growing global awareness of deep poverty in certain places of the world; awareness of this fact, along with the existence of excess resources in other places and the increasing efficiency of transferring such resources, demands a cosmopolitan stance that maintains that they be so transferred.

In addition to philosophical reasons, there are prudential considerations that buttress the view of moral cosmopolitanism, considerations found in the literatures of peace studies and political sociology. Casanova observes that in the advanced modern globalized world, what is good for society is increasingly defined in "global, universal, human terms" because of which the public sphere cannot afford to have "national or state boundaries." Similarly, Lederach observes that in highly conflictual situations the identities of actors—whether of ethnic, religious, geographic, or otherwise—play an indispensable role in the escalation or resolution of conflicts; therefore, identity cannot be confined to the nation-state.[8] In short, in globalized societies consisting of plural identities, resolutions to conflicts are not served well, let alone conceivable, in terms strictly confined to the nation-state.

Another prudential consideration in favor of moral cosmopolitanism is the fact that it balances well the obligations one has both to local loyalties and to global care, obligations that consist in an only apparent contradiction. Indeed, early cosmopolitan thought brooked no such contradiction. For example, Cicero maintained a global outlook and local priority as he wrote in his *De officiis* (*On Duties*) and *De legibus* (*On the Law*), which I quote respectively:

> [The] common bonds [of society] will be best conserved, if kindness be shown to each individual in proportion to the closeness of his relationship[—a hierarchy according to which] country would come first, and parents . . . ; next come children and the whole family . . . ; finally, our kinsmen, with whom . . . our lot is one. . . . [Nevertheless,] to debar foreigners from enjoying the advantages of the city is altogether inhuman.

> The first common possession of human beings and God is reason. . . . [S]ince right reason is Law, we must believe that people have Law [and Justice] also in common with the Gods. [Thus,] those who share these are to be regarded as members of the same commonwealth.[9]

While "law" applies to all human communities, in no way does it preclude a local politics, which is most pragmatically carried out by persons caring for those nearer in proximity and relation; conversely, moral priority to local commitments does not preclude care of humanity. In other words, global moral action is (often best) secured by means of moral action taking place in local contexts. Thus, a global outlook does not preclude local loyalties; rather, it encourages them. That said, a commitment to local moral action does not forestall the global responsibility that individuals bear in virtue of their humanity. For it may be that precisely one's scope of moral responsibility involves relations that are distant in proximity.

Consider, for example, an overseas Filipino worker living in Dubai who has obligations to help financially her relatives in Mindanao: such obligations may rightfully override concerns for those physically nearer. Conversely, an international student from Kenya studying in England may spend—for practical as well as morally fitting reasons—more time volunteering at local homeless charities than assisting similar ones in her homeland. And either of these individuals may devote the majority of her time or money to contributing to the U.S. campaign for the adoption of orphans in Ethiopia, though she may be distant from the situation in terms of both relation and proximity.

For the first time in human history there are in place the conditions needed for a truly global public square, especially when considering the role that can and must be played by religious communities in the global public sphere. Casanova puts it powerfully: "What constitutes the . . . novel aspect of the present global condition is . . . the fact that all world religions can be reconstituted for the first time truly as de-territorialized global imagined communities, detached from the civilizational settings in which they have been traditionally embedded."[10] Thus, moral cosmopolitanism is not only morally required but also increasingly practicable. For these prudential considerations, along with the philosophical reasons discussed above, moral cosmopolitanism ought to be adopted.

COSMOPOLITANISM OVER AGAINST "NATION-NESS"

Here I consider various critiques of cosmopolitan theory. Before proceeding, however, I discuss an important characterization of the nation-state given famously by Benedict Anderson. For this discussion, the *sociology of knowledge* perspective (discussed extensively above) offers important and insightful considerations in analyzing the moral status of nation-states.

Anderson, in his *Imagined Communities*, characterizes nations as "cultural artefacts of a particular kind [whose] creation [was] the distillation of a complex 'crossing' of discrete historical forces." These artifacts are reified such that they produce "profound emotional legitimacy," making "nation-ness . . . inseparable from political consciousness." In short, a nation is "an imagined political community"—an "invention" for which people are "ready to die."

Nations and nationalism arose, Anderson continues, through the course of modernity as a function primarily of neither liberalism nor the Enlightenment per se but of print capitalism, of "national print-languages," and of the territorialization of language. While critiques of the ancien régimes during the Enlightenment had their respective impacts, the sociological forces of the commercialization of print and shared languages most significantly helped to bring about the *imagined community* that is the modern nation-state. Thus, the "concretization" of nations, which carries so much emotive and identitarian force, owes itself to not much more than "peculiar imagining of history and power." In sum, the "well-known arbitrariness of frontiers" that defines national borders has resulted from sociological forces concomitant to the rise of modernity.[11]

OBJECTIONS TO COSMOPOLITANISM CONSIDERED

By contrast, David Miller mounts a thesis in favor of nationalism on the basis of the following three propositions:[12] (1) "that nations really exist, i.e. they are not purely fictitious entities"; (2) that "duties we owe to our fellow nationals are . . . more extensive than [those] we owe to human beings as such"; and (3) "that people who form a national community in a particular territory have a good claim to political self-determination." I turn now to examine and critique Miller's view, considering each proposition in turn.

Regarding the first claim—that nations "really exist," that national identities are "essential"—Miller suggests the following. If in answering the question, "Who are you?," one were to say, "I am Swedish [or] Italian," one would not be saying something "bizarre." Rather, one supposedly is making a claim about something "properly [a] part of []one's identity." Miller analogizes: it is not like "someone who claims without good evidence that she is the illegitimate grandchild of Tsar Nicholas II." The claim, rather, is legitimate—so Miller says. The problem with Miller's position, however, is a false dichotomy: namely, that national identity is either "essential" and thereby legitimate or historically contingent and thereby "bizarre." Pace Miller: Why must one assume that a contingent claim to national identity is bizarre? Rather than being seen as making an unjustified claim to being the grandchild of Tsar Nicholas II, could not one be taken as simply making a bona fide claim to a particular nationality while understanding that this claim does not immediately yield any particular moral status, given that nationality is nonessential to human persons? It seems that one legitimately could do so.

As to Miller's second claim—that "we owe to our fellow-nationals" certain obligations "more extensive than" those owed to "human beings as such"—there is some merit. It seems plausible that one's obligations to those with whom one shares the same political space require certain moral duties over against those owed to members of another polity. But there are two problems with this position if left unqualified. First, precisely which obligations are owed? Miller concedes that "if asked to be . . . specific about the *content* of [national] responsibilities, it would be hard to elicit any determinate general answer." Miller resorts to *imagined communities*, suggesting that the kinds of moral obligations appropriate to a given nation are a function of the "artefact of the public culture of that nation." But such a stance suffers the fate of moral relativism since, as Miller himself writes, this "public culture" will be "reshaped over time."

The second issue is that it merely states the problem and does not solve it. For what is it that makes political states—as characteristically demarcated by national boundaries—such that they are morally insuperable and self-contained spheres of justice? In virtue of what moral fact(s) are national borders the "contour lines in the ethical landscape"? While Miller helpfully lays out principles such as the reciprocity of rights and obligations, the obligations of citizenship, and the like, he says nothing about why these, and not other, principles and obligations carry their putative moral weight—nothing, that is, except to point to the "common ethos [that] takes the form of a public culture." But this is merely to state the problem, not to solve it.

And third, regarding the proposition that a national community has an irreducible right to self-determination, Miller again smuggles in an inherently political dimension to the idea of nationality such that the claim becomes circular. For Miller, nations simply "refer to a community of people with an aspiration to be politically self-determining." However: why think that nations have the right to political self-determination? In virtue of what fact does a group of individuals, characteristically located in a given geographic space, possess such a right? Indeed, Miller himself admits to the "circularity" of his characterization, though without letting it deter his project. In short, I find Miller's proposal for nationalism and against cosmopolitanism unconvincing, indeed unsuccessful in view of a false dichotomy in proposition (1), an unjustified national-centrism in proposition (2), and a circularity in argument in proposition (3).

Anthony Smith is another notable scholar writing in favor of nationalism. Arguing against cosmopolitanism, Smith points out a so-called modernist fallacy among cosmopolitanists that suggests that "nations are essentially recent constructs" and that "ethnic communities, or *ethnies*," are "neither natural nor given." Smith contends that the "images, identities, cultures" of *ethnies* are, on the contrary, ineradicable facts about the human condition, a contention that, if true, would undermine "any vision of a cosmopolitan global order." Indeed, Smith is convinced, as he notes elsewhere, that nationalism "provides the sole vision and rationale of political solidarity" in the modern world. In response to this conclusion, I build on the insights of the international security scholar Mary Kaldor, who points out that there is on Smith's view insuperable conceptual difficulty securing a basis for the universal "civic values" that Smith suggests go beyond all "ethnic" ones. As Kaldor writes, if there is anything to be said about the "main implication of globalization," it is that "territorial sovereignty is no longer viable."[13] Smith, however, refuses to recognize this implication, even though precisely this sort of universal apparatus is what he would need in order to ground his universal "civic values." Smith cannot have his universalist cake and eat it too.

I consider last a third scholar who argues in favor of nationalism, Craig Calhoun.[14] Calhoun observes that the "cosmopolitan ideal of being a citizen of the world" did not arise in opposition to nationalism; rather, "cosmopolitan elites measured their enlightenment by contrast to the rural people around them." For Calhoun, geography and urbanization, more than ideological struggle, have given rise to the modern cosmopolitan. I agree generally with Calhoun's account of the rise of the modern cosmopolitan, a similar account of which I give in chapter 4. Furthermore, Calhoun concedes that theories of cosmopolitanism "grounded in the abstract universality of individual human persons" may indeed provide some insights such as the theoretical basis for civic equality and for universal human rights. That said, in keeping with his overall anti-cosmopolitanist thesis, Calhoun suggests that theories of cosmopolitanism are ultimately "unsound." The main reason for their unsoundness, Calhoun contends, is that they are blind to "the sociological conditions for cosmopolitanism" as well as to "the reasons why national, ethnic, and other groups remain important to most of the world's people." In short, Calhoun's contentions are (1) that cosmopolitanism is itself a "tradition" that arose out of the conditions of modernity; and (2) that cosmopolitan theory discounts group identity and the benefits thereof that matter to people.

There are at least three problems I see with Calhoun's critique. The first is that calling a theory a "tradition" does not, by this fact, make its premises invalid and conclusion unsound. The sociological history of a theory is distinct from its soundness. Second, if the aim of cosmopolitan theory is to ground universal moral equality, then its being "abstract" should not count against it; indeed, arguably its abstractness works in its favor since (at least my version of) cosmopolitanism is about universal public civility. Third, the claim that group identity is vitally important for many people around the world is not anything against which cosmopolitan theory militates. On the contrary, moral cosmopolitanism, though respecting, indeed resourcing theologically, the deep and meaningful differences among human communities, as a theory seeks merely to motivate an appreciation of the human good and its implications for global moral responsibility. In doing so, my goal is not to undercut the meaningfulness of the identities people receive from communities but to underscore the moral obligations that exist across them.

In sum, there are good reasons to hold that national identities derive from contingent and strictly speaking accidental features of history and are thereby technically inessential to human personhood, even if they are (rightly) significant for people's sense of belonging. Thus, moral cosmopolitanism, while not ruling out the significance of political communities, seeks to place an emphasis on the increasingly global scope of moral responsibility that human persons have toward one another qua human persons.

THEOLOGICAL JUSTIFICATIONS FOR MORAL COSMOPOLITANISM

While ultimately aiming to construct a philosophically informed global framework for public civility on the basis of the human good, in order also to keep an eye on the primary context in which we are seeking to construct this framework, in what follows I consider whether there are resources within Islamic and Christian scholarship that support the view of moral cosmopolitanism delineated above. Building on both historical and contemporary thinkers within both traditions, I draw out various theological and historical reflections that align with and indeed justify a cosmopolitan outlook, beginning with Islam.

Muslim Cosmopolitanism Resonances

There is within Islamic traditions the possibility and arguably even the necessity of a moral cosmopolitanism, especially when considering (1) the role that *sharīʿa* plays with respect to Muslims' relationship to geographic boundaries; and (2) the kind of relationship that Muslims are to have with non-Muslims in view of our common humanity.

In this section, I consider Islamic theological resources that align with moral cosmopolitanism. It must be noted at the outset that an Islamic moral cosmopolitanism is different from the "activist revolutionary internationalism" that characterizes the recent "Islamist religionization of politics."[15] Rather, it is entirely possible to be a (non-Islamist) Muslim in favor of moral cosmopolitanism. In this way, contra the Islamist Ayatollah Khomeini—who considers the nation-state a "product of the deficient human [i.e., European imperialist] mind"[16]—an Islamic moral cosmopolitanism merely maintains that, irrespective of the status of political boundaries, the scope of public civility is necessarily global.

Since its early history the Islamic tradition has been marked by a tension between local tribal loyalties and a commitment to the large *ʿumma*, or community of Muslim believers. In order to counteract the human tendency toward local loyalties along with our penchant for boundaries, the Qurʾān emphasizes the primacy of the *ʿumma*, assigning to local loyalties what Sohail Hashmi describes as "a derivative, functional value."[17] In other words, geographic-political boundaries were meant to serve as a means to organize and realize Islam's global vision of a just public order rather than as an obstacle to it. Yet a crucial question arises: If Muslims find themselves in places outside of *dār al-Islām* (the house of Islam), can the requirements of Islam, that is, adherence to *sharīʿa*, still be fulfilled?

Here I note an important point about the distinction between *dār al-Islām* and *dār al-ḥarb* (the house of war). For all of the major schools of Sunnī jurisprudence (except the Ḥanafī), the distinction between the so-called houses was not primarily about geographic territories but about *order* versus *lawlessness*. Since *dār al-Islām* was fundamentally not about territory, fulfillment of the requirements of *sharīʿa* was not confined to geography. That is, the majority of the schools of jurisprudence maintained that the jurisdiction of *sharīʿa* is universal and thereby not tied to a geographic *dār al-Islām*. In summarizing an Islamic view of cosmopolitanism, Hashmi writes, "Human beings establish social boundaries . . . some of which have their place. . . . [So while] religion has to acknowledge and serve both the physical as well as the metaphysical needs of human beings[,] . . . [ultimately t]he Qur'an emphasizes the common ontology of human beings as the creation of God[,] human beings [who] are all essentially the same in their common origin, condition, and fate." There is, for this reason, a priority "on tearing down boundaries rather than erecting them." To be sure, there is a crucial criterion of difference among humans: namely, that of *taqwa*—"the sense of being constantly aware of God's presence in one's life." Thus, if there is any Islamic boundary, it is between those who are religiously earnest and those who are not. In short, an Islamic moral cosmopolitanism, based on the commonality of human persons—that is, *fiṭra*—demotes (without dismissing) the role of national boundaries in favor of global public civility.[18]

Questioning to some extent Hashmi's cosmopolitan bent, Khaled Abou El Fadl asks, "If God's morality is expressed through [law, then would not] God's law need a political community and a plot of land in which it has jurisdiction and sovereignty?" Abou El Fadl argues that the "territorial insularity" of Medina suggests a *dār al-Islām*, for presumably a Muslim could not fulfill the requirements of *sharīʿa* without an "Islamic sovereign" and political boundary. Furthermore, the need for a "*Shariʿah*-based society" is evidenced by the fact that the Quranic mandate to fulfill the *sharīʿa* was given not to individuals but to the collective *ʿumma*; consequently, a polity would be essential to fulfilling this mandate. So Abou El Fadl argues.[19]

Yet Abou El Fadl misses two significant points (aspects of which were discussed in the previous chapter): (1) since *sharīʿa* is not "law" in any modern sense, it does not necessitate a polity in order to be "expressed," let alone fulfilled; and (2) any attempt to connect Islam's universalist ethic with a particular polity would be based on the mistaken idea that the Medinan polity serves as a normative guide to Islamic political theory. As discussed previously, *sharīʿa* is primarily an ethical framework, and thereby not one which befits, let alone necessitates, legal-political implementation.

Indeed, as Abou El Fadl himself notes, Muslim jurists agreed that Muslims needed not to reside only in territories governed by *sharīʿa*. As the classical Muslim scholar al-Māwardī put it, if a Muslim is able to "manifest" his religion in a place among unbelievers, this place becomes *dār al-Islām*, making migration (*hijra*) to *dār al-Islām* unnecessary. Since the requirements of *sharīʿa* "accompany a Muslim wherever he/she may go" and since political boundaries are not necessary for "discharging the obligations of the *Shariʿah*," Abou El Fadl concedes, "this would seem to lend support to the conclusion that moral communities are more essential to the Islamic message than territorial boundaries." He concludes, "Political boundaries threaten to transform the moral communities of Islam to political entities, and to transform the universality . . . of the Islamic message into a . . . parochial reality. . . . Put differently, Muslims run the risk of numbing the moral and universal voice of *Shariʿah* and replacing it with a set of territorially specific legal adjudications and rules."[20] These historical realities and theological reasons justify an Islamic moral cosmopolitanism.

Furthermore, the terms *dār al-Islām* and *dār al-ḥarb* do not actually appear in the Islamic scriptural corpus. Rather, they are a human attempt to provide a "geopolitical scheme" appropriate to the time. Given the contemporary reality of a globalized world, a more appropriate "scheme" is found in what Faysal al-Mawlawi termed *dār al-daʿwa*, "abode of invitation of God"—a global public square of interreligious proselytism based on persuasion.[21] Such a scheme aligns more closely also with the original vision of the Prophet in Mecca and with the Muslims living there, who engaged in a politics of persuasion, not of coercion.

There are other Muslim scholars such as M. Raquibuz Zaman who, in arguing for a thoroughgoing cosmopolitanism, suggest national boundaries are "anathema to Islam." Less extreme but equally insistent is the claim made by a historian of Islamic political thought: "The idea that 'nationality' . . . should be the basis of civic identity . . . was completely alien to Islam."[22] Modestly speaking, there are significant theological resources that motivate an Islamic moral cosmopolitanism, resources that concern the way Muslims relate to physical boundaries as well as to non-Muslims who share a common humanity or *fiṭra*.

Christian Cosmopolitanism Reflections

In an effort to articulate a Christian view of cosmopolitanism, I consider both historical and contemporary Christian thinkers, paying particular attention to aspects of Catholic social thought. A Christian moral cosmopolitanism may be justified, especially when considering the role of land and property in Christian moral theology.

An important discussion about the ethics of geographic boundaries emerged during the period of European exploration. Francisco de Vitoria (d. 1546), expounding on the "commonwealth of humanity" and "the right of natural partnership and communication," provided a vocabulary and a conceptual framework that connotes a Christian view of cosmopolitanism, which is connected to a longer tradition of cosmopolitan Christian thought. Drawing on Aquinas as well as Francisco Suárez (d. 1617), the theologian Anthony Pagden writes, "Contrary to the image that it has acquired since the Enlightenment, the medieval [and I would argue even earlier] Christian world-view was generally cosmopolitan." To be sure, during the crusades of Christendom, there had been abuses (indeed gravely unjust ones) whereby the principle of *prescription* was exploited to justify a conquest of lands then occupied by the Ottoman Empire.[23] Such abuses notwithstanding, the principles of a virtuous, moral cosmopolitanism had long been in place in the Christian tradition, principles to which I now turn.

A Christian theological basis of moral cosmopolitanism can be grounded in the notions of natural dominion (*dominium naturale*) and *imago Dei* as articulated especially by Aquinas.[24] Arguing on the basis of Genesis 1:26—" 'Let us make man in our image, after our likeness. And let them have dominion over the fish of the sea' "—Aquinas writes, "This natural dominion of man over other creatures, which is competent to man in respect of his reason wherein God's image resides, is shown forth in man's creation." In other words, humanity is given a *natural dominion* over all of creation in virtue of being created specially in God's (rational) image. This dominion is one wherein "all things are common property" for all of humanity.

Regarding common property, it is instructive to note that this discussion comes in the context of question 66, "Of Theft and Robbery," in Aquinas's *Summa theologica*, and more specifically in article 7, "Whether it is lawful to steal through stress of need?" Here Aquinas argues that the needs of the poor to subsist take priority over the right of others to private property: "Things which are of human right [*iuris humani*: human law] cannot derogate from natural right or Divine right." That is, one's human right to private property may not "preclude the fact that man's needs have to be remedied by means of these very things"—that is, *natural right*. In other words, natural right is prior to human right. Therefore, "it is lawful for a man to succor his own need by means of another's property," for which reason Aquinas concludes that such an act is not "properly speaking theft or robbery." Put differently, while the right to private property is legitimate with respect to its *use*, it is subject to the prior principle that every earthly thing is ultimately common to all persons with respect to its *nature*. As Brian Tierney sums up, "Property could and should be private and common at the same time; private in the sense that ownership and administration belonged to the individuals, common in the sense that worldly goods had to be shared with others in time of need."[25]

Aquinas's view resonates with the earlier cosmopolitan view of St. John Chrysostom, who contends that "not to share one's possessions [is] theft." Citing the (noncanonical) Jewish scripture Ben Sira 4:1—"Deprive not the poor of his living"—Chrysostom argues that if a rich man "spends more on himself than his need requires," he is guilty of depriving what rightfully belongs to the poor. For Chrysostom, the rich ought to "show mercy" to the needy, owing not to any "virtue" or "misfortune" of the latter but because "need alone is this poor man's worthiness."[26] Similarly, on my view, what motivates the Christian principle of common ownership is a cosmopolitan conception of the human good grounded on the *imago Dei*.

Such cosmopolitan tones also resonate with key aspects of Catholic social thought. *Populorum Progressio* (1967) states, "No one may appropriate surplus goods solely for his own private use when others lack the bare necessities of life." As one commentator on CST observes, "Echoing the view of Aquinas, Paul VI suggests that the needs of humanity outweigh the rights of dominion when these two claims conflict." More recently, U.S. Catholic bishops have maintained that, given the "unity of the human family, the interdependence of peoples and the need for solidarity across national and regional boundaries," this principle must be kept in mind: "The people of far-off lands are not abstract problems, but sisters and brothers. We are called to protect their lives, to preserve their dignity and to defend their rights." As Richard Miller comments, in cases of human rights violations and dire human needs "the cosmopolitan demands of Christianity outweigh the protections normally granted to political autonomy." In sum, the Christian cosmopolitan tradition, which "asserts the metaphysical over the geographical," maintains that national boundaries have "qualified value," in much the same way I have argued above regarding the priorities of global moral responsibility.[27]

There are further instances in CST where a cosmopolitan call is clear: "The fact that he is a citizen of a particular State does not deprive him of membership in the human family, nor of citizenship in that universal society, the common, world-wide fellowship of men" (*PT*, no. 25). Indeed, *Pacem in terris* is rife with language about "the entire human family" (no. 97), "the whole human family" (no. 117), "the world community" (no. 140), and "the universal family of mankind" (no. 145). Fundamentally, the Catholic view of a universal humanity is based on the creation passages in Genesis 1 and 2. Regarding these passages, the Catholic ethicist Lisa Cahill offers an insightful observation that bears on the cosmopolitan dimension of public civility:

> Upon seeing the woman, the man exclaims, "This at last is bone of my bones and flesh of my flesh" (Gen 2:23).
>
> Usually the "one flesh" unity of the first couple is interpreted as [] sexual and reproductive unity. . . . However, . . . at this point in the story the woman and man are the *only* two people that exist. It is the woman's *humanity* that is most significant to Adam, not her gender. . . . [So] we see the "one flesh" unity . . . as the fundamental form of *human* relationship. . . . In other words, co-humanity should be more important to human identity and relationship than any bonds or differences based on family, tribe, race, ethnicity, religion, or national belonging.[28]

In short, based on the doctrine of the *imago Dei*, a Christian moral cosmopolitanism motivates a global scope of public civility. Albert Alejo from Mindanao comments in much the same vein:

> Every time we initiate a person into our community, [we] build . . . by drawing a boundary: "You're in, they're out." [So] should [there] be no boundaries, . . . no walls? No, we need walls because we need security; but let there be windows on the walls. We need fences; but let there be gates and times for opening the gates . . . and let there be bridges [across] our boundaries. . . . Every religion which is worth its name should have resource[s] for giving identity

> and meaning to community, but [also resources for] developing spaces broader than [its] own narrow identities.[29]

In sum, a Christian cosmopolitanism, like an Islamic one, seeks to balance particularity and universality. As Miller puts it, a Christian both affirms location and maintains a universal "unconditional love of others": against boundaries that "privilege local solidarities," a Christian "*agape* [as] exemplified by Jesus's teaching and example [] is . . . cosmopolitan."[30]

My aim in the above sections is rather modest: to point out some historical precedence and theological support for moral cosmopolitanism within both the Christian and Muslim traditions. Thus, the discussion lays down resources that may motivate an *internal dialogue* (see Leguro) about the global scope of public civility among theological leaders and laypersons within respective religious traditions.

I summarize the above sections by underscoring the importance of a moral cosmopolitan, drawing on my interview with Leguro. When asked whether she thought the conflictual situation in Mindanao could be helped by a view of global public civility, Leguro responded, "The wider view of humanity is still very difficult. What I have learned is that people are not able to move forward if the basic issues of survival are not addressed."[31] Here Leguro points to the Lumad as an example of a community who feel their rights have not been represented in the peace process, whose "identity and livelihood are being threatened," such that a "wider view of humanity" is yet foreclosed. That said, Leguro notes the careful balance that CRS is trying to achieve between "respecting distinct identities [and] working toward . . . a spirit of solidarity[, which] can extend beyond Mindanao, beyond Philippines." This "spirit" is exemplified in the Lumads' solidarity with other indigenous peoples (IPs) outside of the Philippines. And such a spirit is grounded in and motivates a moral cosmopolitanism.

I further argue that a cosmopolitan view of public civility would help other groups see the plight of indigenous peoples as the plight of a neighbor, albeit an admittedly distant one for some. In this way, the

Lumads or any group facing grave injustice would not only be right to see their struggle as involving the whole of humanity, but would stand to benefit from seeing it so. In other words, a moral cosmopolitanism, grounded in acknowledgment of the human good inherent in all persons, would motivate a sense of global interconnectedness that results not only in greater solidarity across human communities but also in the alleviation of grave suffering found in any one community.

In addition to this *intergeographic* dimension, I consider in the next section the importance of the *intergenerational* dimension of public civility, which both requires and motivates the cultivation of the virtue of gratitude. These two dimensions—the intergeographic and the intergenerational—are central to the development of a final notion, what I call *global friendships*, which further serve the construction of public civility.[32]

GRATITUDE AS THE GROUND OF GLOBAL FRIENDSHIPS: AN INSIGHT FROM MINDANAO

I bring this chapter to a close by commenting on the virtue of gratitude in developing global friendships, a virtue whose cultivation can be motivated by considering the intergenerational connectedness of humanity. To illustrate this final point, I build on the insights of the social anthropologist Albert Alejo, whom I interviewed in Mindanao. Before doing so, however, I comment briefly on two crucial notions with which I commenced this work in chapter 1: justice and peace.

Alejo observes that lands that once belonged to the IPs in Mindanao have been developed into industrialized cities.[33] "Do we give them back?" Alejo asks. "The indigenous people are not claiming that." Instead, the Lumads seek a "collective recognition of gratitude." (One expression of such collective gratitude, Alejo suggests, might come in the form of scholarship funds for the Lumads.) Many scholars at this point may want to insist on the importance of the arguably more crucial dimensions of reconciliation: political apology and forgiveness.[34] But, Alejo insightfully points out, while apology may be in order, it often can be damaging; that is, while apology recognizes the injustice done, it also implicitly perpetuates the insult. For this reason what Catholic and Muslim settlers in Mindanao need to recognize is the generosity of the Lumads whose land the former were allowed to develop. So rather than a culture of apology and indebtedness, Alejo suggests, "Let's instead develop a culture of gratitude."

Thus, both Muslim and Catholic communities could contribute to the task of public civility by offering a public recognition of gratitude for the work and gifts (largely of land) of the earlier communities in Mindanao. In this way, then, public civility and the virtue of gratitude are related: public recognition and recompense of the history of a given conflictual context can motivate the cultivation of gratitude, which in turn helps to construct public civility across divergent communities. There is, in other words, an undeniably crucial intergenerational dimension to public civility.

To connect this intergenerational dimension of public civility to the intergeographic dimension of moral cosmopolitanism, I draw again on Alejo's observation about the Mindanaoan conflict, this time as it specifically concerns a long view of the history of Christian-Muslim relations. As discussed above, by the thirteenth century Muslim merchants had settled throughout most of Mindanao; then in the sixteenth century, Spanish Catholics conquered nearly all of the Philippines, including Mindanao; finally, in the late twentieth century, under the aegis of various legislative acts, many Catholic Filipinos from Luzon claimed and settled in Mindanaoan lands. What ought to be done about the land? Alejo insightfully points out that the argument currently used by Muslims—that the Catholic settlers should give back the land—is double-edged in that it could have been used in eighth-century Spain by Catholics whose land was taken during the Muslim conquest. Furthermore, both the Catholics and the Muslims are beholden to the Lumads who had settled there long before either group came along.

The solution to the problem does not, then, involve counting as far back as the historical record goes (as if annals of recorded history were the final arbiter of a moral matter). Rather, from a cosmopolitan (intergeographic) and historically deep (intergenerational) perspective, the cultivation of the virtue of gratitude in the context of genuinely global friendships can serve to construct a robust local public civility in the here and now. Put differently, a moral cosmopolitan view, grounded on the idea of the human good, helps to engender and indeed morally demands a cultivation of gratitude-based friendships in the context of which public civility could be constructed. Thus, the intergenerational and intergeographic dimensions of public civility, captured in and motivated by a moral cosmopolitan outlook, require and motivate the cultivation of the virtue of gratitude. And this is how moral cosmopolitanism, friendship, gratitude, and a global public civility are crucially interconnected.

In this final chapter, I discuss the global scope of public civility as based on the universal human good, arguing that such a scope warrants, indeed demands, a robust moral cosmopolitanism. I then consider Islamic and Christian theological resources that seem to comport well with and commend such a global outlook. Next, moving beyond the intergeographic dimension of public civility, I suggest that intergenerational considerations play a crucial role in cultivating gratitude and that such gratitude in turn motivates the kind of global friendships that serve to construct public civility in plural societies.

In the conclusion that follows, I summarize this work as a whole and offer several final remarks on the possibility and need for constructing global public civility as well as the danger of failing to do so.

CONCLUSION

The overarching aim of this study has been to construct a framework of public civility in view of both the ideological forces of modernism (chs. 1 and 2) and the fragmenting nature of modern life (ch. 3), with special reference to Roman Catholic and Islamic theological traditions (chs. 5–7). To this end, I have discussed the significance of and need for public civility and argued against both strictly negative and positive views of human freedom that hinder its construction. I have also considered various constraints on public life, highlighting the secularizing tendency of the modern professional sphere and pointing out the inadequacy of secularist frameworks of public civility found in the leading theories of multiculturalism and legal pluralism.

Furthermore, I have analyzed the need to reframe Catholic and Islamic political theologies on the basis of the human good over against the common good, in view of the theoretical shortcomings of the latter (ch. 4), and suggested the notions of the *imago Dei* and *fiṭra* as conceptually resonant counterparts to the human good. Finally, I have sought to (1) apply my framework of public civility in the religiously divided region of Mindanao, Philippines; (2) consider the extent of the moral implications of this framework as based specifically on the idea of the human good; and (3) commend the plausibility of moral cosmopolitanism within both Catholic and Islamic theological traditions (chs. 8 and 9). To conclude this study, I offer two brief comments on the task of constructing public civility in plural societies and close with a final remark.

First, given the essential attributes of the human good, the task of public civility is *possible*. In his work on civility, the legal scholar Stephen Carter insightfully observes, "Behavior and conversation . . . remain our only tools for distinguishing ourselves from other animals. And distinguishing ourselves from other animals—or . . . displaying our humanity—is what civility is all about."[1] Civility, in other words, which marks humans off from other animals, is possible given the humanness of humanity. But this civility is not merely "personal." The renowned social critic Os Guinness writes, "Genuine civility is more than decorous public manners, or squeamishness about differences. . . . It is a style of public discourse shaped by respect for the humanity and dignity of individuals."[2] Civility in public life involves this discursive respect for the human good and a whole-life commitment to it. Thus, public civility depends on a recovery of the human good and an articulation of its implications for a common life in plural societies.

Second, given the essential attributes of the human good, the task of public civility is *necessary*. Jacques Maritain suggests that, contrary to the tenets of moral relativism, tolerance of others and the pursuit of truth are complementary rather than opposing forces: "There is a [true] tolerance only when a man is firmly and absolutely convinced of a truth, . . . and when he at the same time recognizes the right of those who deny this truth to exist, . . . not because they are free from truth but because they seek truth in their own way [and] because he respects in them human nature and human dignity [which] make them potentially capable of attaining the truth he loves."[3] Tolerance of others, especially of their indomitable dignity, is not an impediment to attaining truth but precisely what ensures its possibility. Given that all human persons seek truth, each in their own way, it is necessary that tolerance be shown in order for truth to be pursued and discovered. Put differently: the rationality of the human mind, the purposiveness with which humans pursue the truth, and the inherent relationality that respects the first and recognizes the second—these three attributes require that tolerance be shown if truth is to be known.

Given the multiple and competing pursuits of truth in plural societies, it has been my aim to consider, for specifically Catholic and Muslim communities, the theological resources available to ground a framework of public civility. Raymond Plant, in the conclusion of his thoroughgoing work on political theory and theology, considers the challenge that remains for plural societies. Given the "particular narratives" of divergent traditions there does not appear to be any "metaphysical assurance" that a "common moral word [*sic*]" should be possible; yet "equally, there is no metaphysical reason why it should not." Accordingly, "we should . . . not give up on the possibility of securing such a common word [*sic*] [in the hope of] creat[ing] a space for the idea of common projects and common interests." And crucial to the task of constructing this "common world of value"—that is, a cosmopolitan framework of public civility—is not only "dialogue and deliberation" but also a recognition (and I would add a reassertion) of "the idea of humanity and the common interest of humanity which can still arise out of our loyalty and location within narrative communities." This task is accomplished, Plant suggests, by "entering through dialogue into a wider witness to the nature of humanity."[4]

And the "nature of humanity," captured in the Christian doctrine of the *imago Dei* and the Islamic idea of *fiṭra*, which I articulate in terms of the human good, is what grounds public civility in plural societies. If we fail to acknowledge the other and articulate in the public square this vital truth, we will not only fail to live up to our humanity. We tragically will both perpetrate and fall victim to our very own uncivil wars.

NOTES

Chapter 1. Religious Diversity and Public Civility

1. Peter Berger, "The Desecularization of the World: A Global Overview," in *Desecularization of World: Resurgent Religion and World Politics*, ed. Peter Berger (Grand Rapids: Eerdmans, 1999), 2.

2. Timothy Shah, *Religious Freedom: Why Now? Defending an Embattled Human Right*, ed. Matthew Franck (Princeton: Witherspoon Institute, 2012), 55.

3. See Monica Toft, Daniel Philpott, and Timothy Shah, *God's Century: Resurgent Religion and Global Politics* (New York: Norton, 2011), 127–28; and Monica Toft, "Getting Religion? The Puzzling Case of Islam and Civil War," *International Security* 31, no. 4 (2007): 97–131, on 113, respectively.

4. Within political theory, see, e.g., John Rawls, *Political Liberalism*, expanded ed. (New York: Columbia University Press, [1993] 2005); Robert Audi and Nicholas Wolterstorff, eds., *Religion in the Public Square* (London: Rowman and Littlefield, 1997). Within social theory, see, e.g., Zygmunt Bauman, *In Search of Politics* (Cambridge: Polity, 1999); Jürgen Habermas, *The Structural Transformation of the Public Sphere* (Cambridge: Polity, 1989); Jürgen Habermas, *Between Naturalism and Religion*, trans. Ciaran Cronin (Cambridge: Polity, 2008); Will Kymlicka, *Multicultural Citizenship* (Oxford: Clarendon, 1995); Will Kymlicka, *Politics in the Vernacular* (Oxford: Oxford University Press, 2001); Tariq Modood, *Multiculturalism: A Civic Idea* (Cambridge: Polity, 2007); Bhikhu Parekh, *Rethinking Multiculturalism: Cultural Diversity and Political Theory*, 2nd ed. (Basingstoke: Palgrave Macmillan, 2006).Within legal theory, see, e.g., Ayelet Shachar, *Multicultural Jurisdictions* (Cambridge: Cambridge University Press, 2001); Ayelet Shachar, "State, Religion, and Family," in *Shariʿa in the West*, ed. Rex Ahdar and Nicholas Aroney (Oxford: Oxford University Press, 2010); Rudolph Peters, *Crime and Punishment in Islamic Law* (Cambridge: Cambridge University Press, 2005); Jeremy Waldron, "One Law for All? The Logic of Cultural Accommodation,"

Washington and Lee Law Review 59, no. 1 (2002): 3–34; Wael Hallaq, *Sharīʿa: Theory, Practice, Transformations* (Cambridge: Cambridge University Press, 2009); Mohammad Hashim Kamali, *Shariʿah Law: An Introduction* (Oxford: Oneworld, 2008); and Sami Zubaida, *Law and Power in the Islamic World* (London: I. B. Tauris, 2003).

5. Habermas, *Naturalism and Religion*, 3.

6. Charles Taylor, "Modes of Civil Society," *Public Culture* 3, no. 1 (1990): 95–118, 98. See also Peter Berger, *Facing up to Modernity* (New York: Basic Books, 1977), 170–73.

7. Zygmunt Bauman, *Liquid Modernity* (Cambridge: Polity, 2000), 104–5.

8. This paragraph builds on the following works: John Ehrenberg, *Civil Society: The Critical History of an Idea* (New York: New York University Press, 1999), esp. ch. 1, "Civil Society and the Classical Heritage"; Michael Edwards, *Civil Society* (Cambridge: Polity, 2004); Thomas Hobbes, *Leviathan*, ed. Michael Oakeshott (Oxford: Blackwell, 1948), esp. pt. 2, ch. 17; and Jean-Jacques Rousseau, *The Social Contract and Discourses*, trans. G. D. H. Cole (London: J. M. Dent and Sons, 1923), esp. bk. 1, ch. 8 (available at http://oll.libertyfund.org/titles/638).

9. See Karl Marx, "Preface to the Critique of Hegel's Philosophy of Right," in *Karl Marx and Friedrich Engels*, ed. Joseph O'Malley (Moscow: Foreign Languages Publishing House, 1962), 362; Karl Marx and Friedrich Engels, *The German Ideology*, trans. S. W. Ryazanskaya (London: Lawrence and Wishart, [1846] 1965), 39; Immanuel Kant, *Perpetual Peace: A Philosophical Essay*, ed. Mary Campbell Smith (London: George Allen and Unwin, 1903), First Suppl., 157; and Baron de Montesquieu, *The Spirit of Laws*, ed. J. V. Prichard, trans. Thomas Nugent (London: G. Bell and Sons, 1914), bk. 20, ch. 2, "Of the Spirit of Commerce."

10. See Adam Ferguson, *An Essay on the History of Civil Society*, ed. Fania Oz-Salzberger (Cambridge: Cambridge University Press, 1995), pt. 1, sec. 6, "Of Moral Sentiment," quotation on 35.

11. Though Hegel himself favored the state's ultimate domination of society; see Georg Wilhelm Friedrich Hegel, *Elements of the Philosophy of Right*, ed. Allen Wood, trans. H. B. Nisbet (Cambridge: Cambridge University Press, 1991), see esp. pt. 3, ch. 2, secs. 182–95.

12. Jean Cohen and Andrew Arato, *Civil Society and Political Theory* (Cambridge, MA: MIT Press, 1992), viii. Cf. Christopher Lasch, *The Revolt of the Elites and the Betrayal of Democracy* (New York: Norton, 1996); Michael

Walzer, "The Idea of Civil Society," in *Community Works: The Revival of Civil Society in America*, ed. E. J. Dionne (Washington, DC: Brookings Institution Press, 1998).

13. Edwards, *Civil Society*, 6.

14. Norbert Elias, *The Civilizing Process*, ed. Eric Dunning et al., rev. ed. (Oxford: Blackwell, [1939] 2000), pt. 2, ch. 1, "The History of the Concept of *Civilité*."

15. Quotations in this paragraph are from Philippe Ariès, *Centuries of Childhood* (Harmondsworth: Penguin Books, 1979), 368–71. Cf. Desiderius Erasmus, *A Lytell Booke of Good Maners for Chyldren* [*De civilitate morum puerilium*], trans. Robert Whittington (London: Wynkyn de Worde, [1530] 1536); cf. Elias, *Civilizing Process*, 47.

16. Except where indicated otherwise, quotations in this paragraph are from Stephen Carter, *Civility: Manners, Morals, and the Etiquette of Democracy* (New York: Basic Books, 1998), 15. For the note about Aristotle, see his *Politics*, trans. Benjamin Jowett (New York: Dover, 2000), bk. 4, ch. 4.

17. Elias, *Civilizing Process*, 34.

18. Kwame Anthony Appiah, *Cosmopolitanism: Ethics in a World of Strangers* (London: Penguin, 2007), xi.

19. John Paul Lederach, *The Moral Imagination: The Art and Soul of Building Peace* (Oxford: Oxford University Press, 2005), 62.

20. See Lederach, *Moral Imagination*, 5 (emphasis original); and R. Scott Appleby, *The Ambivalence of the Sacred: Religion, Violence, and Reconciliation* (Oxford: Rowman and Littlefield, 2000), 13 (emphasis original).

21. See R. Scott Appleby and John Paul Lederach, "Strategic Peacebuilding: An Overview," in *Strategies of Peace: Transforming Conflict in a Violent World*, ed. Daniel Philpott and Gerard Powers (Oxford: Oxford University Press, 2010), 24; and Appleby, *Ambivalence of the Sacred*, 18.

22. Quotations in this paragraph are from Appleby and Lederach, "Strategic Peacebuilding," 22–23 (emphasis added).

23. Quotations in this paragraph are from Fareed Zakaria, *The Future of Freedom: Illiberal Democracy at Home and Abroad* (New York: Norton, 2004), 17.

24. See, e.g., Edwards, *Civil Society*, ch. 3, "Civil Society as the Good Society," esp. 40–49. Quotations in this paragraph are from Edwards, *Civil Society*, 72 and 112.

25. Alasdair MacIntyre famously defines "tradition" as "an historically extended, socially embodied argument" in his *After Virtue: A Study in Moral*

Theory, 3rd ed. (Notre Dame: University of Notre Dame Press, [1981] 2007), 222. It may be the case that nonreligious traditions, of which Enlightenment liberalism is a paragon example, also possess resources to ground normativity; however, given an arguably inherent moral relativism, they do so more tenuously, as I argue below. (For more on liberalism as a "tradition," see Alasdair MacIntyre, *Whose Justice? Which Rationality?* [Notre Dame: University of Notre Dame Press, 1988], esp. chs. 13–17.)

I recognize that "liberalism" does not refer to a monolithic thesis; along with Michael Kenny, I note that "liberalism is a contestable, fluid and complex ideational terrain," exhibiting multiple theoretical forms; see his *The Politics of Identity* (Oxford: Polity, 2004), ix. Yet I concur with Nicholas Wolterstorff that there is a marked resemblance among those who make up a "family of liberal positions"; see his "The Role of Religion in Decision and Discussion of Political Issues," in Audi and Wolterstorff, *Religion in the Public Square*, 74. For a list of such scholars, see Daniel Philpott, *Just and Unjust Peace: An Ethic of Political Reconciliation* (New York: Oxford University Press, 2012), 307 n. 11.

Chapter 2. Modernity's Mayhem and the Need for Moral Political Theory

1. Berger, "Desecularization of the World," 2; Peter Berger, "Pluralism, Protestantization, and the Voluntary Principle," in *Democracy and the New Religious Pluralism*, ed. Thomas Banchoff (Oxford: Oxford University Press, 2007), 20; Berger, "Desecularization of the World," 10; Peter Berger, "The Cultural Dynamics of Globalization," in *Many Globalizations: Cultural Diversity in the Contemporary World*, ed. Peter Berger and Samuel Huntington (Oxford: Oxford University Press, 2002), 4 ff.; and Peter Berger, "Faith and Development," *Society* 46, no. 1 (2009): 69–75, 70, respectively.
2. Talal Asad, *Formations of the Secular: Christianity, Islam, Modernity* (Stanford: Stanford University Press, 2003), 191.
3. For an early study of this phenomenon, see Thomas Luckmann, "The Privatization of Religion and Morality," in *Detraditionalization: Critical Reflections on Authority and Identity*, ed. Paul Heelas, Scott Lash, and Paul Morris (Oxford: Blackwell, 1996), 73.
4. Peter Berger, *A Sacred Canopy* (New York: Doubleday, 1967), 134.
5. José Casanova, *Public Religions in the Modern World* (Chicago: University of Chicago Press, 1994), 15.
6. Robert Audi, "Liberal Democracy and the Place of Religion in Politics," in Audi and Wolterstorff, *Religion in the Public Square*, 25–26.

7. See Rawls, *Political Liberalism*, xix–xx; John Rawls, "The Idea of Public Reason Revisited," *University of Chicago Law Review* 64, no. 3 (1997): 765–807, 766–67, 795, 799, 807.

8. See MacIntyre, *Whose Justice?*, esp. ch. 17, "Liberalism Transformed into a Tradition," and ch. 18, "The Rationality of Traditions." We might note that Rawls offers a "*proviso*"—an allowance of religious reasoning in political matters under specific conditions. Rawls suggests that it would be just ("fair") to bring into political deliberation convictions that arise from religious or nonreligious comprehensive doctrine, "provided that, in due course, we give properly public reasons to support the principles and policies our comprehensive doctrine is said to support." See Rawls, "Public Reason Revisited," 776. (One must wonder whether Rawls's account at this point differs much from Audi's above.) This allowance notwithstanding, the restriction of political speech is only one aspect of the tradition of modern secularism that bears negatively on the prospect of constructing public civility.

9. Quotations in the next two paragraphs are from Jeff Weintraub, "The Theory and Politics of Public/Private Distinction," in *Public and Private in Thought and Practice*, ed. Krisnan Kumar and Jeff Weintraub (Chicago: University of Chicago Press, 1997), 4–6.

10. See, e.g., Peter Berger, *Between Relativism and Fundamentalism* (Grand Rapids: Eerdmans, 2010), "Introduction"; and Toft, Philpott, and Shah, *God's Century*, ch. 3, "The Rise of Politically Assertive Religion."

Charles Taylor draws a similar distinction between two senses of "public." "Public" in one sense refers to that which "affects the whole community ('public affairs')" or the management thereof "('public authority')"; this sense falls under Weintraub's "collectivity" criterion. The second sense has to do with "publicity [qua] a matter of access ('this park is open to the public') or appearance ('the news has been made public')"; this sense aligns with the "visibility" criterion. See his "Modernity and the Rise of the Public Sphere," in *The Tanner Lectures on Human Values*, ed. Grethe Peterson (Salt Lake City: University of Utah Press, 1993), 250.

11. See Rousseau, *Social Contract*; quotation from Dana Villa, *Public Freedom* (Princeton: Princeton University Press, 2008), 2–3; and John Locke, *Two Treatises of Government*, ed. C. B. Macpherson (Cambridge: Cambridge University Press, 1980), respectively. There is some literature on Lockean political thought that suggests a less strictly negative view of liberty whereby the rights of humanity "are always dependent upon prior duties to God entailed in the human beings," and thereby more in line with positive freedom. See Roger Ruston, *Human Rights and the Image of God* (London:

SCM, 2004), 251. See also Jeremy Waldron, *God, Locke, and Equality: Christian Foundations in Locke's Political Thought* (Cambridge: Cambridge University Press, 2002), esp. ch. 3, "Species and the Shape of Equality"; and Brian Tierney, "Historical Roots of Modern Rights," in *Rethinking Rights*, ed. Bruce Frohnen and Kenneth Grasso (Columbia: University of Missouri Press, 2009). Cf. Locke, *Two Treatises of Government*, bk. 2, sec. 6; bk. 1, sec. 86 and 87; bk. 2, sec. 26.

12. Isaiah Berlin, *Four Essays on Liberty* (Oxford: Oxford University Press, [1958] 1969), 121–22.

13. Gerald MacCallum, "Negative and Positive Freedom," in *Freedom: A Philosophical Anthology*, ed. Ian Carter, Matthew Kramer, and Hillel Steiner (Oxford: Blackwell, 2007), 70–78, esp. 70, 71 (originally published as Gerald MacCallum, "Negative and Positive Freedom," *Philosophical Review* 76 [1967]: 312–34).

14. John Stuart Mill, *On Liberty*, ed. Stefan Collini (Cambridge: Cambridge University Press, 1989), 16.

15. Hobbes, *Leviathan*, pt. 2, ch. 21; Locke, *Two Treatises of Government*, bk. 2, ch. 2, sec. 4, p. 8. Though with differences (Hobbes favoring a "sovereign absolute"; Locke, "limited power"), both thinkers argue that the primary function of government is to secure individual freedom.

16. Maureen Ramsay, *What's Wrong with Liberalism? A Radical Critique of Liberal Philosophy* (London: Leicester University Press, 1997), 39.

17. Except where indicated otherwise, the quotations in this paragraph and the next are from Charles Taylor, "What's Wrong with Negative Liberty," in *The Idea of Freedom: Essays in Honour of Isaiah Berlin*, ed. Alan Ryan (Oxford: Oxford University Press, [1979] 1991), 182–83.

18. Jeremy Bentham, "A Manual of Political Economy," in *The Works of Jeremy Bentham*, ed. John Bowring (Edinburgh: Tait, 1843), ch. 1, introd.; John Stuart Mill, *The Principles of Political Economy* (London: Longmans, Green and Dyer, 1990), 924; and Mill, *On Liberty*, 13.

19. Rawls, *Theory of Justice*, 31 ff.

20. Berlin, *Essays on Liberty*, 175.

21. See Rousseau, *Social Contract*, bk. 1, ch. 4; bk. 1, chs. 7 ff.; and bk. 1, ch. 7, respectively.

22. Aristotle, *Politics*, bk. 1, ch. 2.

23. Thomas Green, *Lectures on the Principles of Political Obligation and Other Writings*, ed. Paul Harris and John Morrow (Cambridge: Cambridge University Press, 1986), 199.

24. See Adam Swift, *Political Philosophy* (Cambridge: Polity, 2001), 77–78.

25. Berlin, *Essays on Liberty*, 180.

26. Swift, *Political Philosophy*, 84 and 77–78, respectively (emphasis original).

27. Michael Walzer, "The Communitarian Critique of Liberalism," *Political Theory* 17 (1990): 6–23, 16.

28. Raymond Plant, *Politics, Theology and History* (Cambridge: Cambridge University Press, 2001), 5–6.

29. Michael Sandel, *Democracy's Discontent: America in Search of a Public Philosophy* (Cambridge, MA: Harvard University Press, 1996), 4.

30. Crawford Macpherson, *The Political Theory of Possessive Individualism* (Toronto: University of Toronto Press, 1962).

31. Chandran Kukathas, *The Liberal Archipelago: A Theory of Diversity and Freedom* (Oxford: Oxford University Press, 2003), 15.

32. See, e.g., Charles Taylor, *Sources of the Self: The Making of the Modern Identity* (Cambridge: Cambridge University Press, 1989), 315; and MacIntyre, *After Virtue*, 233–36.

33. Os Guinness, *The Case for Civility: And Why Our Future Depends on It* (New York: HarperCollins, 2008), 125.

34. MacIntyre, *After Virtue*, 50–54.

35. Aristotle, *Politics*, bk. 5, ch. 9, see also bk. 6, chs. 2–4.

36. See Zygmunt Bauman, *Globalization: The Human Consequences* (Cambridge: Polity, 1998), 30–31; Asad, *Formations of the Secular*, 199, 255; and Abdulaziz Sachedina, *Islam and the Challenge of Human Rights* (Oxford: Oxford University Press, 2009), 157, respectively.

Chapter 3. The Decline of Public Life

1. See Reinhart Koselleck, *Critique and Crisis: Enlightenment and the Pathogenesis of Modern Society* (Oxford: Berg, 1988), 103 n. 15; cf. ch. 8, "The Process of Criticism." For secular thinkers, see, e.g., Wendy Brown, Introduction to *Is Critique Secular? Blasphemy, Injury, and Free Speech*, by Talal Asad, Wendy Brown, Judith Butler, and Saba Mahmood (New York: Fordham University Press, 2013), esp. 10–13.

2. Hans-Georg Gadamer, *Truth and Method*, trans. Joel Weinsheimer and Donald Marshall, 2nd ed. (London: Continuum, [1960] 2004), 272–73.

Cf. Saba Mahmood, "Religious Reason and Secular Affect: An Incommensurable Divide?," in Asad et al., *Is Critique Secular?*, 91; and Michael Warner, "Uncritical Reading," in *Polemic: Critical or Uncritical*, ed. Jane Gallop (New York: Routledge, 2004).

3. Elias, *Civilizing Process*, 365–67.

4. Armando Salvatore and Dale Eickelman, *Public Islam and the Common Good* (Leiden: Brill, 2006), xvi (emphasis added).

5. This term was used extensively by the sociologist of knowledge Alfred Schütz when analyzing the "prescientific reality" that the "normal adult simply takes for granted"; see his *The Structures of the Life-World*, ed. Thomas Luckmann (Evanston: Northwestern University Press, 1973), 3.

6. Much of this historical trace relies on Habermas, *Structural Transformation*, see esp. 3–4, 27–31.

7. See Taylor, "Modes of Civil Society," 108; and Salvatore and Eickelman, *Public Islam*, 16–17, respectively. For more on these points and the ones in the following paragraph, see Taylor, "Modernity and Public Sphere."

8. Aristotle, *Politics*, bk. 7, ch. 12; see also bk. 6, ch. 4; and Aristotle, *Ethics*, bk. 5, ch. 5, 1133a2–5. See Bauman, *In Search of Politics*, 87–100.

9. For more on this social history, see Habermas, *Structural Transformation*, 5–7, 9–10.

10. Richard Sennett, *The Fall of Public Man* (London: Penguin, [1976] 2002), 17; for more on this history, see ch. 9, "The Public Men of the 19th Century."

11. Sennett, *Public Man*, 18–19 (emphasis original).

12. See ibid., 64–72, 73–87.

13. On the first point, see Karl Marx and Friedrich Engels, *Capital: A Critique of Political Economy*, trans. Samuel Moore and Edward Aveling (New York: Modern Library, [1867] 1906), esp. pt. 4, ch. 14, "Division of Labour and Manufacture." On the second, see Marx and Engels, *Capital*, 82–85. On the last, see Sennett, *Public Man*, ch. 7, "The Impact of Industrial Capitalism on Public Life," esp. 141–49.

14. See MacIntyre, *After Virtue*, 227–29; Max Weber, *The Protestant Ethic and the Spirit of Capitalism*, trans. Talcott Parsons, ed. Anthony Giddens (London: Routledge, 1992), esp. 75–78; and Max Weber, *The Theory of Social and Economic Organization*, trans. A. M. Henderson and Talcott Parsons (New York: Free Press, 1964), esp. 337–39.

15. See Robert N. Bellah et al., *Habits of the Heart: Individualism and Commitment in American Life* (Berkeley: University of California Press, [1985] 1996), 43–46; and Casanova, *Public Religions*, 64.

16. See Sennett, *Public Man*, 12–16.

17. See Liisa Uusitalo, "Consumption in Postmodernity," in *The Active Consumer*, ed. Marina Bianchi (London: Routledge, 1998), 221; and Georges Benko, "Introduction: Modernity, Postmodernity and Social Sciences," in *Space and Social Theory: Interpreting Modernity and Postmodernity*, ed. Georges Benko and Ulf Strohmayer (Oxford: Blackwell, 1997), 23.

18. See Sennett, *Public Man*, 195, 211–12, 219–21.

19. Quotations in this paragraph are from ibid., 214–18, 25–27, and 99–106, respectively.

20. Ferguson, *Civil Society*, 57.

21. For an early use of this language of colonization, see Jürgen Habermas, *The Theory of Communicative Action*, trans. Thomas McCarthy, 3rd ed. (Boston: Beacon Press, 1987), 2:325 ff.

22. Michael Sandel, *Liberalism and the Limits of Justice*, 2nd ed. (Cambridge: Cambridge University Press, [1982] 1998), 217. On the "right to publicity" and "public acceptability," see Bauman, *In Search of Politics*, 3, 64–65.

23. For more on this point, see Sennett, *Public Man*, 5–12.

24. See Ariès, *Centuries of Childhood*, esp. 381–86.

25. Hannah Arendt, *The Human Condition* (Chicago: University of Chicago Press, 1958), ch. 2, "The Public and the Private Realm," esp. sec. 6, "The Rise of the Social"; quotations from 28–33.

26. Taylor, *Sources of the Self*, 211–12; cf. Aristotle, *Politics*, bk. 1, pt. 2. For a fuller discussion, see Taylor, *Sources of the Self*, ch. 3, "The Affirmation of Ordinary Life."

27. See Arendt, *Human Condition*, see esp. 289–99. On the modern scientific outlook, see John Haldane, *Practical Philosophy: Ethics, Society and Culture* (Exeter: Imprint Academic, 2009), 42–43.

28. Taylor, *Sources of the Self*, 502–8.

29. Bauman, *Liquid Modernity*, 104–9.

30. Ibid., 61, 63, 31, and 134, respectively.

31. Arendt, *Human Condition*, 38.

32. John Seel, "Reading the Post-Modern Self," in *The Question of Identity*, ed. James Davison Hunter (Charlottesville: University of Virginia Press, 1998), 39–40. See also Marina Bianchi, *The Active Consumer* (London: Routledge, 1998), quotation from 6.

33. On the British Airways case, see Eweida v. British Airways plc [2010] EWCA Civ 80 [2010] IRLR 322, CA. As of January 15, 2013, the European Court of Human Rights has overturned this verdict and decided in favor of Nadia Eweida; for the official judgment, see http://bit.ly/EwECHR. The

point remains, however, that the secularizing ethos of the professional sphere is pervasive in advanced modern society. For an illuminating history of religious attire in French public life, see John Bowen, *Why the French Don't Like Headscarves: Islam, the State, and Public Space* (Princeton: Princeton University Press, 2007), quotation from 1. For background and an insightful analysis of the Boston Catholic Charities incident, see Colleen Theresa Rutledge, "Caught in the Crossfire: How Catholic Charities of Boston Was Victim to the Clash between Gay Rights and Religious Freedom," *Duke Journal of Gender Law and Policy* 15, no. 1 (2008): 297–314.

34. See Paolo Ronchi, "Crucifixes, Margin of Appreciation and Consensus: The Grand Chamber Ruling in *Lautsi v. Italy*," *Ecclesiastical Law Journal* 13 (2011): 287–97; and Robyn Ryle, *Questioning Gender: A Sociological Exploration* (Thousand Oaks: Pine Forge Press, 2011).

35. See Sennett, *Public Man*, 89–91, 295–96.

36. Edward Shils, *The Virtue of Civility: Selected Essays on Liberalism, Tradition, and Civil Society*, ed. Steven Grosby (Indianapolis: Liberty Fund, 1997), 351.

Chapter 4. A Case for the Human Good

1. Bassam Tibi, *Islamism and Islam* (New Haven: Yale University Press, 2012), 203.

2. Quotations in this paragraph and the next are from Parekh, *Rethinking Multiculturalism*, 336, 2, 338, 340, 341, 236–37, and 343, respectively.

3. See Kymlicka, *Multicultural Citizenship*, esp. ch. 5, "Justice and Minority Groups"; and Kymlicka, *Politics in the Vernacular*, esp. ch. 2, "Liberal Culturalism: An Emerging Consensus?" For Rawls's view of the state as neutral with respect to "conceptions of the good," see Rawls, *Political Liberalism*, esp. "Introduction."

4. See Modood, *Multiculturalism*, 23–30, quotations from 27–28.

5. See ibid., 37, 43, 140, and 75–78, respectively.

6. See Parekh, *Rethinking Multiculturalism*, 340 and 338, respectively; and Modood, *Multiculturalism*, 7 and 66, respectively. Quotations in the next paragraph are from Modood, *Multiculturalism*, 66.

7. Modood, *Multiculturalism*, 69, 90–91, 94, and 93, respectively.

8. Quotations in this paragraph and the next are from Charles Taylor, "The Politics of Recognition," in *Multiculturalism: Examining the Politics*

of Recognition, ed. Amy Gutmann (Princeton: Princeton University Press, 1994), 28–37, 37–44, 68–69, 71.

9. John Griffiths, "What Is Legal Pluralism?," *Journal of Legal Pluralism* 24 (1986): 1–55, 38.

10. Brian Tamanaha, "The Folly of the 'Social Scientific' Concept of Legal Pluralism," *Journal of Law and Society* 20, no. 2 (1993): 192–217, 192, 202.

11. Quotations in this paragraph and the next are from Waldron, "One Law?," 3, 4, 11–12.

12. Grace Davie, "Law, Sociology and Religion: An Awkward Threesome," *Oxford Journal of Law and Religion* 1, no. 1 (2012): 235–47, 247.

13. For more on this point, see Robert George, *Making Men Moral: Civil Liberties and Public Morality* (Oxford: Clarendon Press, 1993), esp. "Introduction" and ch. 1, "Social Cohesion and the Legal Enforcement of Morals." George argues (inter alia) that laws based on ethics (moral norms) are beneficial and necessary for the proper functioning of society, for only such laws help to (1) prevent self-corruption, which leads to indulgence in immoral conduct; (2) deter immoral examples that others might emulate; (3) preserve society's "moral ecology"; and (4) inform its members about what is "morally right and wrong."

14. See Waldron, "One Law?," 15 (emphasis original). Cf. Brian Barry, *Culture and Equality: An Egalitarian Critique of Multiculturalism* (Cambridge: Polity, 2001), 48–49; Ronald Dworkin, *Taking Rights Seriously* (Cambridge, MA: Harvard University Press, 1978).

15. See Ronald Dworkin, "Is There a Right to Pornography?," *Oxford Journal of Legal Studies* 1, no. 2 (1981): 177–212, esp. 194 ff.

16. People v. Dong Lu Chen, No. 87-7774 (N.Y. Supp. Ct. Dec. 2, 1998), cited in Waldron, "One Law?," 28.

17. This term is taken from R. Mary Hayden Lemmons, who characterizes it as "the virtue that guides the formulation of sound public policy and law as well as just judicial adjudication"; see her "Juridical Prudence and the Toleration of Evil," *University of St. Thomas Law Journal* 4, no. 1 (2006): 25–46, 25.

18. Except where indicated otherwise, quotations in this paragraph and the next are from Waldron, "One Law?," 29 and 32–33 (emphases original).

19. Jeremy Waldron, "Questions about the Reasonable Accommodation of Minorities," in Ahdar and Aroney, *Shariʿa in the West*, 111.

20. Willard Quine, "On Empirically Equivalent Systems of the World," *Erkenntnis* 9, no. 3 (1975): 313–28, 328.

21. Aristotle, *Ethics*, bk. 1, chs. 2–3. For background on the notion of the human good as articulated in Aristotle, see Richard Kraut, *Aristotle on the*

Human Good (Princeton: Princeton University Press, 1989), esp. ch. 4, "The Hierarchy of Ends."

22. Quotations in this paragraph are from Aristotle, *Politics*, bk. 3, chs. 9, 7, and 8, respectively.

23. MacIntyre, *Whose Justice?*, 139 ff.

24. MacIntyre, *After Virtue*, 148; cf. Aristotle, *Politics*, bk. 1, ch. 1, 1252a3. On the "unqualifiedly good," see Haldane, *Practical Philosophy*, 47–48. Taylor calls it the " 'supreme good' (*teleiaon agathon*)" in his *Sources of the Self*, 66. Cf. Aristotle, *Ethics*, bk. 1, ch. 2 ff.

25. Gianni Vattimo, *Nihilism and Emancipation: Ethics, Politics, and Law* (New York: Columbia University Press, 2004), 98–99.

26. Quotations in this paragraph are from Parekh, *Rethinking Multiculturalism*, 115, 117, 119, 122, 124.

27. Richard S. Park, "Fragmented Knowledge Structures: Secularization as Scientization," *Heythrop Journal* 54, no. 4 (2013): 563–73.

28. Quotations of Gewirth in the next two paragraphs are from Alan Gewirth, *Reason and Morality* (Chicago: University of Chicago Press, 1978), x, 64, 48, and 135, respectively (emphasis original).

29. See James Griffin, *On Human Rights* (Oxford: Oxford University Press, 2008), quotations from 149 and 45, respectively; and Nicholas Wolterstorff, "Grounding the Rights We Have as Human Persons," in *Understanding Liberal Democracy*, ed. Terence Cuneo and Nicholas Wolterstorff (Oxford: Oxford University Press, 2012), 207–11. The way in which my account of the human good differs from Wolterstorff's thesis is that whereas Wolterstorff exploits generally the idea of human "worth," the grounding that I identify (the human good) specifies the essential attributes in virtue of which human persons have the worth they do qua human persons. For example, Wolterstorff writes, "On account of possessing certain properties, standing in certain relationships, performing certain actions, each of us has a certain worth." See his *Justice: Rights and Wrongs* (Princeton: Princeton University Press, 2008), 36. I provide an account of that in which these "properties" (essential attributes) consist.

30. See Steffen Stelzer, "Ethics," in *The Cambridge Companion to Classical Islamic Theology*, ed. Tim Winter (Cambridge: Cambridge University Press, 2008), 161.

31. See Aristotle, *Ethics*, bk. 1, chs. 4, 7, 13.

32. See esp. Arendt, *Human Condition*; Charles Taylor, *Human Agency and Language: Philosophical Papers 1* (Cambridge: Cambridge University Press, 1985); Taylor, *Sources of the Self*; and Taylor, "Politics of Recognition." Except where indicated otherwise, quotations in this paragraph and the next

are from Arendt, *Human Condition*, 95, 20, 3–4, and 94–96, respectively. For Aristotle's remark, see his *Politics*, bk. 1, ch. 2.

33. See Taylor, "Politics of Recognition," 32–33 (emphasis original); Taylor, *Human Agency*, 259; and Taylor, "Modernity and Public Sphere," 256.

34. Taylor, *Sources of the Self*, 68.

35. Ibid., 382–83 (emphasis original).

36. Ferguson, *Civil Society*, 64–65. I agree with Ferguson insofar as he means that it is morally impermissible to commit a moral wrong. Arguably, however, there is a legal right that offers protection for one to commit that which may be considered morally wrong (by others). For this distinction between legal and moral rights, I am indebted to a conversation I had with Paul Yowell, Fellow of Law at Oriel College, Oxford.

37. Yasien Mohamed, *Fitrah: The Islamic Concept of Human Nature* (London: Ta-Ha, 1996), 19.

38. See Aristotle, "Metaphysics," trans. Joe Sachs, in *Aristotle's Metaphysics*, ed. Joe Sachs (Santa Fe: Green Lion Press, 1999), bk. 1, ch. 1; and Marcus Tullius Cicero, "On the Laws," trans. Francis Barham, in *The Political Works of Marcus Tullius Cicero* (London: Edmund Spettigue, 1841–42), bk. 1, ch. 10.

39. See Anicius Manlius Severinus Boethius, "A Treatise against Eutyches and Nestorius," trans. Hugh Fraser Stewart and Edward Kennard Rand, in *The Theological Tractates* (Cambridge, MA: Harvard University Press, 1997), ch. 3, p. 85; and Thomas Aquinas, *Summa theologica*, trans. Fathers of the English Dominican Province (Charlottesville: InteLex Corp., 1993), I-I, q. 29, art. 3, 4.

40. Sachedina, *Islam and Human Rights*, 86, 89.

41. See Harrison White, *Identity and Control*, 2nd ed. (Princeton: Princeton University Press, 2008), 197; and Stephan Fuchs, *Against Essentialism* (Cambridge, MA: Harvard University Press, 2001), 6, 16. For an incisive and extensive critique of these works, see Christian Smith, *What Is a Person? Rethinking Humanity, Social Life, and the Moral Good from the Person Up* (Chicago: University of Chicago Press, 2010), esp. ch. 4, "Network Structuralism's Missing Persons."

42. Diana Fritz Cates, *Choosing to Feel: Virtue, Friendship, and Compassion for Friends* (Notre Dame: University of Notre Dame Press, 1997), 204. On the sine qua non of peacebuilding, see Lederach, *Moral Imagination*, 143.

43. For more on this point, see Wolterstorff, *Justice*, 40; cf. Aquinas, *Summa theologica*, I-II, q. 94, art. 2; Taylor, "Politics of Recognition," 41–42.

44. See Smith, *What Is a Person?*, ch. 1, "The Emergence of Personhood," esp. 42–59.

Chapter 5. The Human Good and Catholic Social Thought

1. J. Budziszewski, *Written on the Heart: The Case for Natural Law* (Downers Grove, IL: InterVarsity Press, 1997), 16–18, 33. Aristotle writes, "In justice every virtue is summed up"; see Aristotle, *Ethics*, bk. 5, ch. 1, 1129b26 ff. See also, Aristotle, *Ethics*, bk. 1, ch. 3; and Aristotle, *Politics*, bk. 3, ch. 1, 3, 6–9, 12–13.

2. See Germain Grisez, *Christian Moral Principles*, vol. 1 of *The Way of the Lord Jesus* (Chicago: Franciscan Herald Press, 1983), 184; and Germain Grisez, "The True Ultimate End of Human Beings: The Kingdom, Not God Alone," *Theological Studies* 69, no. 1 (2008): 38–61, 57.

3. John Finnis, *Natural Law and Natural Rights*, 2nd ed. (Oxford: Oxford University Press, 2011), 147.

4. See Aquinas, *Summa theologica*, I-II, q. 96, art. 1; and I-II, q. 91, art. 1–2, I-II, q. 90, art. 4; and I-I, q. 96, art. 3, respectively. Much of my understanding of Thomistic political and ethical theories is drawn from Mary Keys, *Aquinas, Aristotle, and the Promise of the Common Good* (Cambridge: Cambridge University Press, 2006); quotation from 101.

5. See Aquinas, *Summa theologica*, I-II, q. 94, art. 2, 3; q. 63, art. 1; and q. 21, art. 3; and Keys, *Aquinas*, 128.

6. Jacques Maritain, *Man and the State* (Chicago: University of Chicago Press, 1951), 10–12 (emphasis original).

7. "Pastoral Constitution on the Church in the Modern World," http://bit.ly/VatIIGS, last accessed July 1, 2016, no. 26. *Gaudium et spes*, promulgated by Pope Paul VI on December 7, 1965.

8. See Russell Hittinger, *A Critique of the New Natural Law Theory* (Notre Dame: University of Notre Dame Press, 1987), 5. Whether it is *new natural law* or the classical version, which is a more faithful reading of Aquinas, is a disputed matter. For a helpful introduction to this controversy (by one who favors the "new" perspective), see George, *Natural Law*, ch. 2, "Recent Criticisms of Natural Law Theory." For more on "the first principle of practical reason," see Germain Grisez, "The First Principle of Practical Reason: A Commentary on the Summa Theologiae," *Natural Law Forum* 94, no. 2 (1965): 168–201. For a helpful overview of new natural law theory in toto, see George, *Natural Law*, esp. pt. 1, "Theoretical Issues."

To note, there are significant concerns about the natural law tradition that have been discussed by historians such as Richard Tuck and James Tully who argue that (among other things) natural law theory has been adopted by a mutually incompatible set of political arrangements. This performative, if not conceptual, inconsistency problematizes natural law's supposed uniform set of moral deliverances, one that led to no less than the tragedy of civil wars. For more on this subject, see Richard Tuck, *Natural Rights Theories: Their Origin and Development* (Cambridge: Cambridge University Press, 1979), 77–81. The compatibility between natural law theory and a divergent set of politics is one of the overarching arguments of the aforementioned monograph. See also James Tully, *A Discourse on Property* (Cambridge: Cambridge University Press, 1980).

Also, under natural law theory there is the problem concerning the criteria by which to determine rights as properly human, a problem in political theory recognized by Tuck as an intractable one ever since the late Middle Ages. See Tuck, *Natural Rights*, 5–7. My project of constructing a framework of public civility is in part a response to these two problems of natural law theory—namely, the legitimacy of criteria for determining human rights and the moral underdetermination of natural law. That said, there is at least a "core" that is common to all "natural law theories": namely, "that in some sense or other the basic principles or morals and legislation are objective, accessible to reason and based on human nature." Fergus Kerr, *After Aquinas: Versions of Thomism* (Oxford: Blackwell, 2002), 98.

9. See Germain Grisez, Joseph Boyle, and John Finnis, "Practical Principles, Moral Truth, and Ultimate Ends," *American Journal of Jurisprudence* 32 (1987): 99–151, 102; and Finnis, *Natural Law*, 33, respectively.

10. Martin Rhonheimer, *Natural Law and Practical Reason* (New York: Fordham University Press, 2000), 6.

11. See Henry Veatch, "Natural Law and the 'Is'-'Ought' Question," *Catholic Lawyer* 26 (1981): 251–65, 258. On facts functioning as reasons, see David Oderberg, *Moral Theory: A Non-Consequentialist Approach* (Oxford: Blackwell, 2000), 13.

12. David Oderberg, "The Metaphysical Foundations of Natural Law," in *Natural Moral Law*, ed. Holger Zaborowski (Washington, DC: Catholic University of America Press, 2010), 60.

13. John Finnis, "Is Natural Law Theory Compatible with Limited Government?," in *Natural Law, Liberalism, and Morality*, ed. Robert P. George (Oxford: Oxford University Press, 1996), 1–4. For more on Finnis's view on the "political common good," see John Finnis, "Public Good: The Specifically Political Common Good in Aquinas," in *Natural Law and Moral Inquiry*, ed. Robert P. George (Washington, DC: Georgetown University Press, 1998).

14. See Finnis, "Natural Law Theory," 4 (emphasis original). Elsewhere Finnis gives a similar list of "the basic forms of human good": *life, knowledge,*

play, *aesthetic experience*, *friendship*, *practical reasonableness*, and *religion*. See Finnis, *Natural Law*, 85–90.

15. John Finnis, *Human Rights and the Common Good*, ed. John Finnis (Oxford: Oxford University Press, 2011), 1.

16. See Germain Grisez and Joseph Boyle, *Life and Death with Liberty and Justice* (Notre Dame: University of Notre Dame Press, 1979), 36–37 (emphasis original). On their rescission, see Grisez, Boyle, and Finnis, "Practical Principles," 150.

17. See Robert P. George, *In Defense of Natural Law* (Oxford: Clarendon, 1999), esp. 127–36, quotations from 131; and Finnis, *Natural Law*, 155, cited in George, *Natural Law*, 133. Lest one suppose that I am making too much of the relativity of the phrase "for themselves," I note that George, elsewhere commenting on Finnis's definition above, writes, "Under the natural law account . . . , it is important not only that basic human goods be realized, but that people, and peoples, realize these goods *for themselves*, that is, as fruits of their own deliberation, judgment, choice and action." See George, *Natural Law*, 239 (emphasis original).

18. See David Hollenbach, *The Common Good and Christian Ethics* (Cambridge: Cambridge University Press, 2002), 3. Cf. Aristotle, *Ethics*, bk. 1, ch. 3; and Thomas Aquinas, *Summa contra gentiles*, ed. Anton Pegis, 2 vols., vol. 2 of *Basic Writings of Saint Thomas Aquinas* (New York: Random House, 1945), 27. In addition to Hollenbach's reading, my understanding of Aquinas's view on this point is informed largely by Michael Baur, "Law and Natural Law," in *The Oxford Handbook of Aquinas*, ed. Brian Davies and Eleonore Stump (Oxford: Oxford University Press, 2012); and Keys, *Aquinas*, esp. 118–24. Except where indicated otherwise, quotations in the remainder of this section are from Hollenbach, *Common Good*, 69–70, 70, 77, 79, 133, 169, 159, 220, 243, and 135–36, respectively.

19. See Alasdair MacIntyre, "Politics, Philosophy, and the Common Good," in *The Macintyre Reader*, ed. Kelvin Knight (Notre Dame: University of Notre Dame, 1998), 235–39. Except where indicated otherwise, quotations in this paragraph and the next three are from MacIntyre, "Politics," 239–43 and 248 (emphases original).

20. Cf. Budziszewski, *Written on the Heart*, 16.

21. Joshua Hordern, *Political Affections: Civic Participation and Moral Theology* (Oxford: Oxford University Press, 2013), 1. To note, later in this work (see esp. ch. 4, "Affection and Locality"), Hordern suggests there are at some points mutually overlapping common goods with respect to divergent communities.

22. MacIntyre, "Politics," 246–47 (emphases original). See also MacIntyre, *After Virtue*, xiv–xv.

23. Aquinas, *Summa theologica*, I-II, q. 96, art. 3.

24. John XIII, "Establishing Universal Peace in Truth, Justice, Charity and Liberty," http://bit.ly/VatIIPT, last accessed July 1, 2016. *Pacem in terris*, promulgated by Pope John XXIII on May 11, 1963 (abbreviated *PT*); and *Gaudium et spes* (abbreviated *GS*). Citations of these documents appear in the text by section(s) referred to or, where the document is referenced in the immediate context, with only the section(s) referenced: e.g., "*PT*, nos. 1–3"; "nos. 1–3."

Given the aim of this work, some readers may wonder why there is no lengthy discussion of *Nostra aetate*—a Vatican II document that discusses the church's stance on Muslims. Because this document lacks the robust consideration of human nature (inclusive of human dignity and human rights) provided in the other two documents, *Pacem in terris* and *Gaudium et spes*, I focus on what I find the more relevant material for the present work.

25. Karl Rahner, "Membership of the Church," in *Theological Investigations* (London: Darton, Longman & Todd, 1963).

26. David Hollenbach, "A Communitarian Reconstruction of Human Rights," in *Catholicism and Liberalism*, ed. R. Bruce Douglass and David Hollenbach (Cambridge: Cambridge University Press, 1994), 127. Cf. Zachary Calo, "Catholic Social Thought, Political Liberalism, and the Idea of Human Rights," *Journal of Christian Legal Thought* 1, no. 2 (2011): 1–13, esp. 2–3.

27. Calo, "Catholic Social Thought," 8. Cf. *PT*, no. 28; see also nos. 30–33.

28. John Finnis, "Human Rights and Their Enforcement," in *Human Rights and the Common Good: Collected Essays*, vol. 3, ed. John Finnis (Oxford: Oxford University Press, 2011), 34.

29. See Michael Rosen, *Dignity: Its History and Meaning* (Cambridge, MA: Harvard University Press, 2012), 11–19.

30. See Immanuel Kant, *Groundwork of the Metaphysics of Morals*, ed. Mary Gregor, trans. Christine Korsgaard (Cambridge: Cambridge University Press, 1998), 42 [4:434–36], 37 [4:429], and 39 [4:431] (emphasis original).

31. See Rosen, *Dignity*, 63–70, 125 ff.

32. Except where indicated otherwise, the quotations in this paragraph are from *GS*, no. 12.

33. Ethna Regan, *Theology and the Boundary Discourse of Human Rights* (Washington, DC: Georgetown University Press, 2010), 32, 70.

34. Ruston, *Human Rights*, 11. Finnis offers a similar construal of human "identity," which he defines as a "non-fungible distinctness," possessing "truly

intelligible goods" (rationality) attained as one "deliberately intends" their attainment (purposiveness) while realizing that not only do "I matter," but that "others matter" (relationality) and that therefore "it is one's duties to other persons to respect and promote their good." See Finnis, *Human Rights and the Common Good*, 3:6–7.

35. See Christopher McCrudden, "Human Dignity and Judicial Interpretation of Human Rights," *European Journal of International Law* 19, no. 4 (2008): 655–724; and Paolo Carozza, "Human Dignity and Judicial Interpretation of Human Rights: A Reply," *European Journal of International Law* 19, no. 5 (2008): 931–44. The quotations in the next three paragraphs are from Carozza, "Human Dignity," 939, 943–44.

36. See Michael Walzer, *Spheres of Justice* (New York: Basic Books, 1983), xv; and Amartya Sen, *Identity and Violence: The Illusion of Destiny* (London: Allen Lane, 2006), 14 and 5, respectively. See also Michael Walzer, *Thick and Thin: Moral Argument at Home and Abroad* (Notre Dame: University of Notre Dame Press, 1994), ch. 5, "The Divided Self."

37. Walzer, *Thick and Thin*, 9, 11, 17.

38. The quotations in the remainder of this section are from Walzer, *Spheres of Justice*, 5–6, 312, and 4, respectively (emphasis original).

39. See Walzer, *Spheres of Justice*, esp. ch. 12, "Political Power."

Chapter 6. The Human Good within Islamic Political Ethics

1. See Tibi, *Islamism and Islam*, 37, 39, and 31, respectively.

2. See, e.g., Andrew March, "Sources of Moral Obligation to Non-Muslims in the 'Jurisprudence of Muslim Minorities' (Fiqh Al-Aqalliyyat) Discourse," *Islamic Law and Society* 16, no. 1 (2009): 34–94, esp. 36–38; and Sachedina, *Islam and Human Rights*, 188.

3. Thomas Nagel, *Equality and Partiality* (Oxford: Oxford University Press, 1991), 100.

4. See Augustine, *The City of God*, ed. Philip Schaff, trans. Marcus Dods (Edinburgh: T & T Clark, 1886), bk. 16, ch. 26, quotation from bk. 1, ch. 35. Cf. Robert Markus, *Christianity and the Secular* (Notre Dame: University of Notre Dame Press, 2006), 4–6. For more on this point, see Markus, *Christianity and the Secular*, 73. See also Robert Markus, *Saeculum: History and Society in the Theology of St Augustine*, rev. ed. (Cambridge: Cambridge University Press, [1970] 1988), 13–14, 122, 134. Much of my discussion on "the secular"

is indebted to the work of Nigel Biggar, *Behaving in Public: How to Do Christian Ethics* (Cambridge: Eerdmans, 2011), esp. 46 ff.

5. Abdolkarim Soroush, *Reason, Freedom, and Democracy in Islam*, ed. Mahmoud Sadri and Ahmad Sadri (New York: Oxford University Press, 2000), 126. On "rule by the people," see Paul Heck, *Common Ground: Islam, Christianity, and Religious Pluralism* (Washington, DC: Georgetown University Press, 2009), 146.

6. See Ḥasan al-Bannāʾ, *Mudhakkarat al-daʿwa waʾl-daʿiyya* [Treatise on the Ranks of the Righteous and the Devoted] (Cairo: Dar Al-Shihab, ca. 1951), quoted in Richard Mitchell, *The Society of the Muslim Brothers* (New York: Oxford University Press, 1993), 244.

7. Sajjad Rizvi, "A Primordial E Pluribus Unum? Exegeses on Q. 2:213 and Contemporary Muslim Discourses on Religious Pluralism," *Journal of Qurʾanic Studies* 6, no. 1 (2004): 21–42, quotations from 21, 23, and 27.

8. See Abdulaziz Sachedina, *The Qurʾan on Religious Pluralism* (Washington, DC: Georgetown University, 1996); cf. Abdullahi Ahmed An-Naʿim, *Islam and the Secular State* (Cambridge, MA: Harvard University Press, 2008); Mohammad Fadel, "The True, the Good and the Reasonable: The Theological and Ethical Roots of Public Reason in Islamic Law," *Canadian Journal of Law and Jurisprudence* 21, no. 1 (2008): 5–69; and Khaled Abou El Fadl, "Islamic Law and Muslim Minorities," *Islamic Law and Society* 1, no. 2 (1994): 141–87.

9. Bhikhu Parekh, *A New Politics of Identity* (Basingstoke: Palgrave Macmillan, 2008), ch. 6, "European Liberalism and the 'Muslim Question,'" esp. 117–29.

10. For more on this point, see Zubaida, *Law and Power*, 10 ff.

11. These schools are named after their founders: Abū Ḥanīfa, Mālik Ibn Anas, al-Shāfiʿī, and Ibn Ḥanbal, respectively. For a comparative study of the four schools of law, see Wael Hallaq, *Authority, Continuity, and Change in Islamic Law* (Cambridge: Cambridge University Press, 2001).

12. See Ahmad Atif Ahmad, *Structural Interrelations of Theory and Practice in Islamic Law* (Leiden: Brill, 2006), 33–34. For an extended treatment of other "extratextual" sources of Islamic law, see ch. 6, "Extra-Textual Sources of the Law," in the same work.

13. See Tariq Ramadan, *Western Muslims* (Oxford: Oxford University Press, 2004), 32, 37–38; see also Tariq Ramadan, *Islam, the West and the Challenges of Modernity* (Leicester: Islamic Foundation, 2001), 34 ff.

14. See Abdullahi Ahmed An-Naʿim, *Towards an Islamic Reformation* (Syracuse: Syracuse University Press, 1990), 11; Abdullahi Ahmed An-Naʿim,

"Islamic Foundations of Religious Human Rights," in *Religious Human Rights in Global Perspective*, ed. John Witte and Johan van der Vyver (The Hague: Kluwer, 1996), esp. 337, 353 (emphasis original); and An-Naʿim, *Islam and the Secular State*, 13, respectively.

15. Cf. Asma Afsaruddin, "The 'Islamic State': Genealogy, Facts, and Myths," *Journal of Church and State* 48, no. 1 (2006): 153–73; Fuʾād Zakarīyā, *Myth and Reality in the Contemporary Islamist Movement*, trans. Ibrahim M. Abu-Rabiʿ (London: Pluto Press, 2005).

16. For the literal definition, see Joseph Schacht, *An Introduction to Islamic Law* (Oxford: Clarendon, 1964), 211. Some scholars who argue for a promising basis for Muslim civic engagement on the basis of *ijtihād* are Mohammad Hashim Kamali, *Principles of Islamic Jurisprudence*, rev. ed. (Cambridge: Islamic Texts Society, 1991); Abdullah Saeed, "Trends in Contemporary Islam: A Preliminary Attempt at a Classification," *Muslim World* 97, no. 3 (2007): 395–404; and Mashood Baderin, *International Human Rights and Islamic Law* (Oxford: Oxford University Press, 2003).

17. See An-Naʿim, *Islam and the Secular State*, 12–13.

18. Schacht, *Islamic Law*, 70–71. Cf. Wael Hallaq, "Was the Gate of Ijtihad Closed?," *International Journal of Middle East Studies* 16, no. 1 (1984): 3–41, 3.

19. See Kamali, *Islamic Jurisprudence*, 468; and Kamali, *Shariʿah Law*, 31–32, respectively. Cf. Hallaq, "Gate of Ijtihad," 4–5, 8–9.

20. See Peters, *Crime and Punishment*, ch. 5, "Islamic Criminal Law Today," esp. 174–81, quotations from 175; and Erich Kolig, "To Shariʿaticize or Not to Shariʿaticize: Islamic and Secular Law in Liberal Democratic Society," in Ahdar and Aroney, *Shariʿa in the West*, quotations from 269–70.

21. Denis MacEoin, *Sharia Law or "One Law for All"?*, ed. David Green (London: Civitas, 2009), 39, 73, 39–40, and 41, respectively.

22. See Felicitas Opwis, *Maṣlaḥa and the Purpose of the Law: Islamic Discourse on Legal Change from the 4th/10th to 8th/14th Century* (Leiden: Brill, 2010), 1, 4; and Muhammad Qasim Zaman, "The ʿulama of Contemporary Islam and Their Conceptions of the Common Good," in *Public Islam and the Common Good*, ed. Armando Salvatore and Dale Eickelman (Leiden: Brill, 2006), 131–32.

23. See Abū Ḥāmid al-Ghazālī, *Al-Mustaṣfā min ʿilm al-uṣūl*, vol. 1 (Baghdad: Muthanna, 1970), 286–87, quoted in Ramadan, *Radical Reform*, 62, with Arabic annotations suppressed; for commentary on al-Shāṭibī, see Kamali, *Shariʿah Law*, 32–33.

24. Zaman, "The ʿulama and the Common Good," 139.

25. Robert Hefner, "Introduction: Sharīʿa Politics," in *Sharīʿa Politics: Islamic Law and Society in the Modern World*, ed. Robert Hefner (Bloomington: Indiana University Press, 2011).

26. See Kamali, *Islamic Jurisprudence*, 5; and Baderin, *Human Rights and Islamic Law*, 43. See also Yūsuf al-Qaraḍāwī, *Fi fiqh al-aqalliyyat al-muslima* [On the Jurisprudence of Muslim Minorities] (Cairo: Dar al-Shuruq, 2001), cited in Andrew March, "Theocrats Living under Secular Law," *Journal of Political Philosophy* 19, no. 1 (2011): 28–51, 37 n. 25, quotations from 43; and Ṭāhā Jābir Fayyāḍ ʿAlwānī, *Towards a Fiqh for Minorities*, rev. ed. (London: International Institute of Islamic Thought, 2010).

27. Opwis, *Maṣlaḥa*, 1–4.

28. It was pointed out by one of the reviewers of the manuscript that "the doctrine of *maṣlaḥa* ... when it is rendered as public good [of human beings] is derived from the Arabic root '*istislah*,' that is, 'seeking to promote good of humanity,'" and thereby has a wider scope than is argued above. I concur: it is true that there is a sense in which *maṣlaḥa* refers to a wider conception of "public good"—that is, the good of all humanity—and that it derives from the notion of *istiṣlāḥ*—"literally considering something good and beneficial"; see Opwis, *Maṣlaḥa*, 9. However, since its original usage, beginning with the second caliph ʿUmar (d. 634) and continuing with Abū Yūsuf (d. 798), the term *maṣlaḥa* was used to refer to "the good (*khayr*) and general benefit (*ʿumūm al-nafʿ*) of the *Islamic* community"; see Opwis, *Maṣlaḥa*, 9–10 (emphasis added). Even in its earliest instances, the common good of *maṣlaḥa* was specifically Islamic.

29. See Armando Salvatore, "Tradition and Modernity within the Islamic Civilization and the West," in *Islam and Modernity: Key Issues and Debates*, ed. Muhammad Khalid Masud, Armando Salvatore, and Martin van Bruinessen (Edinburgh: Edinburgh University Press, 2009), esp. 18–26, quotations from 18–19.

30. See Hollenbach, *Common Good*, 242.

31. Patricia Crone, *Medieval Islamic Political Thought* (Edinburgh: Edinburgh University Press, 2004), 395.

32. Mark Chapman, *Blair's Britain: A Christian Critique* (London: Darton, Longman & Todd, 2005), 64.

33. See Kamali, *Shariʿah Law*, 16.

34. Frank Griffel, "Al-Ghazālī's Use of 'Original Human Disposition' (Fiṭra) and Its Background," *Muslim World* 102, no. 1 (2012): 1–32, 3. Much of Sachedina's work on *fiṭra* with respect to Islamic political theology can be found especially in Abdulaziz Sachedina, "The Qurʾān and Other Religions,"

in *The Cambridge Companion to the Qur'ān*, ed. Jane Dammen McAuliffe (Cambridge: Cambridge University Press, 2006); and Sachedina, *Islam and Human Rights*.

35. Except where indicated otherwise, quotations of the Qur'ān are from *The Qur'an*, trans. M. A. S. Abdel Haleem (Oxford: Oxford University Press, 2004).

36. See Mohamed Fathi Osman, "The Children of Adam: An Islamic Perspective on Pluralism" (occasional paper presented at the Center for Muslim-Christian Understanding, Washington, DC, 1997), 60–63, http://bit.ly/1dzM1MS, last accessed July 1, 2016; and his "Human Rights in Islam" (occasional paper presented at the Center for Muslim-Jewish Engagement, University of Southern California, Los Angeles, 2012), 4 ff., http://bit.ly/1QcMobW, last accessed July 1, 2016. See also An-Naʿim, "Islamic Foundations"; and Sachedina, *Islam and Human Rights*.

37. See Mohamed, *Fitrah*, 15; and Habib Ali al-Jifri, "Loving God and Loving Neighbour," in *A Common Word: Muslims and Christians on Loving God and Neighbor*, ed. Miroslav Volf, Ghazi bin Muhammad, and Melissa Yarrington (Grand Rapids: Eerdmans, 2010), 80–81, respectively.

38. The Sachedina quotations in this paragraph and the next are from Sachedina, *Islam and Human Rights*, 97, 48, 86, 29, and 60, respectively.

39. See Abdullah Saeed, "Ambiguities of Apostasy and the Repression of Muslim Dissent," *Review of Faith and International Affairs* 9, no. 2 (2011): 31–38, 37; and Kamali, *Shariʿah Law*, 191.

40. Abdullah Saeed, "An Islamic Case for Religious Freedom," in *Religious Freedom: Defending an Embattled Human Right*, ed. Timothy Shah and Matthew Franck (Princeton: Witherspoon Institute, 2012), 41–43. For more on this point, see Abdullah Saeed and Hassan Saeed, *Freedom of Religion, Apostasy, and Islam* (Aldershot: Ashgate, 2004), 72 ff. Religious freedom within Islam is a large and controversial matter, one that I do not intend to address at length here. For a thoroughgoing treatment of this issue that favors a robust view of religious freedom within Islam, see Saeed and Saeed, *Freedom of Religion*, esp. pt. 1.

For a counterperspective, see Crone, *Islamic Political Thought*, ch. 21, "Muslims and Non-Muslims." Despite Crone's generally contrarian stance on this matter, she also notes that "the modernist interpretation of [*sūra* 2:256] may have longer roots than usually assumed." Crone observes that *sūra* 2:256 ("There is no compulsion in religion") was taken initially as an injunction in virtue of which *dhimmī*s (those—typically Jews and Christians—who were granted protected people's status) were left free to exercise their religion, but also one that did not prohibit the warfare (*jihād*) that would result in their becoming *dhimmīs* in the first place. This understanding gradually shifted when by the eleventh century Muslim scholars, in distinguishing between "the spiritual level" of religion and that of "its morality, its law and its war," held that even if external conformance to Islam was demanded of Arab pagans, "inner conviction (*iʿtiqād*)" could not be coerced. Going further, the famed Sunnī theologian Fakhr al-Dīn al-Rāzī argued for the view of noncompulsion of non-Muslims on the basis that coercion would undercut moral responsibility (*taklīf*). Crone concludes, "By this complicated route the verse came to be read in what a modern reader takes to be its prima facie meaning." Quotations in this note are from Crone, *Islamic Political Thought*, 382 n. 101, 373, 378, 380, 381, and 382.

41. Sachedina, *Islam and Human Rights*, 93–95, 48, and 58, respectively. It must be noted that *fiṭra* also involves the idea that anyone who consults her conscience "would recognize that God is one"; for this reason, Muslims often refer to their faith as *din al-fiṭra*, "natural religiousness." See Feisal Abdul Rauf, *What's Right with Islam* (San Francisco: HarperCollins, 2005), 16. The reason that I do not include this aspect of *fiṭra* is that what is being sought in constructing a framework of public civility are the resources within the traditions of Islam and Christianity that focus on interhuman relations, not human-divine ones. At any rate, the Christian tradition too has ways of understanding the *imago Dei* that, like this aspect of the notion of *fiṭra*, involve the idea of a natural inclination to know and worship God.

42. Ibn Qayyim al-Jawziyya, *Shifāʾal-ʿalīl fī masāʾil al-qaḍāʾ wa-al-qadar wa-al-ḥikma wa-al-taʿlīl* [Wrong Concepts about Predetermination and Causality] (1323), ed. al-Ḥalabī (Cairo: al-Maṭbaʿa al-Ḥusayniyya al-Miṣriyya, 1994), 607, quoted in Livnat Holtzman, "Human Choice, Divine Guidance and the Fiṭra Tradition," in *Ibn Taymiyya and His Times*, ed. Yossef Rapoport and Shahab Ahmed (Oxford: Oxford University Press, 2010), 166–67. Cf. Bukhari, *Prophetic Commentary on the Koran*, vol. 6, bk. 60, *ḥadīth* no. 298, http://bit.ly/2ladwAz, last accessed February 22, 2017.

43. Holtzman, "Fiṭra Tradition," 167. For more on this point, see Ramadan, *Western Muslims*, 16, 230 n. 16; and Umar Faruq Abd-Allah, "Theological Dimensions of Islamic Law," in *The Cambridge Companion to Classical Islamic Theology*, ed. Tim Winter (Cambridge: Cambridge University Press, 2008), 248–51.

44. For comments on the second caliph ʿUmar, see Holtzman, "Fiṭra Tradition," 165, 171. See also Abū Yaʿlā, *Kitāb al-muʿtamad fī uṣūl al-dīn*, ed. Wadi Z. Haddad (Beirut: Dār al-Mashriq, 1974), 133; cf. Holtzman, "Fiṭra Tradition," 172–73; and al-Jawziyya, *Predetermination and Causality*, 634, quoted in Holtzman, "Fiṭra Tradition," 175.

45. This insight and much of what follows on Ibn Sīnā, al-Ghazālī, and Ibn Taymiyya draw heavily from Griffel, "Al-Ghazālī's Use of Fiṭra."

46. Ibn Sīnā, *Al-Najāt min al-gharq fī baḥr al-ḍalālāt* [*The Book of Salvation*] (1364), ed. M. T. Dānishpazhūh (Tehran: Intishārāt-i Dānishgāh-i Tihrān, 1985), ch. 9, secs. 4–8, quoted in Griffel, "Al-Ghazālī's Use of Fiṭra," 14; Ibn Sīnā, *Al-Ishārāt wa-al-tanbīhāt* [*Remarks and Admonitions*], ed. Ibn Muḥammad Ṭūsī (Tehran: Daftar Nashr al-Kitāb, 1983), 58–59, quoted in Griffel, "Al-Ghazālī's Use of Fiṭra," 24. Regarding al-Shāṭibī and Ibn Tufayl, see Muhammad Khalid Masud, "The Scope of Pluralism in Islamic Moral Traditions," in *Islamic Political Ethics*, ed. Sohail Hashmi (Princeton: Princeton University Press, 2002), 137.

47. Al-Jawziyya, *Predetermination and Causality*, 634, quoted in Holtzman, "Fiṭra Tradition," 173; Ibn Taymiyya, "The Dispute about the Fiṭra" [in Arabic], in *Majmūʿat al-rasāʾil al-kubrā*, ed. Rashīd Riḍā (Cairo: Maktabat wa-Maṭbaʾat, 1966), 333–49, quoted in Holtzman, "Fiṭra Tradition," 177.

48. See Holtzman, "Fiṭra Tradition," 178. See also Ibn Kathīr, *Tafsīr al-qurʾān al-karīm* (n.p.: Dār al-Turāth al-ʿArabī, n.d.), 2:264, quoted in Holtzman, "Fiṭra Tradition," 185 n. 25.

49. Holtzman, "Fiṭra Tradition," 182.

50. See Joseph Boyle, "Natural Law and International Ethics," in *Traditions of International Ethics*, ed. Terry Nardin and David Mapel (Cambridge: Cambridge University Press, 1992), 7; and Plant, *Politics, Theology and History*, 357–58.

51. See *sūra* 3:110; and Aquinas, *Summa theologica*, I-II, q. 94, art. 2, respectively.

52. Precisely this line of reasoning is taken up in Mohamed, *Fitrah*, 25–32. See also Dominic Keech, *The Anti-Pelagian Christology of Augustine of Hippo* (Oxford: Oxford University Press, 2012), ch. 3, "A Divine Humanity in Sin's Likeness."

53. Regan, *Theology and Discourse*, 33.

54. Lactantius, *Divine Institutes* [*Divinae institutiones*], ed. Anthony Bowen and Peter Garnsey (Liverpool: Liverpool University Press, 2003), bk. 6, sec. 10, 349–50.

Chapter 7. Public Civility and Islamic Political Theology

1. William Cavanaugh and Peter Scott, Introduction to *The Blackwell Companion to Political Theology*, ed. Peter Scott and William Cavanaugh (Malden: Blackwell, 2004), 1.

2. See Massimo Campanini, "Alfarabi and the Foundation of Political Theology in Islam," in *Islam, the State, and Political Authority*, ed. Asma Afsaruddin (Basingstoke: Palgrave Macmillan, 2011); and Abu'l-Hasan al-Mawardi, *The Laws of Islamic Governance* [*al-ahkam al-sultaniyyah*], ed. Assadullah ad-Dhaaki Yate (London: Ta-Ha, 1996), 10.

3. Crone, *Islamic Political Thought*, 396–98. On religious-political rule, see Antony Black, *The History of Islamic Political Thought*, 2nd ed. (Edinburgh: Edinburgh University Press, [2001] 2011), esp. ch. 2, "The Idea of Monarchy" and "Conclusion"; on Islamic legal theory, see Ahmad, *Islamic Law*, 27; on nomocracy, see Nazih Ayubi, *Political Islam* (London: Routledge, 1991).

4. Crone, *Islamic Political Thought*, 13.

5. On the *sūras* given in Mecca, see Kamali, *Shariʿah Law*, 3–4; on the separation, see Tibi, *Islamism and Islam*, 160; on "double administration," see Schacht, *Islamic Law*, 54–55; and on the "fundamentalist cry," see Salvatore and Eickelman, *Public Islam*, xvi.

I note that the force of this claim is given relatively greater weight insofar as one argues against the Islamic doctrine of abrogation (*naskh*) according to which later Medinan passages of the Qurʾān are taken as superseding or abrogating the earlier Meccan ones. (For more on this subject, see David Marshall, *God, Muhammad and the Unbelievers: A Qurʾanic Study* [Surrey: Curzon, 1999], Afterword, 1.) However, for considerations of space, aside from my comments in the section "Revisiting the Role of *Sharīʿa*," I refer readers to the concise yet powerful argument for nonabrogation given in David Bukay, "Peace or Jihad? Abrogation in Islam," *Middle East Quarterly* 14, no. 4 (2007): 3–11.

6. Quotations in this paragraph and the next are from An-Naʿim, *Islam and the Secular State*, 4–5, 137, 36–44, and 276, respectively.

7. Quotations in this paragraph are from An-Naʿim, *Islam and the Secular State*, 279, 16–20, 284–85, and 52–53, respectively.

8. An-Naʿim, *Islam and the Secular State*, 276, 290.

9. Quotations in this paragraph from Toft, Philpott, and Shah, *God's Century*, 132, 109, and 50, respectively (emphasis original). For the discussion on religious terrorism, see ch. 5, "The 'Glocal' Dimensions of Religious Terrorism"; on democratization, see ch. 4, "Religion and Global Democratization."

10. See Noah Feldman, *The Fall and Rise of the Islamic State* (Princeton: Princeton University Press, 2008), pt. 3, "The Rise of the New Islamic State"; and Hefner, "Introduction: Shariʿa Politics," 23–27, respectively.

11. Quotations in this paragraph are from An-Naʿim, *Islam and the Secular State*, 55, 277.

12. Quotations in this paragraph are from Sachedina, *Islam and Human Rights*, 23, 43, 52. While I build on Sachedina's idea of an "inclusive political theology," I do not agree that "exclusionary theology," which makes "exclusive religious truth" claims, stands in diametric opposition to it (see p. 186). A pluralistic political theology does not entail a relativism about religious truth: political pluralism is one thing; religious pluralism, another.

13. An earlier version of this controversy between the "Traditionalists (*Ahl al-ḥadīth*)" and "Rationalists (*Ahl al-Ra'y*)" had taken place (ca. seventh century) over the question about the role of "personal reasoning" regarding *fiqh*. See Kamali, *Shariʿah Law*, 247–48. It is worth noting here the key roles played by the traditionalist Ibn Ḥanbal, who vigorously championed the "Partisans of Sunna (ahl al-Sunna)" or Sunnism—nomenclature that highlights its revelationist bent—as well as by his successor al-Ashʿarī in Ashʿarī theology's takeover. See Majid Khadduri, *The Islamic Conception of Justice* (Baltimore: Johns Hopkins University Press, 1984), 53–58, quotation on 54. And again, a controversy parallel to the Muʿtazilī-Ashʿarī one erupted during the classical period between Islamic philosophy, which prioritized human reason, on the one hand, and *fiqh* jurisprudence, which represented the revelationist tradition, on the other. This controversy resulted in noted thinkers such as Ibn Rushd and Ibn Khaldūn favoring the former and the majority of Sunnī scholars pursuing "*shariʿa* reasoning"; hence, the long history of Sunnī juridical enterprising.

14. Quotations in this paragraph are from Sachedina, *Islam and Human Rights*, 59–60 and 129–31.

15. See, e.g., Masud, "The Scope of Pluralism"; Kamali, *Shariʿah Law*; Rahman, "Law and Ethics in Islam," in *Ethics in Islam*, ed. Richard Hovannisian (Malibu: Undena, 1985); and Sohail Hashmi, "Islamic Ethics and International Society," in Hashimi, *Islamic Political Ethics*.

16. See Sachedina, *Islam and Human Rights*, 61. See also, e.g., Khaled Abou El Fadl, *Speaking in God's Name: Islamic Law, Authority and Women* (Oxford: Oneworld, 2001).

17. On the first point, see Wael Hallaq, Introduction to *The Formation of Islamic Law*, ed. Wael Hallaq (Aldershot: Ashgate Variorum, 2003), xix–xx; and Joseph Schacht, *The Origins of Muhammadan Jurisprudence* (Oxford: Clarendon, 1950), respectively. On the second point, see Kamali, *Shariʿah Law*, ch. 5, "Disagreement (*Ikhtilāf*) and Pluralism in *Sharīʿah*"; ch. 4, "The

Leading Schools of Law (*Madhāhib*)," esp. 68–70; and Ahmad, *Islamic Law*, 43. On the third point, see Wael Hallaq, *A History of Islamic Legal Theories* (New York: Cambridge University Press, 1997), quotation from 162. See also Berkey, *Formation of Islam*, ch. 22, "Modes of Justice"; and Patricia Crone, *Roman, Provincial, and Islamic Law* (Cambridge: Cambridge University Press, 1987). On the fourth and final point, see Ahmad, *Islamic Law*, 157–58.

18. See Sachedina, *Islam and Human Rights*, 42–44, 75–79, 86, 244, 246; and Hashmi, "Islamic Ethics," 154. Cf. Berkey, *Formation of Islam*, 148.

19. Quotations in this paragraph are from Sachedina, *Islam and Human Rights*, 166, 172, 81, 79–80, 167, and 14–15, respectively.

20. Sachedina, *Islam and Human Rights*, 69.

21. See Sachedina, *Islam and Human Rights*, 93 ff. On the "great and inspiring sources," see Feldman, *Fall and Rise*, 108. On the "governing law," see Ayubi, *Political Islam*; and Tibi, *Islamism and Islam*, 158.

22. See Ayubi, *Political Islam*, 13. On "Islamized constitutional arrangements" see Feldman, *Fall and Rise*, 105–17, quotations on 111.

23. Yūsuf al-Qaraḍāwī, *al-Hall al-Islami*, vol. 2 (Beirut: Mu'assasat al-Risalah, 1980), 82–83, quoted in Tibi, *Islamism and Islam*, 159.

24. For more on this point, see Kamali, *Shariʿah Law*, 3–4.

25. See Tibi, *Islamism and Islam*, 158, 173, 167, 160–61, and 175.

26. See ʿAli ʿAbd al-Raziq, "Message Not Government, Religion Not State," in Kurzman, *Liberal Islam*, 30–31. This piece originally comes from his monograph *Islam and the Basis of Government*, bk. 2, pt. 3. For Crone quotations, see her *Islamic Political Thought*, 11, 16, 44–53, and 246–49, respectively.

27. Afsaruddin, "'Islamic State,'" 163–64.

28. Zubaida, *Law and Power*, 10; Hallaq, *Sharīʿa*, 549.

29. Rahman, "Law and Ethics in Islam," 8, 11.

30. See Tabrizi, *Mishkāt*, vol. 3, *ḥadīth* no. 5097, cited in Kamali, *Shariʿah Law*, 48. For more on *sūra* 45:18, see Kamali, *Shariʿah Law*, 2–4.

31. Kamali, *Shariʿah Law*, ch. 11, "Beyond the Sharīʿah: An Analysis of Sharīʿah-Oriented Policy."

32. On "*fatwā* making," see Kamali, *Shariʿah Law*, 174–77; on "etatization," see Hefner, "Introduction: Shariʿa Politics," 28–29; on "ethicalized" *sharīʿa* and "scholastic fanaticism," see Hefner, "Introduction: Shariʿa Politics," 32–34; and ʿAbd al-Wahhāb Abū Sulaymān, *Al-fikr al-uṣūlī* (Jiddah: Dār al-Shurūq, 1984), cited in Kamali, *Shariʿah Law*, 73.

Chapter 8. The Prospects of Public Civility

1. Much of this historical sketch relies on Carmen Abubakar, "The Advent and Growth of Islam in the Philippines," in *Islam in Southeast Asia*, ed. K. S. Nathan and Mohammad Hashim Kamali (Singapore: Institute of Southeast Asian Studies, 2005). The term *moro*, used by the Spaniards to identify Muslim Filipinos, was later adopted by local Muslims and is not considered derogatory. See Salvatore Schiavo-Campo and Mary Judd, *The Mindanao Conflict in the Philippines* (Washington, DC: World Bank, 2005), 1 n. 3. Strictly speaking, not all Muslims are *moros* since "Muslim" carries a religious denotation while *moro* concerns political identity. See Miriam Ferrer, "The Case of the Autonomous Region in Muslim Mindanao," *Ethnic and Racial Studies* 35, no. 12 (2011): 1–19, 14 n. 3. I use the terms interchangeably in accordance with the standard practice in the literature.

2. "Agreement between the Government of the Republic of the Philippines and the Moro National Liberation Front with the Participation of the Quadripartite Ministerial Commission Members of the Islamic Conference and the Secretary General of the Organization of the Islamic Conference," Tripoli, December 23, 1976.

3. Terms of Reference of the "Memorandum of Agreement on the Ancestral Domain"; sec. 2, para. 6.

4. Jan Stark, "Muslims in the Philippines," *Journal of Muslim Minority Affairs* 23, no. 1 (2003): 195–209, 198–99. On "past injustice," see Timothy Williams, "The MOA-AD Debacle—an Analysis of Individuals' Voices, Provincial Propaganda and National Disinterest," *Journal of Current Southeast Asian Affairs* 29, no. 1 (2009): 121–44, 137–41, quotation from 134; cf. Michael Mastura, "Legal Pluralism in the Philippines," *Law and Society Review* 28, no. 3 (1994): 462–75, 467–68. On third party mediation, see Temario Rivera, "The Crisis of Philippine Democracy," in *Asian New Democracies*, ed. Hsin-Huang Michael Hsiao (Taipei: Taiwan Foundation for Democracy, 2006), 32.

5. On land, see, e.g., Schiavo-Campo and Judd, *Mindanao Conflict*; and Astrid Tuminez, "This Land Is Our Land: Moro Ancestral Domain and Its Implications for Peace and Development in the Southern Philippines," *School of Advanced International Studies Review* 27, no. 2 (2007): 77–91. On economic causes, see, e.g., Wan Kadir Che Man, *Muslim Separatism* (Singapore: Oxford University Press, 1990); and Thayil Jacob Sony George, *Revolt in Mindanao* (Kuala Lumpur: Oxford University Press, 1980). On the Lumads, see, e.g., Shamsuddin Taya, "The Politicization of Ethnic Sentiments in the

Southern Philippines: The Case of the Bangsamoro," *Journal of Muslim Minority Affairs* 30, no. 1 (2010): 19–34. Cf. Steven Rood, *Forging Sustainable Peace in Mindanao: The Role of Civil Society* (Washington, DC: East-West Center, 2005), 4; and Hannah Neumann, "Identity-Building and Democracy in the Philippines," *Journal of Current Southeast Asian Affairs* 29, no. 3 (2010): 61–90.

6. Rood, *Forging Sustainable Peace*, 7.

7. This observation is corroborated by Lederach, who notes more generally that the "mid-level" actors of peacebuilding are most often the key to constructing an enduring and just peace. See John Paul Lederach, *Building Peace: Sustainable Reconciliation in Divided Societies* (Washington, DC: United States Institute of Peace Press, 1997), ch. 5, "Structure: Lenses for the Big Picture," esp. 46–51.

8. Much of my discussion in this paragraph draws on Thomas McKenna, *Rulers and Rebels: Everyday Politics and Armed Separatism in the Southern Philippines* (Berkeley: University of California Press, 1998), ch. 9, "Unarmed Struggle," quotations from 213 and 232. On the Lumads, see Taya, "Politicization of Ethnic Sentiments."

9. Muhammad Qasim Zaman, *The Ulama in Contemporary Islam: Custodians of Change* (Princeton: Princeton University Press, 2002), 174; and Fr. Albert E. Alejo, in-person interview, Zamboanga City, November 25, 2012.

10. See Michael Barnes, *Theology and the Dialogue of Religions* (Cambridge: Cambridge University Press, 2002), 230–54.

11. E.g., the Tripoli Agreement states that "the Muslims shall have the right to set up their own Courts which implement the Islamic Shari'ah laws"; the Organic Act made provision for a "Shari'ah Appellate Court"; the 1996 Peace Agreement states, "The Regional Legislative Assembly . . . shall establish Shari'ah Courts"; and the MOA-AD makes allowance for the "Bangsamoro Juridical Entity (BJE)" to be based on *sharīʿa*.

12. See McKenna, *Rulers and Rebels*, 249; and Hallaq, *Authority, Continuity, and Change*, 7–14. This description of *sharīʿa* is given by MILF peace panel chair, Mr. Mohagher Iqbal. MILF peace panel chair Mohagher Iqbal, Skype interview, Manila, December 5, 2012.

13. Fr. Angel C. Calvo, CMF, immigrated to become the first Catholic bishop assigned to the diocese of Zamboanga, Mindanao, where he has helped to found several interreligious initiatives, including the highly successful Peace Advocates Zamboanga. The quotations and discussion that follow in this paragraph and the next are drawn from Fr. Angel C. Calvo, in-person interview, Zamboanga City, November 26, 2012.

14. Fr. Sebastiano D'Ambra, PIME, is founder of the Silsilah Dialogue Movement (established in 1984), which is arguably the most successful interreligious dialogue effort in Mindanao. D'Ambra served as a key negotiator in the 1996 Peace Agreement between GPH and MNLF. The quotations and discussion that follow in this paragraph and the next are drawn from Fr. Sebastiano D'Ambra, in-person interview, Zamboanga City, November 27, 2012.

15. Amado Picardal, "Christian-Muslim Dialogue in Mindanao," *Asian Christian Review* 2, no. 2 (2008): 54–72, 60.

16. Fr. Albert E. Alejo, SJ, received his PhD in social anthropology from the School of Oriental and African Studies (SOAS) at the University of London. Alejo has been actively involved with the peace process in Mindanao over the past thirty years at the national, civil society, and grassroots levels. The quotations and discussion that follow in this paragraph and the next are drawn from Alejo, in-person interview, November 25, 2012.

17. In an article he wrote for the inaugural edition of *Our Mindanao*, Alejo outlines twenty-five points to consider in effecting vertical peace communication; see his "Let the People Understand," *Our Mindanao* 1, no. 1 (2010): 15–19.

18. Picardal, "Christian-Muslim," 55–56.

19. Retired Archbishop Fernando R. Capalla, DD, is co-convenor/founder of the Bishops-Ulama Conference, which began as a government mandate to implement key measures of the 1996 Peace Agreement. BUC consists of 24 Catholic bishops, 24 Muslim *ʿulamāʾ/ustadzes*, and 18 Protestant pastors. The quotations and discussion that follow in this paragraph and the next are drawn from Archbishop Fernando R. Capalla, in-person interview, Davao City, November 28, 2012.

20. For more on this point, see Lederach, *Moral Imagination*, ch. 11, "On Serendipity: The Gift of Accidental Sagacity."

21. See John Paul II, "The Fiftieth General Assembly of the United Nations Organization," http://bit.ly/JPII50UN, last accessed May 28, 2015, no. 3. *Apostolic Journey of His Holiness John Paul II to the United States of America*, promulgated by Pope John Paul II on October 5, 1995.

22. With a graduate degree from the Kroc Institute for International Peace Studies at the University of Notre Dame and two decades of work at Catholic Relief Services, Myla Leguro founded and continues to advise two major peace organizations, Mindanao Peacebuilding Institute and Grassroots Peace Learning Center. The quotations and discussion that follow in this paragraph and

the next two are drawn from Myla Leguro, in-person interview, Davao City, November 28, 2012. For more on the indispensability of contributions from the NGO sector, see Lederach, *Building Peace*, chs. 4 and 5; Lederach, *Moral Imagination*, ch. 8.

23. With graduate degrees from Al-Azhar University and International Islamic University, Moner Bajunaid is professor of Islamic studies and director of the Center for Peace Studies at Mindanao State University, where he once served as chancellor. Amina Rasul, previously a Philippine Government cabinet member and currently a member of the Brookings Institution Task Force on U.S. Foreign Policy Towards the Islamic Countries, serves as the lead convener of the Philippine Center for Islam and Democracy. She earned a graduate degree from the John F. Kennedy School of Government at Harvard University. The quotations and discussion that follow in this paragraph and the next two are from Moner Bajunaid, in-person interview, Manila, December 3, 2012; and Amina Rasul, in-person interview, Manila, December 3, 2012.

24. The distinction that Bajunaid seems to have in mind here is that between *maqāṣid al-sharīʿa* (the aims and purposes of the Lawgiver) and *maqāṣid al-mukallaf* (the human goals and purposes), respectively. See Kamali, *Shariʿah Law*, 134.

25. Mohagher Iqbal is the official representative of the Muslim communities for peace talks with GPH, which until recently was represented by peace panel chair Marvic Leonen. The quotations and discussion that follow in this paragraph and the next are from Iqbal, in-person interview, December 5, 2012.

26. Lederach, *Moral Imagination*, ch. 8, "On Space: Life in the Web," esp. 78–80; Lederach, *Building Peace*, ch. 4, "Structure: Lenses for the Big Picture," esp. 41–43.

27. Tibi, *Islamism and Islam*, 169–71.

28. The following are some examples: (1) Section 13 of Act No. 787 (1903); (2) the Civil Code (1950); (3) the Barangay Justice Law (1978); and (4) the Family Code of the Philippines (1987). These examples are drawn largely from Mastura, "Legal Pluralism," 474–75. The quotations in this paragraph are from pp. 463, 468–69, 469–70, and 472 of the same work.

29. At any points of interpretive conflict, the predominant Shāfiʿī school took precedence.

30. See Rocco Viviano, "Christian-Muslim Relations in the Philippines: Between Conflict, Reconciliation and Dialogue," in *Christian Responses to Islam: Muslim-Christian Relations in the Modern World*, ed. Anthony

O'Mahony and Emma Loosley (Manchester: Manchester University Press, 2008), 133–38.

Chapter 9. The Human Good and the Scope of Public Civility

1. See Charles Beitz, *Political Theory and International Relations*, 2nd ed. (Princeton: Princeton University Press, [1979] 1999), esp. pt. 3, ch. 1, "Social Cooperation, Boundaries, and the Basis of Justice"; Charles Beitz, "Cosmopolitan Ideals and National Sentiment," *Journal of Philosophy* 80, no. 10 (1983): 591–600, quotation from 595; Walzer, *Spheres of Justice*, esp. ch. 2, "Membership"; Joseph Carens, "Aliens and Citizens: The Case for Open Borders," *Review of Politics* 49, no. 2 (1987): 251–73, 269; and Martha Nussbaum, "Patriotism and Cosmopolitanism," in *For Love of Country*, ed. Martha Nussbaum and Joshua Cohen (Boston: Beacon Press, 1996).

2. Amartya Sen, "Global Justice," in *Global Public Goods*, ed. Inge Kaul, Isabelle Grunberg, and Marc Stern (New York: Oxford University Press, 1999), 121.

3. See Walzer, *Thick and Thin*, ch. 4, "Justice and Tribalism: Minimal Morality in International Politics," quotations from 78, 82, 83.

4. Quotations in this paragraph and the next are from Nussbaum, "Patriotism and Cosmopolitanism," 14, 13, 9, 15, and 6, respectively.

5. Diogenes Laertius, *The Lives and Opinions of Eminent Philosophers*, trans. Charles Yonge (London: H. G. Bohn, 1853), 240–41; Plutarch, *On the Fortune and Virtue of Alexander the Great* [*De Alexandri fortuna aut virtute*], 329ab, quoted in Tad Brennan, *The Stoic Life* (Oxford: Oxford University Press, 2005), 162.

6. Arendt, *Human Condition*, 198.

7. See Nussbaum, "Reply," in Nussbaum and Cohen, *Love of Country*, 135.

8. Casanova, *Public Religions*, 229; and Lederach, *Building Peace*, 12–13.

9. See Marcus Tullius Cicero, *On Duties* [*De officiis*], trans. Walter Miller, Loeb ed. (Cambridge, MA: Harvard University Press, 1913), bk. 1, ch. 50; bk. 1, ch. 17; bk. 3, ch. 11, respectively; and Cicero, "On the Laws," bk. 1, ch. 7.

10. José Casanova, "Public Religions Revisited," in *Religion: Beyond a Concept*, ed. Hent de Vries (New York: Fordham University Press, 2008), 116.

11. Quotations from Anderson, *Imagined Communities*, 4, 135, 5–6, and 141, respectively.

12. Quotations in this paragraph and the next four are from David Miller, *On Nationality* (Oxford: Oxford University Press, 1997), 10–11, 68–70, 71–74, 19, and 12, respectively.

13. See Anthony Smith, *Nations and Nationalism in a Global Era* (Cambridge: Polity, 1995), 24–29; and Anthony Smith, *National Identity* (Reno: University of Nevada Press, 1991), 176 ff. Mary Kaldor cites *Nations and Nationalism* in her *New and Old Wars*, 2nd ed. (Cambridge: Polity, 2006), 207 n. 30; see also p. 91.

14. See Craig Calhoun, *Nationalism* (Minneapolis: University of Minnesota Press, 1997), 89; and his *Nations Matter: Culture, History, and the Cosmopolitan Dream* (Abingdon: Routledge, 2007), 17–24.

15. Tibi, *Islamism and Islam*, 34, 40.

16. Quoted in Hashmi, "Islamic Ethics," 158.

17. For this discussion, I draw heavily on Sohail Hashmi, "Political Boundaries and Moral Communities: Islamic Perspectives," in *States, Nations, and Borders: The Ethics of Making Boundaries*, ed. Allen Buchanan and Margaret Moore (Cambridge: Cambridge University Press, 2003), quotations from 186.

18. Hashmi, "Political Boundaries," 206 and 197–98, respectively. Cf. Hashmi, "Islamic Ethics," 159; and Khaled Abou El Fadl, "The Unbounded Law of God and Territorial Boundaries," in Buchanan and Moore, *States, Nations, and Borders*, 222 ff.

19. See Abou El Fadl, "Unbounded Law," 214, and "Islamic Law," 181.

20. See Abou El Fadl, "Unbounded Law," 218, 222, 255, 226; and Abū Zakarīyā᾽ al-Nawawī, *Al-Majmū*ʿ *sharḥ al-muhadhdhab* (1421), vol. 19 (Beirut: Dār al-Fikr, 2000), 262–63, quoted in Abou El Fadl, "Islamic Law," 150.

21. See Ramadan, *Western Muslims*, 69; and Faysal Al-Mawlawi, *Al-Usus al-shariyya lil-alaquat bayna al-muslimin wa-ghayr al-muslimin* (Paris: UOIF, 1987), 104, quoted in Ramadan, *Western Muslims*, 72. The famed medieval theologian Fakhr al-Dīn al-Rāzī similarly articulated this idea of *dār al-da*ʿ*wa*; see Fakhr al-Dīn al-Rāzī, *Al-Tafsīr al-kabīr* [The Great Commentary] (Cairo: al-Maṭbaʿah al Bahiyyah al-Miṣriyyah, 1938), cited in ʿAlwānī, *Fiqh for Minorities*, 29.

22. Zaman, "Territorial Boundaries," 87–88; and Black, *Islamic Political Thought*, 342.

23. See Anthony Pagden, "The Christian Tradition," in Buchanan and Moore, *States, Nations, and Borders*, 105, 114–17. For more on this point, see Anthony Pagden and Jeremy Lawrance, eds., *Vitoria: Political Writings*

(Cambridge: Cambridge University Press, 1991), 3.4, "On Civil Power"; and 3.1, "On the American Indians."

24. See Aquinas, *Summa theologica*, quotations that follow are from II-II, q. 66, art. 1–2 and 7. My discussion of Aquinas on this point draws heavily on Ruston, *Human Rights*, 40–51; and Tuck, *Natural Rights*, 17–24.

25. Brian Tierney, *The Idea of Natural Rights* (Grand Rapids: Eerdmans, [1997] 2001), 72–73.

26. See John Chrysostom, *On Wealth and Poverty*, trans. Catharine Roth (Crestwood: St. Vladimir's Seminary Press, 1984), 49–55.

27. See Paul VI, "On the Development of Peoples," no. 23, http://bit.ly/VatIIPP, last accessed July 1, 2016. *Populorum Progressio*, promulgated by Pope Paul VI on March 26, 1967; and U.S. Catholic Conference International Policy Committee, "American Responsibilities in a Changing World," *Origins* 22 (1992): 337–41, 339 and 341. Comments from Richard Miller, "Christian Attitudes towards Boundaries: Metaphysical and Geographical," in Coleman, *Christian Political Ethics*, 76, 85, 86.

28. Lisa Cahill, "A Theology for Peacebuilding" (paper presented at the Catholic Peacebuilding Network conference, University of Notre Dame, 2008, 7 (emphasis original).

29. Alejo, in-person interview, November 25, 2012.

30. R. Miller, "Christian Attitudes," 69.

31. Leguro, in-person interview, November 28, 2012.

32. The subject of friendship is a large, complex, and important one; and my use of the term here represents an admittedly idiosyncratic gloss. For example, a simple but most important point in Cates's study of the Aristotelian-Thomistic ideal of friendship is that there is a categorical difference between "friends" on the one hand and "strangers" (and "enemies") on the other. See Cates, *Choosing to Feel*, chs. 10 and 11, esp. 204–6, 230–35. By contrast, my use of "friendship" would include those "strangers" who are farther away in both distance and time. That said, given the phrase from the seventeenth-century theologian Jeremy Taylor—"Christian charity is friendship to all the world"—perhaps my use, at least in certain theological circles, is less idiosyncratic than suspected. See Jeremy Taylor, *A Discourse of the Nature, Offices, and Measures of Friendship* (London: Printed for R. Royston, 1657). (This quotation from Taylor and my understanding thereof come from Liz Carmichael, *Friendship: Interpreting Christian Love* [London: T & T Clark, 2004], 136–46.)

33. Quotations in this paragraph are from Alejo, in-person interview, November 25, 2012.

34. Such a case made with philosophical precision and substantive case studies is found in Philpott, *Just and Unjust Peace*, 54–62, 181–91, 198–206, and ch. 12, "Forgiveness."

Conclusion

1. Carter, *Civility*, 19.
2. Guinness, *Case for Civility*, 151.
3. Jacques Maritain, "Truth and Human Fellowship," in *On the Use of Philosophy: Three Essays* (Princeton: Princeton University Press, 1961), 24.
4. The quotations in this paragraph are from Plant, *Politics, Theology and History*, 358.

BIBLIOGRAPHY

Abd-Allah, Umar Faruq. "Theological Dimensions of Islamic Law." In *The Cambridge Companion to Classical Islamic Theology*, edited by Tim Winter. Cambridge: Cambridge University Press, 2008.

Abou El Fadl, Khaled. *Islam and the Challenge of Democracy: A "Boston Review" Book*. Edited by Joshua Cohen and Deborah Chasman. Princeton: Princeton University Press, 2004.

———. "Islamic Law and Muslim Minorities." *Islamic Law and Society* 1, no. 2 (1994): 141–87.

———. *Speaking in God's Name: Islamic Law, Authority and Women*. Oxford: Oneworld, 2001.

———. "The Unbounded Law of God and Territorial Boundaries." In *States, Nations, and Borders: The Ethics of Making Boundaries*, edited by Allen Buchanan and Margaret Moore. Cambridge: Cambridge University Press, 2003.

Abubakar, Ayesah Uy. "The Philippines: Challenges to Peacebuilding." In *Islam and Violent Separatism*, edited by Ashok Swain. London: Kegal Paul, 2007.

Abubakar, Carmen. "The Advent and Growth of Islam in the Philippines." In *Islam in Southeast Asia*, edited by K. S. Nathan and Mohammad Hashim Kamali. Singapore: Institute of Southeast Asian Studies, 2005.

Abuza, Zachary. *Militant Islam in Southeast Asia*. Boulder: Lynne Rienner, 2003.

Afsaruddin, Asma. "The 'Islamic State': Genealogy, Facts, and Myths." *Journal of Church and State* 48, no. 1 (2006): 153–73.

Ahmad, Ahmad Atif. *Structural Interrelations of Theory and Practice in Islamic Law*. Leiden: Brill, 2006.

Alejo, Albert. "Let the People Understand." *Our Mindanao* 1, no. 1 (2010): 15–19.

ʿAlwānī, Ṭāhā Jābir Fayyāḍ. *Towards a Fiqh for Minorities*. Rev. ed. London: International Institute of Islamic Thought, 2010.

An-Na'im, Abdullahi Ahmed. *Islam and the Secular State*. Cambridge, MA: Harvard University Press, 2008.

———. "Islamic Foundations of Religious Human Rights." In *Religious Human Rights in Global Perspective*, edited by John Witte and Johan van der Vyver. The Hague: Kluwer, 1996.

———. *Towards an Islamic Reformation*. Syracuse: Syracuse University Press, 1990.

Anderson, Benedict. *Imagined Communities: Reflections on the Origin and Spread of Nationalism*. Rev. ed. London: Verso, [1983] 1991.

Appiah, Kwame Anthony. *Cosmopolitanism: Ethics in a World of Strangers*. London: Penguin, 2007.

Appleby, R. Scott. *The Ambivalence of the Sacred: Religion, Violence, and Reconciliation*. Oxford: Rowman and Littlefield, 2000.

———. "Building Sustainable Peace: The Roles of Local and Transnational Religious Actors." In *Religious Pluralism, Globalization, and World Politics*, edited by Thomas Banchoff. New York: Oxford University Press, 2008.

Appleby, R. Scott, and John Paul Lederach. "Strategic Peacebuilding: An Overview." In *Strategies of Peace: Transforming Conflict in a Violent World*, edited by Daniel Philpott and Gerard Powers. Oxford: Oxford University Press, 2010.

Aquinas, Thomas. *Summa contra gentiles*. Vol. 2. Basic Writings of Saint Thomas Aquinas. Edited by Anton Pegis. 2 vols. New York: Random House, 1945.

———. *Summa theologica* (1265–74). Translated by Fathers of the English Dominican Province. Charlottesville: InteLex Corporation, 1993.

Arendt, Hannah. *The Human Condition*. Chicago: University of Chicago Press, 1958.

Ariès, Philippe. *Centuries of Childhood*. Harmondsworth: Penguin Books, 1979.

Aristotle. "Metaphysics." Translated by Joe Sachs. In *Aristotle's Metaphysics*, edited by Joe Sachs. Santa Fe: Green Lion Press, 1999.

———. *Nicomachean Ethics*. Translated by David Ross, edited by Lesley Brown. Oxford: Clarendon Press, 2009.

———. *Politics*. Translated by Benjamin Jowett. New York: Dover, 2000.

Asad, Talal. *Formations of the Secular: Christianity, Islam, Modernity*. Stanford: Stanford University Press, 2003.

———. "Free Speech, Blasphemy, and Secular Criticism." In *Is Critique Secular? Blasphemy, Injury, and Free Speech*, by Talal Asad, Wendy Brown,

Judith Butler, and Saba Mahmood. New York: Fordham University Press, 2013.

Asad, Talal, Wendy Brown, Judith Butler, and Saba Mahood. *Is Critique Secular? Blasphemy, Injury, and Free Speech.* New York: Fordham University Press, 2013.

Audi, Robert. "Liberal Democracy and the Place of Religion in Politics." In *Religion in the Public Square,* edited by Robert Audi and Nicholas Wolterstorff. London: Rowman and Littlefield, 1997.

Audi, Robert, and Nicholas Wolterstorff, eds. *Religion in the Public Square.* London: Rowman and Littlefield, 1997.

Augustine. *The City of God.* Translated by Marcus Dods. Edited by Philip Schaff. Edinburgh: T & T Clark, 1886.

Ayubi, Nazih. *Political Islam.* London: Routledge, 1991.

Baderin, Mashood. *International Human Rights and Islamic Law.* Oxford: Oxford University Press, 2003.

Banchoff, Thomas, and Robert Wuthnow, eds. *Religion and the Global Politics of Human Rights.* Oxford: Oxford University Press, 2011.

Bannā᾽, Ḥasan al-. *Mudhakkarat al-daʿwa wa᾽l-daʿiyya* [Treatises on the Ranks of the Righteous and the Devoted]. Cairo: Dar Al-Shihab, ca. 1951.

Barnes, Michael. *Theology and the Dialogue of Religions.* Cambridge: Cambridge University Press, 2002.

Barry, Brian. *Culture and Equality: An Egalitarian Critique of Multiculturalism.* Cambridge: Polity, 2001.

Barthes, Roland. "The Death of the Author." Translated by Stephen Heath. In *Image-Music-Text,* edited by Stephen Heath. London: Fontana, 1977.

Bauman, Zygmunt. *Globalization: The Human Consequences.* Cambridge: Polity, 1998.

———. *In Search of Politics.* Cambridge: Polity, 1999.

———. *Liquid Modernity.* Cambridge: Polity, 2000.

Baur, Michael. "Law and Natural Law." In *The Oxford Handbook of Aquinas,* edited by Brian Davies and Eleonore Stump. Oxford: Oxford University Press, 2012.

Bautista, Cynthia. "Democratic Consolidation and the Challenge of Poverty in the Philippines." In *Asian New Democracies,* edited by Michael Hsiao. Taipei: Taiwan Foundation for Democracy, 2006.

Bazargan, Mehdi. "Religion and Liberty." In *Liberal Islam,* edited by Charles Kurzman. Oxford: Oxford University Press, 1998.

Beck, Ulrich. *The Cosmopolitan Vision.* Cambridge: Polity, 2006.

Beitz, Charles. "Cosmopolitan Ideals and National Sentiment." *Journal of Philosophy* 80, no. 10 (1983): 591–600.

———. *Political Theory and International Relations*. 2nd ed. Princeton: Princeton University Press, [1979] 1999.

Bellah, Robert N. *The Broken Covenant: American Civil Religion in Time of Trial*. New York: Seabury, 1975.

———. "Confronting Modernity." In *Varieties of Secularism in a Secular Age*, edited by Michael Warner, Jonathan VanAntwerpen, and Craig Calhoun. Cambridge, MA: Harvard University Press, 2010.

Bellah, Robert N., et al. *Habits of the Heart: Individualism and Commitment in American Life*. Berkeley: University of California Press, [1985] 1996.

Benko, Georges. "Introduction: Modernity, Postmodernity and Social Sciences." In *Space and Social Theory: Interpreting Modernity and Postmodernity*, edited by Georges Benko and Ulf Strohmayer. Oxford: Blackwell, 1997.

Bentham, Jeremy. "A Manual of Political Economy." In *The Works of Jeremy Bentham*, edited by John Bowring. Edinburgh: Tait, 1843.

Berger, Peter. *Between Relativism and Fundamentalism*. Grand Rapids: Eerdmans, 2010.

———. "The Cultural Dynamics of Globalization." In *Many Globalizations: Cultural Diversity in the Contemporary World*, edited by Peter Berger and Samuel Huntington. Oxford: Oxford University Press, 2002.

———. "The Desecularization of the World: A Global Overview." In *The Desecularization of World: Resurgent Religion and World Politics*, edited by Peter Berger. Grand Rapids: Eerdmans, 1999.

———, ed. *The Desecularization of the World: Resurgent Religion and World Politics*. Grand Rapids: Eerdmans, 1999.

———. *Facing up to Modernity*. New York: Basic Books, 1977.

———. "Faith and Development." *Society* 46, no. 1 (2009): 69–75.

———. *The Heretical Imperative*. New York: Doubleday, 1979.

———. "Pluralism, Protestantization, and the Voluntary Principle." In *Democracy and the New Religious Pluralism*, edited by Thomas Banchoff. Oxford: Oxford University Press, 2007.

———. *A Sacred Canopy*. New York: Doubleday, 1967.

———. "Secularism in Retreat." *National Interest* 46 (1996–97): 3–12.

———. *The Social Reality of Religion*. Harmondsworth: Penguin, 1973.

Berger, Peter, Brigitte Berger, and Hansfried Kellner. *The Homeless Mind*. Harmondsworth: Penguin, 1974.

Berger, Peter, Grace Davie, and Effie Fokas. *Religious America, Secular Europe?* Aldershot: Ashgate, 2008.

Berger, Peter, and Thomas Luckmann. *The Social Construction of Reality: A Treatise in the Sociology of Knowledge*. London: Allen Lane, 1967.

Berkey, Jonathan. *The Formation of Islam*. Cambridge: Cambridge University Press, 2003.

Berkman, John. Introduction to *The Pinckaers Reader: Renewing Thomistic Moral Theology*, by Servais Pinckaers, OP. Translated by John Berkman and Craig Titus. Washington, DC: Catholic University of America Press, 2005.

Berlin, Isaiah. *Four Essays on Liberty*. Oxford: Oxford University Press, [1958] 1969.

Bianchi, Marina. *The Active Consumer*. London: Routledge, 1998.

Bielefeldt, Heiner. "Freedom of Religion or Belief—a Human Right under Pressure." *Oxford Journal of Law and Religion* 1, no. 1 (2012): 15–35.

———. "Misperceptions of Freedom of Religion or Belief." *Human Rights Quarterly* 35, no. 1 (2013): 33–68.

Biggar, Nigel. *Behaving in Public: How to Do Christian Ethics*. Cambridge: Eerdmans, 2011.

———. "Not Translation, but Conversation: Theology in Public Debate About Euthanasia." In *Religious Voices in Public Places*, edited by Nigel Biggar and Linda Hogan. Oxford: Oxford University Press, 2009.

———. "Peace and Justice: A Limited Reconciliation." *Ethical Theory and Moral Practice* 5, no. 2 (2002): 167–79.

———. "The Value of Limited Loyalty: Christianity, the Nation, and Territorial Boundaries." In *Christian Political Ethics*, edited by John Coleman. Princeton: Princeton University Press, 2008.

Black, Antony. *The History of Islamic Political Thought*. 2nd ed. Edinburgh: Edinburgh University Press, [2001] 2011.

Boethius, Anicius Manlius Severinus. "A Treatise against Eutyches and Nestorius." Translated by Hugh Fraser Stewart and Edward Kennard Rand. In *The Theological Tractates*. Cambridge, MA: Harvard University Press, 1997.

Bowen, John. *Why the French Don't Like Headscarves: Islam, the State, and Public Space*. Princeton: Princeton University Press, 2007.

Boyle, Joseph. "Natural Law and International Ethics." In *Traditions of International Ethics*, edited by Terry Nardin and David Mapel. Cambridge: Cambridge University Press, 1992.

Brennan, Tad. *The Stoic Life*. Oxford: Oxford University Press, 2005.

Brown, Nathan. "Egypt: Cacophony and Consensus." In *Sharī'a Politics: Islamic Law and Society in the Modern World*, edited by Robert Hefner. Bloomington: Indiana University Press, 2011.

Brown, Wendy. Introduction to *Is Critique Secular? Blasphemy, Injury, and Free Speech,* by Talal Asad, Wendy Brown, Judith Butler, and Saba Mahood. New York: Fordham University Press, 2013.

Bruce, Steve. *Fundamentalism*. Cambridge: Polity, 2008.

———. *God Is Dead: Secularization in the West*. Oxford: Blackwell, 2002.

Budziszewski, J. *Written on the Heart: The Case for Natural Law*. Downers Grove, IL: InterVarsity Press, 1997.

Bukay, David. "Peace or Jihad? Abrogation in Islam." *Middle East Quarterly* 14, no. 4 (2007): 3–11.

Bukhari. *Prophetic Commentary on the Koran*. http://bit.ly/2ladwAz.

Būṭī, Muḥammad Sa'īd Ramaḍān. *The Jurisprudence of the Prophetic Biography*. Translated by Nancy Roberts, edited by Anas al-Rifā'ī. Damascus: Dar al-Fikr, 2001.

Cahill, Lisa. "A Theology for Peacebuilding." Paper presented at the Catholic Peacebuilding Network Conference, University of Notre Dame, 2008.

Calhoun, Craig. *Nationalism*. Minneapolis: University of Minnesota Press, 1997.

———. *Nations Matter: Culture, History, and the Cosmopolitan Dream*. Abingdon: Routledge, 2007.

Calo, Zachary. "Catholic Social Thought, Political Liberalism, and the Idea of Human Rights." *Journal of Christian Legal Thought* 1, no. 2 (2011): 1–13.

Campanini, Massimo. "Alfarabi and the Foundation of Political Theology in Islam." In *Islam, the State, and Political Authority*, edited by Asma Afsaruddin. Basingstoke: Palgrave Macmillan, 2011.

Carens, Joseph. "Aliens and Citizens: The Case for Open Borders." *Review of Politics* 49, no. 2 (1987): 251–73.

Carmichael, Liz. *Friendship: Interpreting Christian Love*. London: T & T Clark, 2004.

Carozza, Paolo. "Human Dignity and Judicial Interpretation of Human Rights: A Reply." *European Journal of International Law* 19, no. 5 (2008): 931–44.

Carter, Ian. "Positive and Negative Liberty." In *The Stanford Encyclopedia of Philosophy*, edited by Edward Zalta. Fall 2010 ed. http://stanford.io/18Dkvtt.

Carter, Stephen. *Civility: Manners, Morals, and the Etiquette of Democracy.* New York: Basic Books, 1998.

Casanova, José. *Public Religions in the Modern World.* Chicago: University of Chicago Press, 1994.

———. "Public Religions Revisited." In *Religion: Beyond a Concept*, edited by Hent de Vries. New York: Fordham University Press, 2008.

———. "The Return of Religion to the Public Sphere: A Global Perspective." Blackfriars Hall, Oxford University, 2011.

———. "A Secular Age: Dawn or Twilight?" In *Varieties of Secularism in a Secular Age*, edited by Michael Warner, Jonathan VanAntwerpen, and Craig Calhoun. Cambridge, MA: Harvard University Press, 2010.

Cates, Diana Fritz. *Choosing to Feel: Virtue, Friendship, and Compassion for Friends.* Notre Dame: University of Notre Dame Press, 1997.

Cavanaugh, William, and Peter Scott. Introduction to *The Blackwell Companion to Political Theology*, edited by Peter Scott and William Cavanaugh. Malden: Blackwell, 2004.

Chadwick, Henry. *Boethius: The Consolations of Music, Logic, Theology and Philosophy.* Oxford: Clarendon Press, 1981.

Chadwick, Owen. *The Secularization of the European Mind.* Cambridge: Cambridge University Press, [1975] 1990.

Chapman, Mark. *Blair's Britain: A Christian Critique.* London: Darton, Longman & Todd, 2005.

———. *Doing God: Religion and Public Policy.* London: Darton, Longman & Todd, 2008.

Chittick, William. *Imaginal Worlds: Ibn al-ʿArabī and the Problem of Religious Diversity.* Albany: State University of New York Press, 1994.

Chrysostom, John. *On Wealth and Poverty.* Translated by Catharine Roth. Crestwood: St. Vladimir's Seminary Press, 1984.

Cicero, Marcus Tullius. *On Duties* [*De officiis*]. Translated by Walter Miller. Loeb ed. Cambridge, MA: Harvard University Press, 1913.

———. "On the Laws." Translated by Francis Barham. In *The Political Works of Marcus Tullius Cicero.* London: Edmund Spettigue, 1841–42.

Cohen, Jean, and Andrew Arato. *Civil Society and Political Theory.* Cambridge, MA: MIT Press, 1992.

Comte, Auguste. *System of Positive Polity.* London: Longmans, Green and Co., [1851–54] 1876.

Crone, Patricia. *Medieval Islamic Political Thought.* Edinburgh: Edinburgh University Press, 2004.

———. *Roman, Provincial, and Islamic Law*. Cambridge: Cambridge University Press, 1987.

Davie, Grace. "Law, Sociology and Religion: An Awkward Threesome." *Oxford Journal of Law and Religion* 1, no. 1 (2012): 235–47.

Diogenes Laertius. *The Lives and Opinions of Eminent Philosophers*. Translated by Charles Yonge. London: H. G. Bohn, 1853.

Donohue, John, and John Esposito, eds. *Islam in Transition: Muslim Perspectives*. 2nd ed. Oxford: Oxford University Press, 2007.

Durkheim, Émile. *The Division of Labour in Society*. Translated by W. D. Halls. Edited by Lewis Coser. Basingstoke: Macmillan, [1893] 1984.

———. *The Elementary Forms of the Religious Life*. Translated by Karen Fields. New York: Free Press, [1912] 1995.

Dworkin, Ronald. "Is There a Right to Pornography?" *Oxford Journal of Legal Studies* 1, no. 2 (1981): 177–212.

———. *Taking Rights Seriously*. Cambridge, MA: Harvard University Press, 1978.

Edwards, Michael. *Civil Society*. Cambridge: Polity, 2004.

Ehrenberg, John. *Civil Society: The Critical History of an Idea*. New York: New York University Press, 1999.

Eisenstadt, Shmuel. "Concluding Remarks: Public Sphere, Civil Society, and Political Dynamics in Islamic Societies." In *The Public Sphere in Muslim Societies*, edited by Miriam Hoexter, Shmuel Eisenstadt, and Nehemia Levtzion. Albany: State University of New York Press, 2002.

———. "Multiple Modernities in an Age of Globalization." *Canadian Journal of Sociology* 24, no. 2 (1999): 283–95.

Elias, Norbert. *The Civilizing Process*. Edited by Eric Dunning et al. Rev. ed. Oxford: Blackwell, [1939] 2000.

Elshtain, Jean Bethke. "Religion, the Enlightenment, and a Common Good." In *Religion, the Enlightenment, and the New Global Order*, edited by John Owen and J. Judd Owen. New York: Columbia University Press, 2010.

Erasmus, Desiderius. *A Lytell Booke of Good Maners for Chyldren* [*De civilitate morum puerilium*]. Translated by Robert Whittington. London: Wynkyn de Worde, [1530] 1536.

Esack, Farid. *Qur'ān, Liberation and Pluralism*. Oxford: Oneworld, 1997.

Esposito, John, and John Voll. *Islam and Democracy*. Oxford: Oxford University Press, 1996.

Fadel, Mohammad. "The True, the Good and the Reasonable: The Theological and Ethical Roots of Public Reason in Islamic Law." *Canadian Journal of Law and Jurisprudence* 21, no. 1 (2008): 5–69.

Fakhry, Majid. *Averroes, Aquinas, and the Rediscovery of Aristotle in Western Europe*. Washington, DC: Georgetown University Press, 1997.
Feldman, Noah. *The Fall and Rise of the Islamic State*. Princeton: Princeton University Press, 2008.
———. "The Intellectual Origins of the Establishment Clause." *New York University Law Review* 77 (2002): 346–428.
Ferguson, Adam. *An Essay on the History of Civil Society* (1782). Edited by Fania Oz-Salzberger. Cambridge: Cambridge University Press, 1995.
Ferguson, Harvie. *Phenomenological Sociology: Insight and Experience in Modern Society*. London: Sage, 2006.
Ferrer, Miriam. "The Case of the Autonomous Region in Muslim Mindanao." *Ethnic and Racial Studies* 35, no. 12 (2011): 1–19.
Finnis, John, ed. *Human Rights and the Common Good: Collected Essays*. Vol. 3. Oxford: Oxford University Press, 2011.
———. "Human Rights and Their Enforcement." In *Human Rights and Common Good: Collected Essays*, vol. 3, edited by John Finnis. Oxford: Oxford University Press, 2011.
———. "Is Natural Law Theory Compatible with Limited Government?" In *Natural Law, Liberalism, and Morality*, edited by Robert P. George. Oxford: Oxford University Press, 1996.
———. *Natural Law and Natural Rights*. 2nd ed. Oxford: Oxford University Press, 2011.
———. "Public Good: The Specifically Political Common Good in Aquinas." In *Natural Law and Moral Inquiry*, edited by Robert P. George. Washington, DC: Georgetown University Press, 1998.
Foot, Philippa. "Moral Beliefs." In *Virtues and Vices*, edited by Philippa Foot. Oxford: Oxford University Press, 2002.
Fuchs, Stephan. *Against Essentialism*. Cambridge, MA: Harvard University Press, 2001.
Gadamer, Hans-Georg. *Truth and Method*. Translated by Joel Weinsheimer and Donald Marshall. 2nd ed. London: Continuum, [1960] 2004.
Galtung, Johan. "Introduction: Peace by Peaceful Conflict Transformation." In *Handbook of Peace and Conflict Studies*, edited by Charles Webel and Johan Galtung. London: Routledge, 2007.
Gellner, Ernest. *Conditions of Liberty*. London: Penguin, 1996.
George, Robert P. *In Defense of Natural Law*. Oxford: Clarendon, 1999.
———. *Making Men Moral: Civil Liberties and Public Morality*. Oxford: Clarendon Press, 1993.

———. “Natural Law and International Order.” In *In Defense of Natural Law*. Oxford: Clarendon, 1999.

George, Thayil Jacob Sony. *Revolt in Mindanao*. Kuala Lumpur: Oxford University Press, 1980.

Gewirth, Alan. *Reason and Morality*. Chicago: University of Chicago Press, 1978.

Ghazālī, Abū Ḥāmid al-. *Al-Mustaṣfā min ʿilm al-uṣūl*. Vol. 1. Baghdad: Muthanna, 1970.

Giddens, Anthony. *Central Problems in Social Theory*. London: Macmillan Press, 1979.

Gorski, Philip, and Ateş Altınordu. “After Secularization?” *Annual Review of Sociology* 34 (2008): 55–85.

Gramsci, Antonio. *Selections from the Prison Notebooks*. Edited by Quintin Hoare and Geoffrey Nowell-Smith. London: Lawrence and Wishart, 1971.

Greeley, Andrew. *Unsecular Man: The Persistence of Religion*. New York: Schocken, 1972.

Green, Thomas. *Lectures on the Principles of Political Obligation and Other Writings* (1895). Edited by Paul Harris and John Morrow. Cambridge: Cambridge University Press, 1986.

Griffel, Frank. “Al-Ghazālī’s Use of ‘Original Human Disposition’ (Fiṭra) and Its Background.” *Muslim World* 102, no. 1 (2012): 1–32.

Griffin, James. *On Human Rights*. Oxford: Oxford University Press, 2008.

Griffiths, John. “What Is Legal Pluralism?” *Journal of Legal Pluralism* 24 (1986): 1–55.

Grisez, Germain. *Christian Moral Principles*. Vol. 1 of *The Way of the Lord Jesus*. 3 vols. Chicago: Franciscan Herald Press, 1983.

———. “The First Principle of Practical Reason: A Commentary on the *Summa Theologiae*.” *Natural Law Forum* 94, no. 2 (1965): 168–201.

———. “The True Ultimate End of Human Beings: The Kingdom, Not God Alone.” *Theological Studies* 69, no. 1 (2008): 38–61.

Grisez, Germain, and Joseph Boyle. *Life and Death with Liberty and Justice*. Notre Dame: University of Notre Dame Press, 1979.

Grisez, Germain, Joseph Boyle, and John Finnis. “Practical Principles, Moral Truth, and Ultimate Ends.” *American Journal of Jurisprudence* 32 (1987): 99–151.

Guinness, Os. *The Case for Civility: And Why Our Future Depends on It*. New York: HarperCollins, 2008.

Habermas, Jürgen. *Between Naturalism and Religion*. Translated by Ciaran Cronin. Cambridge: Polity, 2008.

———. *The Inclusion of the Other: Studies in Political Theory*. Edited by Ciaran Cronin and Pable De Greiff. Cambridge, MA: MIT Press, 1998.

———. *The Postnational Constellation: Political Essays*. Translated by Max Pensky. Cambridge, MA: MIT Press, 2001.

———. "Religion in the Public Sphere." In *Between Naturalism and Religion*. Cambridge: Polity, 2008.

———. *The Structural Transformation of the Public Sphere*. Cambridge: Polity, 1989.

———. *The Theory of Communicative Action*. Translated by Thomas McCarthy. 3rd ed. Vol. 2. Boston: Beacon Press, 1987.

Hadden, Jeffrey. "Desacralizing Secularization Theory." In *Secularization and Fundamentalism Reconsidered*, edited by Jeffrey Hadden and Anson Shupe. New York: Paragon House, 1989.

———. "Toward Desacralizing Secularization Theory." *Social Forces* 65 (1987): 587–611.

Haldane, John. *Faithful Reason: Essays Catholic and Philosophical*. London: Routledge, 2004.

———. *Practical Philosophy: Ethics, Society and Culture*. Exeter: Imprint Academic, 2009.

Hallaq, Wael. *Authority, Continuity, and Change in Islamic Law*. Cambridge: Cambridge University Press, 2001.

———. *A History of Islamic Legal Theories*. New York: Cambridge University Press, 1997.

———. Introduction to *The Formation of Islamic Law*, edited by Wael Hallaq. Aldershot: Ashgate Variorum, 2003.

———. "On the Authoritativeness of Sunni Consensus." *International Journal of Middle East Studies* 18, no. 1 (1986): 427–54.

———. *The Origins and Evolution of Islamic Law*. Cambridge: Cambridge University Press, 2005.

———. *Sharīʿa: Theory, Practice, Transformations*. Cambridge: Cambridge University Press, 2009.

———. "Was the Gate of Ijtihad Closed?" *International Journal of Middle East Studies* 16, no. 1 (1984): 3–41.

Häring, Bernard. "Dynamism and Continuity in a Personalistic Approach to Natural Law." In *Norm and Context in Christian Ethics*, edited by Gene Outka and Paul Ramsey. New York: Charles Scribner's Sons, 1968.

Harris, Albert. "Peace Processes under Conditions of Uncertain Sovereignty." *International Negotiation* 12, no. 2 (2007): 175–205.

Hashemi, Nader. *Islam, Secularism, and Liberal Democracy*. New York: Oxford University Press, 2009.

Hashmi, Sohail. "Interpreting the Islamic Ethics of War and Peace." In *Islamic Political Ethics*, edited by Sohail Hashmi. Princeton: Princeton University Press, 2002.

———. "Islamic Ethics and International Society." In *Islamic Political Ethics*, edited by Sohail Hashmi. Princeton: Princeton University Press, 2002.

———. "Political Boundaries and Moral Communities: Islamic Perspectives." In *States, Nations, and Borders: The Ethics of Making Boundaries*, edited by Allen Buchanan and Margaret Moore. Cambridge: Cambridge University Press, 2003.

Hayek, Friedrich. *Law, Legislation and Liberty*, vol. 2: *The Mirage of Social Justice*. London: Routledge, 1976.

———. *Law, Legislation and Liberty*, vol. 3: *The Political Order of a Free People*. London: Routledge, 1979.

Heck, Paul. *Common Ground: Islam, Christianity, and Religious Pluralism*. Washington, DC: Georgetown University Press, 2009.

Hefner, Robert. *Civil Islam: Muslims and Democratization in Indonesia*. Princeton: Princeton University Press, 2000.

———. "Introduction: Shariʿa Politics." In *Shariʿa Politics: Islamic Law and Society in the Modern World*, edited by Robert Hefner. Bloomington: Indiana University Press, 2011.

Hegel, Georg Wilhelm Friedrich. *Elements of the Philosophy of Right* (1821). Translated by H. B. Nisbet, edited by Allen Wood. Cambridge: Cambridge University Press, 1991.

Higton, Mike. "Scriptural Reasoning." *Conversations in Religion and Theology* 7, no. 2 (2009): 129–33.

Hittinger, Russell. *A Critique of the New Natural Law Theory*. Notre Dame: University of Notre Dame Press, 1987.

Hobbes, Thomas. *Leviathan* (1651). Edited by Michael Oakeshott. Oxford: Blackwell, 1948.

Hobsbawm, Eric. *Nations and Nationalism since 1780*. Cambridge: Cambridge University Press, 1990.

Hollenbach, David. *The Common Good and Christian Ethics*. Cambridge: Cambridge University Press, 2002.

———. "A Communitarian Reconstruction of Human Rights." In *Catholicism and Liberalism*, edited by R. Bruce Douglass and David Hollenbach. Cambridge: Cambridge University Press, 1994.

Holtzman, Livnat. "Human Choice, Divine Guidance and the Fiṭra Tradition." In *Ibn Taymiyya and His Times*, edited by Yossef Rapoport and Shahab Ahmed. Oxford: Oxford University Press, 2010.

Hooft, Stan van. *Cosmopolitanism: A Philosophy for Global Ethics*. Stocksfield: Acumen, 2009.

Hordern, Joshua. *Political Affections: Civic Participation and Moral Theology*. Oxford: Oxford University Press, 2013.

Hornsby-Smith, Michael. *An Introduction to Catholic Social Thought*. Cambridge: Cambridge University Press, 2006.

Husserl, Edmund. *The Crisis of European Sciences and Transcendental Phenomenology*. Translated by David Carr. Evanston: Northwestern University Press, [1913] 1970.

Jawziyya, Ibn Qayyim al-. *Shifāʾ al-ʿalīl fī masāʾil al-qaḍāʾ wa-al-qadar wa-al-ḥikma wa-al-taʿlīl* (1323) [Wrong Concepts about Predetermination and Causality]. Edited by al-Ḥalabī. Cairo: al-Maṭbaʿa al-Ḥusayniyya al-Miṣriyya, 1994.

Jifri, Habib Ali al-. "Loving God and Loving Neighbour." In *A Common Word: Muslims and Christians on Loving God and Neighbor*, edited by Miroslav Volf, Ghazi bin Muhammad, and Melissa Yarrington. Grand Rapids: Eerdmans, 2010.

Ibn Kathīr. *Tafsīr al-qurʾān al-karīm*. N.p.: Dār al-Turāth al-ʿArabī, n.d.

Ibn Sīnā. *Al-Ishārāt wa-al-tanbīhāt* [*Remarks and Admonitions*]. Edited by Ibn Muḥammad Ṭūsī. Tehran: Daftar Nashr al-Kitāb, 1983.

———. *Al-Najāt min al-gharq fī baḥr al-ḍalālāta* [*The Book of Salvation*]. Edited by M. T. Dānishpazhūh Tehran: Intishārāt-i Dānishgāh-i Tihrān, [1364] 1985.

Ibn Taymiyya. "The Dispute about the Fiṭra" [in Arabic]. In *Majmūʿat al-rasāʾil al-kubrā*, edited by Rashīd Riḍā. Cairo: Maktabat wa-Maṭbaʿat, 1966.

"International Religious Freedom Report 2010—Philippines." Edited by U.S. State Department. Washington, DC: Bureau of Democracy, Human Rights, and Labor.

Iqbal, Muhammad. *The Reconstruction of Religious Thought in Islam*. Lahore: Sh. Muhammad Ashraf, 1968.

Ishay, Micheline. *The History of Human Rights*. Berkeley: University of California Press, 2008.

Islam, Syed Serajul. "Ethno-Communal Conflict in the Philippines." In *Ethnic Conflict and Secessionism*, edited by Rajat Ganguly and Ian Macduff. London: Sage, 2003.

———. "Islamic Independence Movements." *Asian Survey* 38, no. 5 (1998): 441–56.

John XXIII. "Establishing Universal Peace in Truth, Justice, Charity and Liberty." Libreria Editrice Vaticana. http://bit.ly/VatIIPT.

John Paul II. "The Fiftieth General Assembly of the United Nations Organization." Libreria Editrice Vaticana. http://bit.ly/JPII50UN.

Jones, Charles. *Global Justice: Defending Cosmopolitanism*. Oxford: Oxford University Press, 1999.

———. "Global Liberalism: Political or Comprehensive?" *University of Toronto Law Journal* 54, no. 2 (2004): 227–48.

Kaldor, Mary. *New and Old Wars*. 2nd ed. Cambridge: Polity, 2006.

Kamali, Mohammad Hashim. *The Dignity of Man: An Islamic Perspective*. Cambridge: Islamic Texts Society, 2002.

———. *Principles of Islamic Jurisprudence*. Rev. ed. Cambridge: Islamic Texts Society, 1991.

———. *Shariʿah Law: An Introduction*. Oxford: Oneworld, 2008.

Kant, Immanuel. *Groundwork of the Metaphysics of Morals* (1785). Translated by Christine Korsgaard, edited by Mary Gregor. Cambridge: Cambridge University Press, 1998.

———. *Perpetual Peace: A Philosophical Essay*. Edited by Mary Campbell Smith. London: George Allen and Unwin, 1903.

———. *Theory and Practice* (1793). Translated by H. B. Nisbet. Kant: Political Writings, edited by Hans Reiss. Cambridge: Cambridge University Press, 1970.

Keech, Dominic. *The Anti-Pelagian Christology of Augustine of Hippo*. Oxford: Oxford University Press, 2012.

Kelsay, John. *Arguing the Just War in Islam*. Cambridge, MA: Harvard University Press, 2007.

Kenny, Michael. *The Politics of Identity*. Oxford: Polity, 2004.

Kepel, Gilles. *The Revenge of God*. Cambridge: Polity, [1991] 1994.

Kerr, Fergus. *After Aquinas: Versions of Thomism*. Oxford: Blackwell, 2002.

Keys, Mary. *Aquinas, Aristotle, and the Promise of the Common Good*. Cambridge: Cambridge University Press, 2006.

Khadduri, Majid. *The Islamic Conception of Justice*. Baltimore: Johns Hopkins University Press, 1984.

Kolig, Erich. "To Shariʿaticize or Not to Shariʿaticize: Islamic and Secular Law in Liberal Democratic Society." In *Shariʿa in the West*, edited by Rex Ahdar and Nicholas Aroney. Oxford: Oxford University Press, 2010.

Koselleck, Reinhart. *Critique and Crisis: Enlightenment and the Pathogenesis of Modern Society*. Oxford: Berg, 1988.

Kraut, Richard. *Aristotle on the Human Good*. Princeton: Princeton University Press, 1989.

Kukathas, Chandran. *The Liberal Archipelago: A Theory of Diversity and Freedom*. Oxford: Oxford University Press, 2003.

Kymlicka, Will. *Liberalism, Community and Culture*. Oxford: Clarendon, 1989.

———. *Multicultural Citizenship*. Oxford: Clarendon, 1995.

———. *Politics in the Vernacular*. Oxford: Oxford University Press, 2001.

Lactantius. *Divine Institutes* [*Divinae institutiones*]. Edited by Anthony Bowen and Peter Garnsey. Liverpool: Liverpool University Press, 2003.

Langan, John. "The Common Good: Catholicism, Pluralism, and Secular Society." In *Building a Better Bridge: Muslims, Christians and the Common Good*, edited by Michael Ipgrave. Washington, DC: Georgetown University Press, 2008.

Lasch, Christopher. *The Revolt of the Elites and the Betrayal of Democracy*. London: Norton, 1996.

Lederach, John Paul. *Building Peace: Sustainable Reconciliation in Divided Societies*. Washington, DC: U.S. Institute of Peace Press, 1997.

———. "Justpeace: The Challenge of the 21st Century." In *People Building Peace*. Utrech: European Centre for Conflict Prevention, 1999.

———. *The Moral Imagination: The Art and Soul of Building Peace*. Oxford: Oxford University Press, 2005.

Lemmons, R. Mary Hayden. "Juridical Prudence and the Toleration of Evil." *University of St. Thomas Law Journal* 4, no. 1 (2006): 25–46.

Lévinas, Emmanuel. *Otherwise than Being*. The Hague: Nijhoff, [1974] 1981.

———. *Totality and Infinity: An Essay on Exteriority*. Translated by Alphonso Lingis. Pittsburgh: Duquesne University Press, [1961] 2007.

Locke, John. *Two Treatises of Government* (1690). Edited by C. B. Macpherson. Cambridge: Cambridge University Press, 1980.

Long, Graham. *Relativism and the Foundations of Liberalism*. Exeter: Imprint Academic, 2004.

Lowry, Joseph. *Early Islamic Legal Theory*. Leiden: Brill, 2007.

Luckmann, Thomas. *The Invisible Religion*. New York: Macmillan, 1967.

———. "The Privatization of Religion and Morality." In *Detraditionalization: Critical Reflections on Authority and Identity*, edited by Paul Heelas, Scott Lash, and Paul Morris. Oxford: Blackwell, 1996.

———. "Shrinking Transcendence, Expanding Religion?" *Sociological Analysis* 50, no. 2 (1990): 127–38.

MacCallum, Gerald. "Negative and Positive Freedom." *Philosophical Review* 76 (1967): 312–34.

———. "Negative and Positive Freedom." In *Freedom: A Philosophical Anthology*, edited by Ian Carter, Matthew Kramer, and Hillel Steiner. Oxford: Blackwell, 2007.

MacEoin, Denis. *Sharia Law or "One Law for All"?* Edited by David Green. London: Civitas, 2009.

MacIntyre, Alasdair. *After Virtue: A Study in Moral Theory*. 3rd ed. Notre Dame: University of Notre Dame Press, [1981] 2007.

———. "Politics, Philosophy and the Common Good." In *The MacIntyre Reader*, edited by Kelvin Knight. Notre Dame: University of Notre Dame, 1998.

———. *Secularization and Moral Change*. London: Oxford University Press, 1967.

———. *Whose Justice? Which Rationality?* Notre Dame: University of Notre Dame Press, 1988.

Macpherson, Crawford. *The Political Theory of Possessive Individualism*. Toronto: University of Toronto Press, 1962.

Mahmood, Saba. "Religious Reason and Secular Affect: An Incommensurable Divide?" In *Is Critique Secular? Blasphemy, Injury, and Free Speech*, by Talal Asad, Wendy Brown, Judith Butler, and Saba Mahmood. New York: Fordham University Press, 2013.

Mahoney, John. *The Making of Moral Theology: A Study of the Roman Catholic Tradition*. Oxford: Clarendon, 1987.

Man, Wan Kadir Che. *Muslim Separatism*. Singapore: Oxford University Press, 1990.

March, Andrew. "Sources of Moral Obligation to Non-Muslims in the 'Jurisprudence of Muslim Minorities' (Fiqh al-aqalliyyāt) Discourse." *Islamic Law and Society* 16, no. 1 (2009): 34–94.

———. "Theocrats Living under Secular Law." *Journal of Political Philosophy* 19, no. 1 (2011): 28–51.

Maritain, Jacques. *Man and the State*. Chicago: University of Chicago Press, 1951.

———. "Truth and Human Fellowship." In *On the Use of Philosophy: Three Essays*. Princeton: Princeton University Press, 1961.

Markus, Robert. *Christianity and the Secular*. Notre Dame: University of Notre Dame Press, 2006.

———. *Saeculum: History and Society in the Theology of St Augustine*. Rev. ed. Cambridge: Cambridge University Press, [1970] 1988.

Marshall, David. *God, Muhammad and the Unbelievers: A Qur'anic Study*. Surrey: Curzon, 1999.

Martin, David. *The Future of Christianity: Reflections on Violence and Democracy, Religion and Secularisation*. Farnham: Ashgate, 2011.

———. *A General Theory of Secularization*. New York: Harper and Row, 1978.

———. *On Secularization: Towards a Revised General Theory*. Aldershot: Ashgate, 2005.

———. "Towards Eliminating the Concept of Secularization." In *Penguin Survey of the Social Sciences*, edited by Julius Gould. Harmondsworth: Penguin, 1965.

Marx, Karl. *Contribution to a Critique of Hegel's Philosophy of Right* (1843). Selected Works, edited by Karl Marx and Frederick Engels. New York: International Publishers, 1968.

———. "Preface to the Critique of Hegel's Philosophy of Right." Translated by Annette Jolin and Joseph O'Malley. In *Karl Marx and Friedrich Engels*, edited by Joseph O'Malley. Moscow: Foreign Languages Publishing House, 1962.

Marx, Karl, and Friedrich Engels. *Capital: A Critique of Political Economy*. Translated by Samuel Moore and Edward Aveling. New York: Modern Library, [1867] 1906.

———. *The German Ideology*. Translated by S. W. Ryazanskaya. London: Lawrence and Wishart, [1846] 1965.

Mastura, Michael. "Legal Pluralism in the Philippines." *Law and Society Review* 28, no. 3 (1994): 462–75.

Masud, Muhammad Khalid. "The Scope of Pluralism in Islamic Moral Traditions." In *Islamic Political Ethics*, edited by Sohail Hashmi. Princeton: Princeton University Press, 2002.

Mawardi, Abu'l-Hasan al-. *The Laws of Islamic Governance* [*Al-ahkam al-sultaniyyah*]. Edited by Assadullah ad-Dhaaki Yate. London: Ta-Ha, 1996.

Mawlawi, Faysal al-. *Al-Usus al-shariyya lil-alaquat bayna al-muslimin wa-ghayr al-muslimin*. Paris: UOIF, 1987.

McCrudden, Christopher. "Human Dignity and Judicial Interpretation of Human Rights." *European Journal of International Law* 19, no. 4 (2008): 655–724.

McKenna, Thomas. *Rulers and Rebels: Everyday Politics and Armed Separatism in the Southern Philippines*. Berkeley: University of California Press, 1998.

Mill, John Stuart. *On Liberty* (1859). Edited by Stefan Collini. Cambridge: Cambridge University Press, 1989.

———. *The Principles of Political Economy* (1869). London: Longmans, Green and Dyer, 1990.

Miller, David. *On Nationality*. Oxford: Oxford University Press, 1997.

Miller, Richard. "Christian Attitudes towards Boundaries: Metaphysical and Geographical." In *Christian Political Ethics*, edited by John Coleman. Princeton: Princeton University Press, 2008.

Mitchell, Richard. *The Society of the Muslim Brothers*. New York: Oxford University Press, 1993.

Modood, Tariq. *Multiculturalism: A Civic Idea*. Cambridge: Polity, 2007.

Mohamed, Yasien. *Fitrah: The Islamic Concept of Human Nature*. London: Ta-Ha, 1996.

Montesquieu, Baron de. *The Spirit of Laws* (1752). Translated by Thomas Nugent, edited by J. V. Prichard. London: G. Bell and Sons, 1914.

Nagel, Thomas. *Equality and Partiality*. Oxford: Oxford University Press, 1991.

———. *The View from Nowhere*. Oxford: Oxford University Press, 1986.

Nathan, K. S., and Mohammad Hashim Kamali. "Addressing the Challenge of Political Islam in Southeast Asia." In *Islam in Southeast Asia*, edited by K. S. Nathan and Mohammad Hashim Kamali. Singapore: Institute of Southeast Asian Studies, 2005.

Nawawī, Abū Zakarīyāʾ al-. *Al-Majmūʿ sharḥ al-muhadhdhab* (1421). Vol. 19. Beirut: Dār al-Fikr, 2000.

Neumann, Hannah. "Identity-Building and Democracy in the Philippines." *Journal of Current Southeast Asian Affairs* 29, no. 3 (2010): 61–90.

Noble, Lela. "The Moro National Liberation Front in the Philippines." *Pacific Affairs* 49, no. 3 (1976): 405–24.

Norris, Pippa, and Ronald Inglehart. *Sacred and Secular: Religion and Politics Worldwide*. Cambridge Cambridge University Press, 2004.

Nozick, Robert. *Anarchy, State and Utopia*. Oxford: Blackwell, 1974.

Nussbaum, Martha. "Patriotism and Cosmopolitanism." In *For Love of Country*, edited by Martha Nussbaum and Joshua Cohen. Boston: Beacon Press, 1996.

Nussbaum, Martha, and Joshua Cohen, eds. *For Love of Country*. Boston: Beacon Press, 1996.

Nyang, Sulayman. "Religion and the Maintenance of Boundaries." In *Islamic Political Ethics*, edited by Sohail Hashmi. Princeton: Princeton University Press, 2002.

Oderberg, David. "The Metaphysical Foundations of Natural Law." In *Natural Moral Law*, edited by Holger Zaborowski. Washington, DC: Catholic University of America Press, 2010.

———. *Moral Theory: A Non-Consequentialist Approach*. Oxford: Blackwell, 2000.

O'Donovan, Oliver. *Resurrection and Moral Order*. 2nd ed. Grand Rapids: Eerdmans, 1994.

O'Neill, Onora. "Bounded and Cosmopolitan Justice." *Review of International Studies* 26, no. 5 (2000): 45–60.

———. *Bounds of Justice*. Cambridge: Cambridge University Press, 2000.

Opwis, Felicitas. *Maṣlaḥa and the Purpose of the Law: Islamic Discourse on Legal Change from the 4th/10th to 8th/14th Century*. Leiden: Brill, 2010.

Osman, Mohamed Fathi. "The Children of Adam: An Islamic Perspective on Pluralism." Occasional paper, Center for Muslim-Christian Understanding, Georgetown University, Washington, DC, 1997.

———. "Human Rights in Islam." Occasional paper, Center for Muslim-Jewish Engagement, University of Southern California, Los Angeles, 2012.

Oz-Salzberger, Fania. Introduction to *Adam Ferguson's "An Essay on the History of Civil Society."* Cambridge: Cambridge University Press, 1995.

Pagden, Anthony. "The Christian Tradition." In *States, Nations, and Borders: The Ethics of Making Boundaries*, edited by Allen Buchanan and Margaret Moore. Cambridge: Cambridge University Press, 2003.

Pagden, Anthony, and Jeremy Lawrance, eds. *Vitoria: Political Writings*. Cambridge: Cambridge University Press, 1991.

Parekh, Bhikhu. *A New Politics of Identity*. Basingstoke: Palgrave Macmillan, 2008.

———. *Rethinking Multiculturalism: Cultural Diversity and Political Theory*. 2nd ed. Basingstoke: Palgrave Macmillan, 2006.

Park, Richard S. "Fragmented Knowledge Structures: Secularization as Scientization." *Heythrop Journal* 54, no. 4 (2013): 563–73.

"Pastoral Constitution on the Church in the Modern World." Libreria Editrice Vaticana. http://bit.ly/VatIIGS.

Paul VI. "On the Development of Peoples." Libreria Editrice Vaticana. http://bit.ly/VatIIPP. March 26, 1967.

Peters, Rudolph. *Crime and Punishment in Islamic Law*. Cambridge: Cambridge University Press, 2005.

"The Philippines: Religious Conflict Resolution on Mindanao." In *Case Studies*. Washington, DC: Berkley Center for Religion, Peace, and World Affairs, 2011.

Philpott, Daniel. *Just and Unjust Peace: An Ethic of Political Reconciliation*. New York: Oxford University Press, 2012.

Picardal, Amado. "Christian-Muslim Dialogue in Mindanao." *Asian Christian Review* 2, no. 2 (2008): 54–72.

Pinckaers, Servais, OP. *The Pinckaers Reader: Renewing Thomistic Moral Theology*. Translated by John Berkman and Craig Titus. Washington, DC: Catholic University of America Press, 2005.

Plant, Raymond. *Politics, Theology and History*. Cambridge: Cambridge University Press, 2001.

Plato. *The Republic*. Edited by Ivor Richards. Cambridge: Cambridge University Press, 1966.

Pogge, Thomas. "Priorities of Global Justice." In *Global Justice*, edited by Thomas Pogge. Oxford: Blackwell, 2001.

———. *World Poverty and Human Rights: Cosmopolitan Responsibilities and Reforms*. Cambridge: Polity, 2002.

"Population and Annual Growth Rates: Autonomous Region in Muslim Mindanao: 1995, 2000 and 2007—Appendix D." National Statistics Office. http://bit.ly/CensusGovPh.

Porter, Jean. *Nature as Reason: A Thomistic Theory of the Natural Law*. Grand Rapids: Eerdmans, 2005.

Qaraḍāwī, Yūsuf al-. *Al-Ḥall al-Islāmi*. Vol. 2. Beirut: Muʾassasat al-Risalah, 1980.

———. *Fi fiqh al-aqalliyyāt al-muslima* [On the Jurisprudence of Muslim Minorities]. Cairo: Dar al-Shuruq, 2001.

Quine, Willard. "On Empirically Equivalent Systems of the World." *Erkenntnis* 9, no. 3 (1975): 313–28.

The Qurʾan. Translated by M. A. S. Abdel Haleem. Oxford: Oxford University Press, 2004.

Rahman, Fazlur. "Law and Ethics in Islam." In *Ethics in Islam*, edited by Richard Hovannisian. Malibu: Undena, 1985.

Rahner, Karl. "Membership of the Church." In *Theological Investigations*. London: Darton, Longman & Todd, 1963.

Ramadan, Tariq. *Islam, the West and the Challenges of Modernity*. Leicester: Islamic Foundation, 2001.

———. "Islamic Views of the Collective." In *Building a Better Bridge: Muslims, Christians, and the Common Good*, edited by Michael Ipgrave. Washington, DC: Georgetown University Press, 2008.

———. *Radical Reform: Islamic Ethics and Liberation*. Oxford: Oxford University Press, 2009.

———. *Western Muslims*. Oxford: Oxford University Press, 2004.

Ramsay, Maureen. *What's Wrong with Liberalism? A Radical Critique of Liberal Philosophy*. London: Leicester University Press, 1997.

Rauf, Feisal Abdul. *What's Right with Islam*. San Francisco: HarperCollins 2005.

Rawls, John. "The Idea of Public Reason Revisited." *University of Chicago Law Review* 64, no. 3 (1997): 765–807.

———. *Political Liberalism*. Expanded ed. New York: Columbia University Press, [1993] 2005.

———. *A Theory of Justice*. Rev. ed. Cambridge, MA: Harvard University Press, [1971] 1999.

Raz, Joseph. *The Morality of Freedom*. Oxford: Oxford University Press, 1988.

Rāzī, Fakhr al-Dīn al-. *Al-Tafsīr al-kabīr* [The Great Commentary]. Cairo: al-Maṭbaʿah al Bahiyyah al-Miṣriyyah, 1938.

Raziq, ʿAli ʿAbd al-. "Message Not Government, Religion Not State." Translated by Joseph Massad. In *Liberal Islam*, edited by Charles Kurzman. Oxford: Oxford University Press, 1998.

Regan, Ethna. *Theology and the Boundary Discourse of Human Rights*. Washington, DC: Georgetown University Press, 2010.

Rhonheimer, Martin. *Natural Law and Practical Reason*. New York: Fordham University Press, 2000.

Rivera, Temario. "The Crisis of Philippine Democracy." In *Asian New Democracies*, edited by Hsin-Huang Michael Hsiao. Taipei: Taiwan Foundation for Democracy, 2006.

Rizvi, Sajjad. "A Primordial E Pluribus Unum? Exegeses on Q. 2:213 and Contemporary Muslim Discourses on Religious Pluralism." *Journal of Qur'anic Studies* 6, no. 1 (2004): 21–42.

Ronchi, Paolo. "Crucifixes, Margin of Appreciation and Consensus: The Grand Chamber Ruling in *Lautsi v. Italy*." *Ecclesiastical Law Journal* 13 (2011): 287–97.

Rood, Steven. *Forging Sustainable Peace in Mindanao: The Role of Civil Society*. Washington, DC: East-West Center, 2005.

Rosen, Michael. *Dignity: Its History and Meaning*. Cambridge, MA: Harvard University Press, 2012.

Rousseau, Jean-Jacques. *The Social Contract and Discourses* (1762). Translated by G. D. H. Cole. London and Toronto: J. M. Dent and Sons, 1923.

Roy, Olivier. *Secularism Confronts Islam*. Translated by George Holoch. New York: Columbia University Press, 2007.

Russell, Susan, and Rey Ty. "Conflict Transformation Efforts in the Southern Philippines." In *Conflict Resolution and Peace Education*, edited by Candice Carter. Basingstoke: Palgrave Macmillan, 2010.

Ruston, Roger. *Human Rights and the Image of God*. London: SCM, 2004.

Rutledge, Colleen Theresa. "Caught in the Crossfire: How Catholic Charities of Boston Was Victim to the Clash between Gay Rights and Religious Freedom." *Duke Journal of Gender Law and Policy* 15, no. 1 (2008): 297–314.

Ryle, Robyn. *Questioning Gender: A Sociological Exploration*. Thousand Oaks: Pine Forge Press, 2011.

Sachedina, Abdulaziz. *Islam and the Challenge of Human Rights*. Oxford: Oxford University Press, 2009.

———. *The Islamic Roots of Democratic Pluralism*. New York: Oxford University Press, 2001.

———. "The Qur'ān and Other Religions." In *The Cambridge Companion to the Qur'ān*, edited by Jane Dammen McAuliffe. Cambridge: Cambridge University Press, 2006.

———. *The Qur'an on Religious Pluralism*. Washington, DC: Georgetown University, 1996.

———. "Reason and Revelation in Islamic Political Ethics." In *Religion, the Enlightenment, and the New Global Order*, edited by John Owen and J. Judd Owen. New York: Columbia University Press, 2010.

Saeed, Abdullah. "Ambiguities of Apostasy and the Repression of Muslim Dissent." *Review of Faith and International Affairs* 9, no. 2 (2011): 31–38.

———. "An Islamic Case for Religious Freedom." In *Religious Freedom: Defending an Embattled Human Right*, edited by Timothy Shah and Matthew Franck. Princeton: Witherspoon Institute, 2012.

———. "Trends in Contemporary Islam: A Preliminary Attempt at a Classification." *Muslim World* 97, no. 3 (2007): 395–404.

Saeed, Abdullah, and Hassan Saeed. *Freedom of Religion, Apostasy and Islam*. Aldershot: Ashgate, 2004.

Salvatore, Armando. "Tradition and Modernity within the Islamic Civilization and the West." In *Islam and Modernity: Key Issues and Debates*, edited by Muhammad Khalid Masud, Armando Salvatore, and Martin van Bruinessen. Edinburgh: Edinburgh University Press, 2009.

Salvatore, Armando, and Dale Eickelman, eds. *Public Islam and the Common Good.* Leiden: Brill, 2006.

Sandel, Michael. *Democracy's Discontent: America in Search of a Public Philosophy.* Cambridge, MA: Harvard University Press, 1996.

———. *Liberalism and the Limits of Justice.* 2nd ed. Cambridge: Cambridge University Press, [1982] 1998.

Schacht, Joseph. *An Introduction to Islamic Law.* Oxford: Clarendon, 1964.

———. *The Origins of Muhammadan Jurisprudence.* Oxford: Clarendon, 1950.

Schiavo-Campo, Salvatore, and Mary Judd. *The Mindanao Conflict in the Philippines.* Washington, DC: World Bank, 2005.

Schütz, Alfred. *The Structures of the Life-World.* Edited by Thomas Luckmann. Evanston: Northwestern University Press, 1973.

Seel, John. "Reading the Post-Modern Self." In *The Question of Identity*, edited by James Davison Hunter. Charlottesville: University of Virginia Press, 1998.

Sen, Amartya. "Global Justice." In *Global Public Goods*, edited by Inge Kaul, Isabelle Grunberg, and Marc Stern. New York: Oxford University Press, 1999.

———. *Identity and Violence: The Illusion of Destiny.* London: Allen Lane, 2006.

Sennett, Richard. *The Fall of Public Man.* London: Penguin, [1976] 2002.

Shachar, Ayelet. *Multicultural Jurisdictions.* Cambridge: Cambridge University Press, 2001.

———. "State, Religion, and Family." In *Shari'a in the West*, edited by Rex Ahdar and Nicholas Aroney. Oxford: Oxford University Press, 2010.

Shah, Timothy. *Religious Freedom: Why Now? Defending an Embattled Human Right.* Edited by Matthew Franck. Princeton: Witherspoon Institute, 2012.

Shaw, Martin. "Civil Society and Global Politics." *Millennium: Journal of International Studies* 23, no. 3 (1994): 647–67.

Shils, Edward. *The Virtue of Civility: Selected Essays on Liberalism, Tradition, and Civil Society.* Edited by Steven Grosby. Indianapolis: Liberty Fund, 1997.

Shupack, Martin. "The Churches and Human Rights: Catholic and Protestant Human Rights Views as Reflected in Church Statements." *Harvard Human Rights Journal* 6 (1993): 127–57.

Sidgwick, Henry. *The Elements of Politics.* London: Macmillan, 1891.

Silliman, Sidney, and Lela Noble. *Organizing for Democracy: Ngos, Civil Society, and the Philippine State.* Honolulu: University of Hawai'i Press, 1998.

Simmel, Georg. *The Sociology of Georg Simmel.* Translated by Kurt H. Wolff. Glencoe: Free Press, 1950.

Simonsohn, Uriel. *A Common Justice: The Legal Allegiances of Christians and Jews under Early Islam.* Philadelphia: University of Pennsylvania Press, 2011.

Smith, Anthony. *National Identity.* Reno: University of Nevada Press, 1991.

———. *Nations and Nationalism in a Global Era.* Cambridge: Polity, 1995.

Smith, Christian. *What Is a Person? Rethinking Humanity, Social Life, and the Moral Good from the Person Up.* Chicago: University of Chicago Press, 2010.

Smith, Michael. *Human Dignity and the Common Good in the Aristotelian-Thomistic Tradition.* Lewiston: Mellen University Press, 1995.

Soroush, Abdolkarim. *Reason, Freedom, and Democracy in Islam.* Edited by Mahmoud Sadri and Ahmad Sadri New York: Oxford University Press, 2000.

Stackhouse, Max. *Public Theology and Political Economy.* Grand Rapids: Eerdmans, 1987.

Stark, Jan. "Muslims in the Philippines." *Journal of Muslim Minority Affairs* 23, no. 1 (2003): 195–209.

Stark, Rodney, and William Bainbridge. *The Future of Religion.* Berkeley: University of California Press, 1985.

Stelzer, Steffen. "Ethics." In *The Cambridge Companion to Classical Islamic Theology*, edited by Tim Winter. Cambridge: Cambridge University Press, 2008.

Sullivan, Winnifred, Robert Yelle, and Mateo Taussig-Rubbo, eds. *After Secular Law.* Stanford: Stanford University Press, 2011.

Swift, Adam. *Political Philosophy.* Cambridge: Polity, 2001.

Tamanaha, Brian. "The Folly of the 'Social Scientific' Concept of Legal Pluralism." *Journal of Law and Society* 20, no. 2 (1993): 192–217.

Tamir, Yael. *Liberal Nationalism.* Princeton: Princeton University Press, 1993.

Taya, Shamsuddin. "The Politicization of Ethnic Sentiments in the Southern Philippines: The Case of the Bangsamoro." *Journal of Muslim Minority Affairs* 30, no. 1 (2010): 19–34.

Taylor, Charles. *Human Agency and Language: Philosophical Papers 1.* Cambridge: Cambridge University Press, 1985.

———. *Modern Social Imaginaries.* Durham: Duke University Press, 2004.

———. "Modernity and the Rise of the Public Sphere." In *The Tanner Lectures on Human Values*, edited by Grethe Peterson. Salt Lake City: University of Utah Press, 1993.

———. "Modes of Civil Society." *Public Culture* 3, no. 1 (1990): 95–118.
———. "Modes of Secularism." In *Secularism and Its Critics*, edited by Rajeev Bhargava. Oxford: Oxford University Press, 1999.
———. "The Politics of Recognition." In *Multiculturalism: Examining the Politics of Recognition*, edited by Amy Gutmann. Princeton: Princeton University Press, 1994.
———. *Sources of the Self: The Making of the Modern Identity*. Cambridge: Cambridge University Press, 1989.
———. "What's Wrong with Negative Liberty." In *The Idea of Freedom: Essays in Honour of Isaiah Berlin*, edited by Alan Ryan. Oxford: Oxford University Press, 1991.
Taylor, Jeremy. *A Discourse of the Nature, Offices, and Measures of Friendship*. London: Printed for R. Royston, 1657.
Thomson, Judith. *The Realm of Rights*. Cambridge, MA: Harvard University Press, 1990.
Tibi, Bassam. *Islamism and Islam*. New Haven: Yale University Press, 2012.
———. "War and Peace in Islam." In *Islamic Political Ethics*, edited by Sohail Hashmi. Princeton: Princeton University Press, 2002.
Tierney, Brian. "Historical Roots of Modern Rights." In *Rethinking Rights*, edited by Bruce Frohnen and Kenneth Grasso. Columbia: University of Missouri Press, 2009.
———. *The Idea of Natural Rights*. Grand Rapids: Eerdmans, [1997] 2001.
———. "Religious Rights: An Historical Perspective." In *Religious Human Rights in Global Perspective*, edited by John Witte and Johan David Van der Vyver. The Hague: Martinus Nijhoff, 1996.
Toft, Monica. "Getting Religion? The Puzzling Case of Islam and Civil War." *International Security* 31, no. 4 (2007): 97–131.
Toft, Monica, Daniel Philpott, and Timothy Shah. *God's Century: Resurgent Religion and Global Politics*. New York: Norton, 2011.
Tuck, Richard. *Natural Rights Theories: Their Origin and Development*. Cambridge: Cambridge University Press, 1979.
Tully, James. *A Discourse on Property*. Cambridge: Cambridge University Press, 1980.
Tuminez, Astrid. "This Land Is Our Land: Moro Ancestral Domain and Its Implications for Peace and Development in the Southern Philippines." *School of Advanced International Studies Review* 27, no. 2 (2007): 77–91.
U.S. Catholic Conference International Policy Committee. "American Responsibilities in a Changing World." *Origins* 22 (1992): 337–41.

Uusitalo, Liisa. "Consumption in Postmodernity." In *The Active Consumer*, edited by Marina Bianchi. London: Routledge, 1998.

Vattimo, Gianni. *Nihilism and Emancipation: Ethics, Politics, and Law*. New York: Columbia University Press, 2004.

Veatch, Henry. "Natural Law and the 'Is'-'Ought' Question." *Catholic Lawyer* 26 (1981): 251–65.

Vickers, Lucy. *Religious Freedom, Religious Discrimination and the Workplace*. Oxford: Hart, 2008.

Villa, Dana. *Public Freedom*. Princeton: Princeton University Press, 2008.

Viviano, Rocco. "Christian-Muslim Relations in the Philippines: Between Conflict, Reconciliation and Dialogue." In *Christian Responses to Islam: Muslim-Christian Relations in the Modern World*, edited by Anthony O'Mahony and Emma Loosley. Manchester: Manchester University Press, 2008.

Vogel, Frank. *Islamic Law and Legal System*. Leiden: Brill, 2000.

Vries, Hent de. Introduction to *Political Theologies: Public Religions in a Post-Secular World*, edited by Hent de Vries and Lawrence Sullivan. New York: Fordham University Press, 2006.

Waldron, Jeremy. *God, Locke, and Equality: Christian Foundations in Locke's Political Thought*. Cambridge: Cambridge University Press, 2002.

———. "One Law for All? The Logic of Cultural Accommodation." *Washington and Lee Law Review* 59, no. 1 (2002): 3–34.

———. "Questions about the Reasonable Accommodation of Minorities." In *Shariʿa in the West*, edited by Rex Ahdar and Nicholas Aroney. Oxford: Oxford University Press, 2010.

Wallace, Anthony. *Religion: An Anthropological View*. New York: Random House, 1966.

Wallis, Roy, and Steve Bruce. "Secularization: The Orthodox Model." In *Religion and Secularization*, edited by Steve Bruce. Oxford: Oxford University Press, 1992.

Walzer, Michael. "The Communitarian Critique of Liberalism." *Political Theory* 17 (1990): 6–23.

———. "The Idea of Civil Society." In *Community Works: The Revival of Civil Society in America*, edited by E. J. Dionne. Washington, DC: Brookings Institution Press, 1998.

———. *Spheres of Justice*. New York: Basic Books, 1983.

———. *Thick and Thin: Moral Argument at Home and Abroad*. Notre Dame: University of Notre Dame Press, 1994.

Warner, Michael. "Uncritical Reading." In *Polemic: Critical or Uncritical*, edited by Jane Gallop. New York: Routledge, 2004.

Warren, David, and Christine Gilmore. "Rethinking Neo-Salafism through an Emerging Fiqh of Citizenship." *New Middle Eastern Studies* 2 (2012): 1–7.

Weber, Max. *General Economic History*. Translated by Frank Knight. New York: Greenberg, 1927.

———. *The Protestant Ethic and the Spirit of Capitalism* (1930). Translated by Talcott Parsons, edited by Anthony Giddens. London: Routledge, 1992.

———. *The Theory of Social and Economic Organization*. Translated by A. M. Henderson and Talcott Parsons. New York: Free Press, 1964.

Weintraub, Jeff. "The Theory and Politics of Public/Private Distinction." In *Public and Private in Thought and Practice*, edited by Krisnan Kumar and Jeff Weintraub. Chicago: University of Chicago Press, 1997.

White, Harrison. *Identity and Control*. 2nd ed. Princeton: Princeton University Press, 2008.

Williams, Rowan. "Civil and Religious Law in England: A Religious Perspective." Paper presented at the Temple Festival series at the Royal Courts of Justice, London, February 2008. http://bit.ly/RWCivRelLaw.

Williams, Timothy. "The MOA-AD Debacle—an Analysis of Individuals' Voices, Provincial Propaganda and National Disinterest." *Journal of Current Southeast Asian Affairs* 29, no. 1 (2009): 121–44.

Wilson, Bryan. "Secularization: The Inherited Model." In *The Sacred in a Secular Age*, edited by Philip Hammond. Berkeley: University of California Press, 1985.

Wolterstorff, Nicholas. "Grounding the Rights We Have as Human Persons." In *Understanding Liberal Democracy*, edited by Terence Cuneo and Nicholas Wolterstorff. Oxford: Oxford University Press, 2012.

———. Introduction to *Understanding Liberal Democracy*, edited by Terence Cuneo and Nicholas Wolterstorff. Oxford: Oxford University Press, 2012.

———. *Justice: Rights and Wrongs*. Princeton: Princeton University Press, 2008.

———. "The Role of Religion in Decision and Discussion of Political Issues." In *Religion in the Public Square*, edited by Robert Audi and Nicholas Wolterstorff. London: Rowman and Littlefield, 1997.

Wood, Nicholas. *Confessing Christ in a Plural World*. Oxford: Whitley Publications, 2002.

———. *Faiths and Faithfulness: Pluralism, Dialogue and Mission in the Work of Kenneth Cragg and Lesslie Newbigin*. Bletchley: Paternoster, 2009.

Yaʿlā, Abū. *Kitāb al-muʿtamad fī uṣūl al-dīn*. Edited by Wadi Z. Haddad. Beirut: Dār al-Mashriq, 1974.

Zakaria, Fareed. *The Future of Freedom: Illiberal Democracy at Home and Abroad*. New York: Norton, 2004.

Zakarīyā, Fuʾād. *Myth and Reality in the Contemporary Islamist Movement*. Translated by Ibrahim M. Abu-Rabiʿ. London: Pluto Press, 2005.

Zaman, M. Raquibuz. "Islamic Perspectives on Territorial Boundaries and Autonomy." In *Islamic Political Ethics*, edited by Sohail Hashmi. Princeton: Princeton University Press, 2002.

Zaman, Muhammad Qasim. *The Ulama in Contemporary Islam: Custodians of Change*. Princeton: Princeton University Press, 2002.

———. "The ʿulama of Contemporary Islam and Their Conceptions of the Common Good." In *Public Islam and the Common Good*, edited by Armando Salvatore and Dale Eickelman. Leiden: Brill, 2006.

Zubaida, Sami. *Law and Power in the Islamic World*. London: I. B. Tauris, 2003.

INDEX

Bishops-Ulama Conference (BUC), 153, 160–61, 224n19
Boethius, 75
Boston Catholic Charities, 51, 203n33
Boyle, Joseph, 88–89, 127

Cahill, Lisa, 186
Calhoun, Craig, 178–79
Calvo, Angel, 157–58, 223n13
Capalla, Fernando, 160–61, 224n19
Carens, Joseph, 170
Carozza, Paolo, 100–101
Carter, Stephen, 10–11, 192
Casanova, José, 173, 175
Cates, Diana Fritz, 228n32
Catholic Relief Services (CRS), 161–63, 224n22
Catholic social teaching
  cosmopolitanism in, 185–86
  on human dignity, 95, 96, 97, 98–100
  on human rights, 96–97, 100
  imago Dei concept in, 95–100, 128
  Islamic resonance with, 127–29
  on positive and negative rights, 99
  Vatican II and, 84, 95, 211n24
  See also Christian theology
Cavanaugh, William, 131
Centuries of Childhood (Ariès), 46
Chapman, Mark, 118
Christian cosmopolitanism, 183–88
Christian theology, 117
  on common good, 82, 83, 90, 94–95
  Islamic parallels to, 128–29
  moral relationality in, 75–76
  See also Catholic social teaching
Chrysostom, John. *See* John Chrysostom, Saint
Cicero, 75, 174
civic republican tradition, 22, 26
civility
  civil society and, 7–9
  critique and, 33–35
  personal, 9, 10–11
  vertical and horizontal, 6–7, 8–9, 37
  virtues of, 8, 9–10, 52–53
  See also public civility
civil liberties, 26, 63, 68
civil society, 6, 14–15
  brief history of, 7–9
  in Mindanao, 153, 154, 155, 161–62, 166
Code of Muslim Personal Laws, 151–52, 166–67
collectivity criterion, 20, 199n10
common good
  aggregate view of, 92
  Aquinas on, 82, 83, 90, 94–95
  Aristotle on, 82–83
  associative view of, 92–94
  constructing a just society and, 2, 15, 84, 88, 90
  as ensemble of diverse goods, 89–92
  human good and, 13, 95, 117–18
  maṣlaḥa as, 82, 95, 115–19, 129, 164
  mutually overlapping, 91, 210n21
  natural law theory and, 82–84
  new natural law theory and, 85–89, 210n17
  plural societies and, 93–94, 97
  relativism and, 14, 84, 93, 94, 101, 118
common property, 184–85

individualized justice, 62
Iqbal, Mohagher, 164–66, 225n25
Islam and the Challenge of Human Rights (Sachedina), 121–22
Islamic law and jurisprudence
distinction between *dār al-Islām* and *dār al-ḥarb* in, 181
establishment of principles of, 133
fiqh jurisprudence and, 110, 112, 122, 140, 141, 143, 144, 146, 220n13
legal pluralism in, 112, 114–15, 156, 164, 167
main sources of jurisprudence in, 110
maqāṣid al-sharīʿa in, 95, 115–16, 129, 167
maqāṣid in, 115–17, 146, 167
nonmonolithic character of, 140–41
public civility within, 109
Qurʾān and, 110, 112, 140, 144
sharīʿa, contextualizability within, 109–12
uṣūl al-fiqh in, 109–10, 113, 118
See also sharīʿa
Islamic political ethics and theology
An-Naʿim on, 111, 113, 132, 133–38
Christianity's conceptual resonance with, 127–29
cosmopolitanism and, 180–83
democracy and, 106, 163
fiṭra concept in, 105, 118, 119–22, 123–26, 128, 137, 140, 143, 146–47, 191, 193
on free will, 122, 124–26, 128, 139
on human dignity, 121, 122
on human nature, 76–77, 78, 121, 131, 140, 141–42
on human reason, 76, 121–22, 139, 141, 220n13
on human rights, 121, 137
on human teleology, 76, 105, 138–39, 141–42
ijtihād concept in, 112–15, 116, 117, 118, 146
inclusiveness and, 138–43
Islamism and, 106, 143–44
on justice, 13, 139–40, 146
maṣlaḥa doctrine in, 82, 95, 115–19, 129, 164, 215n28
moral cosmopolitanism and, 180–81, 182–83, 191–92
on morality, 118–19, 145–46, 182
pluralism and, 109, 138, 140, 142, 144
prioritization of ethics in, 118–19, 132, 138, 140, 141, 143, 145–47, 165
on rationality and relationality, 76, 122, 147
religion-politics relation in, 108, 133–38, 142
Sachedina on, 76, 109, 119, 121–22, 137, 138, 139–40, 142
Islamism, 106, 143–44, 180–81

Jabarites, 139
Jabidah Massacre, 151, 154, 155
Jadʿān, Fahmī, 140
John Chrysostom, Saint, 185
John Paul II, 161
Jones, Charles, 170
Judaism, 117

Richard S. Park is assistant professor of religion at Vanguard University.

CPSIA information can be obtained
at www.ICGtesting.com
Printed in the USA
BVOW06*0816180817
491695BV00014B/11/P

9 780268 102739